Britain in the European Union today

Colin Pilkington

Manchester University Press
Manchester and New York

distributed exclusively in the USA and Canada by St. Martin's Press

Copyright © Colin Pilkington 1995

Published by Manchester University Press
Oxford Road, Manchester M13 9NR, UK
and Room 400, 175 Fifth Avenue, New York, NY 10010, USA

Distributed exclusively in the USA and Canada
by St Martin's Press, Inc., 175 Fifth Avenue, New York, NY 10010, USA

British Library Cataloguing-in-Publication Data
A catalogue record for this book is available from the British Library

Library of Congress Cataloging-in-Publication Data
Pilkington, Colin
  Britain in the European Union today/Colin Pilkington
     p.   cm. — (Politics today)
  ISBN 0–7190–4561–4 — ISBN 0–7190–4562–2 (pbk. alk.paper)
  1. European Union—Great Britain. 2. Great Britain—Politics and
government—1979– I. Title. II. Series: Politics today (Manchester,
England)
JN30.P55   1995
327.4104'09'049—dc20   95–4958
                                                                            CIP

ISBN   0 7190 4561 4 *hardback*
       0 7190 4562 2 *paperback*

00 99 98 97 96   10 9 8 7 6 5 4 3 2 1

Typeset in Great Britain
by Northern Phototypesetting Co Ltd, Bolton

Printed in Great Britain
by Bell & Bain Ltd, Glasgow

Britain in the European Union today

Politics today
Series editor: Bill Jones

Of related interest

Contents

Preface

There are a handful of subjects, present in all Politics syllabuses, that are inadequately dealt with, generally speaking. Of these, the political implications of British involvement in Europe is probably the area about which students are most ill-informed and badly prepared. As an examiner, I see questions on Europe answered in a totally unsatisfactory manner; as a producer of resource materials, Europe is always the first to be mentioned when I ask what areas my clients would like me to cover. There are a number of reasons for this – apathy and ignorance of European issues on the part of both students and teachers play their part, but of even greater importance is the lack of correctly targeted information, for the teachers as much as for the students. At the moment there are a number of textbooks dealing with the European Community itself, but for the most part they either concentrate on the history and institutions of the Community or they discuss the economic or constitutional aspects of the Community in a very technical sense, and without any specific British dimension. Alternatively, there are mentions of Europe in general textbooks on British politics but these are restricted at best to a single chapter or, more often, are just a few paragraphs in a section headed 'Britain and the World' or 'International Relations'.

The European dimension is of increasing importance in British politics: the change to the European Union post-Maastricht and the Single Market means that there are constraints placed on many aspects of British legislation and decision-making; the problems of the European Monetary System (EMS) and the long debate over Maastricht has raised the profile of European issues, especially the question of sovereignty; and possibly most important is the impact Europe is having on the political parties, a divisive issue comparable to the effects of the Corn Laws or Home Rule in the past. In the light of that growing importance it is certain that A-level and university examiners will extend and intensify their expectation that the European dimension will be included in students' examination responses.

A-level syllabuses do no contain specific sections on European politics but all now contain references to Europe in the syllabus outlines. Take, for example, the AEB revision of the syllabus for 1994, which amends the Aims to read

> the study of government and politics of the UK at local, national and European Community levels' ... Candidates will not be expected to reveal extensive knowledge of European institutions but should be able to refer to such events as elections to the European Parliament, the impact of Europe on UK political parties etc. ... Throughout the syllabus credit will be given to candidates who make relevant references to the EC.

For the NEAB these explicit references have been present for some time, so that each of the three sections of the Core syllabus contains its own mention of Europe. On the constitution it says 'a knowledge will be expected of ... the impact of British membership of the European Community and the fact that Britain is a signatory of the European Convention of Human Rights'; on representation it says 'knowledge of local, national and European Parliament elections and electoral systems'; and on the governmental process it says that 'a detailed knowledge of European institutions is not required but candidates will be expected to appreciate the influence of these institutions on the British machinery of government'.

It can be seen that a knowledge of the relations between the UK and Europe has been useful to A-level candidates for some time, but that with the increased emphasis on European issues in recent years, examiners are likely to lay even more stress and importance on this aspect of a candidate's answer. It is not particularly relevant to quote past questions because in the new circumstances the questions are also likely to be new, but students will be expected to comment on the European dimension in questions that heretofore were exclusively about domestic issues.

All that has been said above about A-level students is equally applicable to those first- and second-year degree students following a course in government or politics at universities or other institutions of higher education. Since my aim has been to write a clear, concise and accessible account I would also suggest that this book could be of use to students of GCSE Politics or to members of the general public looking for clarification over British membership of the European Union.

I should like to thank Dr Bill Jones and Richard Purslow of Manchester University Press, both for the trust and confidence they showed when they commissioned me to write this work and for the help and encouragement they provided during the writing process. Acknowledgements are also due to my friends and colleagues, Dr Robert Gibson of Didcot Sixth Forms and Dennis Harrigan of Framwellgate School in Durham, both of whom helped with support, encouragement and an insight into the current thinking of A-level students. For their unwitting service as guinea-pigs in pilot-testing the material in this book my thanks have to go to my students at the Liverpool Institute of Higher Education, and to the eighty centres or so who purchased my resource packs from Fulcrum Publishing. For a wealth of information, often about areas that are not generally as widely-known as they should be, I am indebted to the information services of both the European Commission and the European Parliament, and in particular to the European Information Centre North West, based in the Liverpool Central Libraries.

We have just completed a period of major changes to the European Union and, within the next few years, we are to be plunged into a fresh round of growth and development. I trust that this book might help students to understand just what is happening in Europe and what impact that is having on the British political scene.

Colin Pilkington
November 1994

Abbreviations

The European Communities are littered with acronyms for the various institutions, treaties, agencies, political groupings, etc. The following is a glossary of the acronyms used in the text of this book.

ACP	African, Caribbean and Pacific countries associated with the EC
BBQ	British Budgetary Question (1979–84), aka the Bloody British Question
BEUC	European Bureau of Consumers' Organisations
CAP	Common Agricultural Policy
CCC	Consumers' Consultative Council
CECG	Consumers in the European Community Group (UK organisations)
CEDEFOP	European Centre for the development of vocational education
CEEP	European Centre of Public Enterprises
CFP	Common Fisheries Policy
CFSP	Common Foreign and Security Policy (one pillar of the TEU)
Coface	Confederation of Family Organisations in the EC
COPA	Committee of Professional Agricultural Organisations
COR	Committee of the Regions
COREPER	Committee of Permanent Representatives
DG	Directorate-General of the Commission (there are

	23, differentiated by Roman numerals, e.g. DGVI, Directorate-General for agriculture)
EC	European Community, merger of EEC + ECSC + Euratom (1967)
ECJ	European Court of Justice
Ecofin	Economics and finance (Council of Ministers)
ECSC	European Coal and Steel Community (Treaty of Paris 1951)
ECU	European Currency Unit (currently used only for accountancy purposes but representing a putative common currency)
EDA	European Democratic Alliance (Gaullist Centre-Right)
EDC	European Defence Community, aborted in 1954
EEA	European Economic Area – applicant members of EFTA
EEB	European Environmental Bureau
EEC	European Economic Community – the original Common Market 1957
EFTA	European Free Trade Area, rival to EEC founded 1959
EIICA	European Inter-regional Institute for Consumer Affairs
EMS	European Monetary System
EMU	Economic and Monetary Union
ENEL	Italian nationalised electricity industry
EP	European Parliament
EPP	European People's Party (Christian Democrat grouping)
ERA	European Radical Alliance (non-socialist Left)
ERM	Exchange Rate Mechanism, within the EMS
ERP	European Recovery Program, part of the Marshall Aid Plan 1947
ESC	Economic and Social Committee
ETUC	European Trade Union Confederation
EU	European Union, made up of EC plus defence and security 'pillars'

EUL	European United Left (former Communist parties)
Euratom	European Atomic Community (Treaty of Rome 1957)
Eurocoop	EC Consumer Co-operatives
Europol	European Police Office
FE	Forza Europa (Berlusconi's Forza Italia in EP)
FCO	(the British) Foreign and Commonwealth Office
GATT	General Agreement on Tariffs and Trade
IGC	Intergovernmental Conference
IMF	International Monetary Fund (of the United Nations)
LDR	Liberal, Democratic and Reformist Group (Centre-Right party group)
MEP	Member of the European Parliament
NATO	North Atlantic Treaty Organisation
NE	Nations of Europe (grouping of anti-Europe MEPs)
OEEC	Organisation for European Economic Co-operation
OECD	Organisation for Economic Co-operation and Development
PES	Party of European Socialists
QMV	Qualified Majority Voting (in the Council of Ministers)
SCA	Special Committee on Agriculture (like COREPER but for agriculture)
SEA	Single European Act of 1987
TEU	Treaty for European Union (Maastricht)
TREVI	anti-terrorism group within the Council of Ministers
UNICE	Union of Industries of the European Community (employers group)
WCED	World Commission on Environment and Development
WEU	Western European Union, defence arm of the Council of Europe

Introduction

Early in the nineteenth century the great Austrian statesman
Metternich, faced with rampant Italian nationalism, stated contemptuously 'Italien ist ein geographischer Begrifft' – that is to
say, 'Italy is no more than a geographical expression'. And yet the
term 'Italian' was always rather more than merely geographical.
The concept of being Italian may not have been a statement of
nationality but it did make a statement about culture, language
and a way of life, even though there was no cohesive political
entity called Italy at that time.

What was true for Italy in the first half of the nineteenth century was equally true of Europe in the first half of the twentieth
– 'European' meant an indication of geographical origin and could
also be a statement of cultural identity, but had very little meaning other than that. There have always been latter-day Metter-
nichs who dismiss the idea of European integration with as much
contempt as Metternich showed for Italian nationalism. Nevertheless, despite Metternich's dismissal of the idea, Italians over-
came their internal differences and achieved political union.
Similarly, in the present century, there were those who ignored
the sceptics and, through their personal vision of a European
identity, sought ways in which Europe might be encouraged to
develop its own political and economic union, just as the frag-
mented states of Italy and Germany had achieved unification in
the late nineteenth century. As Hallstein, first President of the
European Commission, said in his memoirs, 'Europe shares a

sense of values: of what is good and bad; of what a man's rights should be and what are his duties; of how society should be ordered; of what is happiness and what disaster. Europe shares many things such as its memories that we call history ...' (Hallstein, 1972). This book is about Europe and it is about politics, but it is not necessarily about European politics. Aimed at the student of British Government and Politics, the intention is to study the impact which a movement towards European integration has had upon the British peoples, on the British political system and on the constitution of the United Kingdom.

One factor emerges very clearly from any consideration of the European Union's history and present structure. Contrary to public perceptions, the debate over Europe has not been primarily about membership or non-membership, but about what the politicians of the component states hope to gain from membership. Over the years there have been at least two perspectives governing attitudes towards what is seen as European co-operation, and these two – often diametrically opposed – perspectives thread themselves through its historical development, lay constraints upon the functioning of European institutions and determine the degree of British commitment to the European ideal. To the casual and uninformed onlooker the impression is sometimes given that the only argument over Europe is as to whether Britain or any other country should ever have joined. In fact, although there always has been, and continues to be, a strong anti-European body of opinion in this and other countries of the Union, the real arguments that have influenced development over the years, and which continue to dominate discussions, are over different views as to the nature of EU membership:

- Should Europe be a federation or a confederation?
- Are politicians federalists or functionalists?
- Should the institutions of the EU be supranational or inter-governmental?

It must be stressed that the position on these matters adopted by individuals, parties, or even entire countries does not follow a consistent pattern but tends to move according to the political climate or economic realities of the time. The labels given to these conflicting attitudes and institutions are terms that will be used throughout this book, so it may well be advisable to clarify their meaning at this point.

Federalists is the name given to those who have, as their ultimate aim, a full political and economic union of Europe, with the creation of something in the nature of a United States of Europe, with considerable powers in the hands of a federal government. On the whole federalists believe that the national interests of component states should be subordinated to the general good of the European Union as a whole. Used as a pejorative term by opponents, the 'f-word' is sometimes replaced by the term 'Eurocentrism' to suggest the overthrow of national liberties by authoritarian centralisation in Brussels.

Functionalists or pragmatists are those who, to put it crudely, are members of the Union for what they can get out of it. For them the institutions of the Union should be meetings of equals which negotiate the agreed outcomes that will best satisfy the individual needs of member states. Functionalists are unwilling to surrender any aspect of national sovereignty, but for reasons of history, chauvinistic pride or for some other cause, believe in the supremacy of the centralised nation-state. The functionalists adhere to the Union for the pragmatic reason that it is more effective to co-operate than to face cut-throat competition in the modern industrial and commercial world. The reverse view is that functionalists ignore the general good in favour of self-interested nationalism.

Supranational institutions are the bodies favoured by the federalists. The officials staffing the institutions are encouraged to think of themselves as loyal only to the Union, ignoring their former national loyalties; the policies they advocate are in the interests of all and take precedence over national positions. The Commission and Parliament of the EU are supranational institutions.

Intergovernmental institutions are institutions where members discuss and negotiate as representatives of their national governments, retaining their national loyalties. These institutions are seen by functionalists as places where they can defend their national interests against the encroachment of federalist ideas. The Council of Ministers and, even more so, the European Council are intergovernmental bodies.

Subsidiarity is a concept that attempts to reconcile the federalist and functionalist positions, evolved, largely at the behest of John Major, in the immediate aftermath of the Maastricht agreement to show that functionalists can adhere to the European ideal without embracing federalist beliefs. Subsidiarity agrees that Community policy decisions should be made at the centre but that the way in which those policies are implemented should be decided as close to the people as possible. In other words, the Union-wide policy is decided in Brussels but each individual national government can interpret that policy in the way which best suits the individual state's interests. Ironically, since subsidiarity was evoked to challenge federalism, this definition of subsidiarity is what many people understand by a federal system. It is important that these perspectives are borne in mind while reading this book because the behaviour of those involved, whether individuals, parties or governments, whether in the past or today, can only be properly understood in relation to their stance on the nature of Europe.

Finally, while still considering terminology, it might be worth mentioning the use of the terms 'European Union' and 'European Community'. The Union, as established by the Maastricht Treaty with its defence and security 'pillars', is the wider of the two and all citizens of member states making up the European Community are citizens of the European Union. But all the institutions we think of as European, from the Commission and European Parliament to the Court of Justice, belong to the European Community rather than to the European Union. When the terms 'Union' or 'Community' are used in this book there is a very subtle distinction between them, but as far as the reader is concerned, they both essentially refer to the same thing and should be regarded as interchangeable terms.

I

The growth of the European Union

1

Origins and growth of European institutions, 1945–79

The idea of an integrated Europe has a long history, dating from at least 1789, but it only began to be taken seriously some fifty years ago. There were some stirrings of integrationist thought following the First World War, when a Pan-European Union was founded by Count Coudenhove-Kalergi. Gustav Stresemann, German Foreign Minister from 1923 to 1929, advocated European co-operation in an attempt to extricate Germany from restrictions imposed by the Treaty of Versailles. Similarly, Aristide Briand, French Foreign Minister from 1925 to 1932 and ardent member of the Pan-European Union, also promoted the idea of European co-operation; in 1929, Jean Monnet, a Frenchman who had been working for the League of Nations since 1919, drew up on his behalf the 'Briand Plan' for the Federal Union of European States. The plan was presented to European governments in 1930 but nothing came of it. However, the idea had a practical edge for the young Monnet and proved seminal to a career which would result, thirty years later, in Monnet being called 'The Father of Europe'.

Despite these moves towards unity nothing happened, because the idea went against the prevailing mood. With the fragmentation of the former Habsburg and Ottoman Empires into a patchwork of small competitive states; with the growth of jingoistic nationalism in Italy and Germany, and with Britain still preoccupied by imperial visions, the dream of European unity was held by only a small minority and was to be shattered by the outbreak of the Second World War.

Moves towards integration prior to 1948

The inspiration for post-war movements towards European union was a speech made by Winston Churchill in Zurich on 19 September 1946. The main theme of his argument was the threat posed by the atomic bomb, but he went on to claim that the best way to counter that threat was through the unity of the 'European family'. The best guarantee of that unity would be reconciliation between France and Germany, who could then work together for the revival of Europe: 'The fighting has stopped; but the dangers have not stopped. If we are to form the United States of Europe, or whatever name or form it may take, we must begin now.'[1]

The Zurich speech was rapturously received by all those in favour of European unity. 'You have lit a torch to give a message of hope to a shattered world,' wrote Leo Amery, 'You have done few bigger things'.[2] The pre-war founder of the European Movement, Count Coudenhove-Kalergi, acknowledged the prestige gained for the European cause by Churchill's advocacy: 'Now *you* have raised the European question, the Governments can no longer ignore it.'[3] A more cautious approach came from *The Times*, which described his suggestions as 'outrageous propositions', asked if the idea was one 'to which Europe, in its present situation, will submit' and concluded that 'there is little to suggest that the unity so much spoken of, and indeed so much desired, is on the way.'[4]

Eager Europeans read far more into Churchill's speech than the former prime minister had intended. One has only to look back at what Churchill was saying in the 1930s to see the real nature of his view of Europe: 'We see nothing but good and hope in a richer, freer, more contented European commonalty. But we have our own dreams and our own task. We are with Europe but not of it. We are linked but not compromised. We are interested and associated but not absorbed.'

Churchill's position was made even clearer in 1949, in a speech about the newly-founded Council of Europe:

The French Foreign Minister, M. Schuman, declared in the French Parliament this week that 'Without Britain there can be no Europe' … But our friends on the Continent need have no misgivings. Britain is an integral part of Europe, and we mean to play our part.

But Britain cannot be thought of as a single state in isolation. She is the founder and centre of a world-wide Empire and Commonwealth. We shall never do anything to weaken the ties of blood, of sentiment and tradition and common interest which unite … the British family of nations.[5]

The truth was that Churchill was a federalist as far as Europe was concerned but did not necessarily see Britain as forming part of that federation. In Churchill's eyes Britain held an important and unique position, as the Western world faced the Soviet bloc in an emerging Cold War. Churchill believed that there would be three important groupings in the non-Soviet world:

1 an Atlantic alliance linking North America to Europe
2 a united Europe
3 the British Empire and Commonwealth.

Within that tripartite vision of the future Britain was the only nation with a foot in all three camps, thereby acting as a linchpin in the post-war settlement.

The first tangible agreement to be signed between European countries was the Treaty of Dunkirk, signed in March 1947 by Britain and France as a military alliance against a possible resurgence of German aggression. Even as the treaty was signed it as out of date and contrary to current European opinion: the treaty is virtually forgotten today. More in tune with the European movement was an agreement on economic union reached, also in March 1947, between Belgium, the Netherlands and the Grand Duchy of Luxembourg. An informal agreement on economic cooperation between the three had been in force before the war, so the move was not innovative, but it still led the way as a concrete gesture of integration between European states. An economic union of the three countries, known collectively as 'the Benelux countries', came into force in October 1947 and a customs union, with a common external tariff, was established on 1 January 1948.

The next step was for the signatories of the Treaty of Dunkirk and the Benelux countries to reach an agreement. This was the Treaty of Brussels, signed on 17 March 1948. The treaty pledged mutual assistance if any one of the signatories were attacked, but the signatories went beyond this in undertaking to examine the idea of a Western European Union, which would provide a common defence policy and military alliance for the non-Communist countries of Europe. There was a major shift of attitude in the Treaty of Brussels, a movement away from the intrinsically anti-German stance of the Treaty of Dunkirk to a position which acknowledged Soviet encroachment as the main threat to Western Europe.

There is no doubt that 1948 was a major turning-point in the process of European integration. Before 1948, European union was seen as either an aid to post-war re-construction or as a means of preventing the resurgence of an aggressive Germany. After 1948 these views changed in response to what was seen as Soviet expansionism in the Greek Civil War, in the confrontation in Trieste, through the Berlin blockade and by the *coup d'état* against Jan Masaryk in Czechoslovakia. As Russian puppet governments assumed power in more and more Eastern European countries, the integration of Western Europe was seen as a necessary safeguard against this expansion; furthermore, if Western Europe were to combine against the Soviet threat, West Germany, in the front line of East-West confrontation, would have to be included. As the Cold War intensified, the need emerged for some kind of united Europe to be a third world force, interposed between the growing world super-states of the USA and USSR. In that interposition there would be both a defensive and an economic dimension.

The Truman Doctrine

In 1947 recovery in Europe was faltering as countries which had attempted to rebuild their economies too rapidly found it difficult to meet the cost of their imports, creating massive balance of payments crises and deficits in European gold and dollar reserves. Britain, still impoverished by the cost of the war, was doubly affected. There was not only the problem of rebuilding the domestic economy, but Britain was still attempting to play a role as a world power. In 1947, the British government, worried by the cost of its involvement in Greece, by the continuing crisis in Trieste and by the near-revolutionary activities of the French and Italian Communist Parties, appealed to the United States, more or less saying that unless America was ready to see Western Europe fall victim to Soviet Communism, then aid, both military and economic, was urgently required.

The American President, Harry Truman, proved receptive to the appeal and in March 1947 pronounced the Truman Doctrine. This promised, among other things, to give full support and assistance to 'those free peoples who are resisting attempted subjugation by armed minorities or by outside pressures'. The first tangible evidence of support came on 5 June 1947 when the US Secretary of State, George Marshall, proposed a programme of financial aid to Europe in what was known as the Marshall Plan.

It was understood that any aid offered under the Marshall Plan came with a proviso that countries accepting that aid must work together in planning its use and distribution. In July 1947 the representatives of eighteen non-Communist European countries met in Paris to formulate the European Recovery Program and to devise the institutions that would execute it. By April 1948, with the beginning of Marshall Aid, a body known as the Organisation for European Economic Co-operation (OEEC) had been set up to administer the ERP. This was essentially an intergovernmental organisation whose ruling body was a Council, with one representative from each member state. Beneath the Council was a network of committees and agencies whose task it was to prepare reports for decisions by the Council.

The OEEC's tasks were

- to distribute Marshall Aid
- to reduce trade tariffs between member states
- to fix currency exchange rates

- to restore economic recovery in Europe.

The OEEC carried out these tasks very successfully, achieving its main objectives in three years. By the mid-1950s the OEEC had achieved its purpose in transforming the economic situation in Western Europe and Britain. The organisation and co-operation involved in setting up an administering the OEEC as the source of much inspiration to European federalists.

The OEEC could have been a force for European integration, but always intergovernmental in scope and organisation, and with strong links to the USA, it belonged more to the Atlantic Community than to Europe. Ernest Bevin, the British Foreign Secretary, found federalist enthusiasm 'embarrassing' and he opposed any attempts to make the OEEC supranational by turning it into a customs union, claiming that world trade was more important than purely European trade. In 1960 the international nature of the OEEC was recognised by the admission of the United States and Canada to membership and by a change of name, to Organisation for Economic Co-operation and Development (OECD). In 1964 the membership widened beyond the Atlantic Community with the entry of Japan. Since then other members, such as Australia and New Zealand, have joined, making the OECD a fully international body, albeit one with a formative influence on European development.

The other organisation spawned as a result of the Truman Doctrine was intended to be international from the start, even though its headquarters and the focus of its attentions were firmly European. The North Atlantic Treaty Organisation (NATO), was formed for the purpose of collective defence and security in a treaty signed on 4 April 1949. The membership was made up of the five signatories of the Treaty of Brussels together with Denmark, Iceland, Italy, Norway and Portugal in Europe, and the United States and Canada in North America. The purpose of NATO was to defend Western Europe against what was seen as the Soviet threat, but not being restricted to European membership, the place of NATO was always in the Atlantic Community rather than in Western Europe alone.

The Council of Europe

In December 1947 the International Committee of the Movements for European Unity was formed. More simply referred to as the European Movement, the Committee took up an idea which had been put forward in a 1943 speech by Winston Churchill. This was the idea of a Council for Europe; a forum for European nations to discuss their problems and difficulties, which would break down the distrust of centuries through the frank exchange of views and mutual programmes of action.

In May 1948, 663 delegates from sixteen European states attended a Congress of Europe in The Hague. It was this Congress which first issued an explicit call for moves towards the political and economic union of Europe. What was proposed was an open debating assembly guided by a council of ministers. With the initial agreement of ten governments – Belgium, Denmark, France, Great Britain, Ireland, Italy, Luxembourg, Netherlands, Norway and Sweden – the Statute of the Council of Europe was signed in London in May 1949:

The aim of the Council of Europe is to achieve a greater unity between its Members for the purpose of safeguarding and realising the ideals and principles which are their common heritage and facilitating their economic and social progress.

This aim shall be pursued through the organs of the Council by discussion of questions of common concern and by agreements and common action in economic, social, cultural, scientific, legal and administrative matters and in the maintenance and further realisation of human rights and fundamental freedoms.[6]

The Council was set up in Strasbourg with an Assembly of 150 members, open to the public, and a guiding committee made up of a Council of Ministers, consisting of Foreign Ministers who met in closed session twice a year. In 1952 the ministers appointed permanent deputies to provide continuity between meetings of the ministers themselves.

The Council of Europe plays an important role in the development of European institutions but it was never central to the integration process. Its structure was always intergovernmental and its decision-making weak, in that decisions were not binding on members. The Assembly is very much a talking-shop with no powers, but it remains useful for airing issues of European importance. With a current membership of twenty-six states it is by far the largest pan-European organisation.

One important product of the Council of Europe was the framing of the European Convention of Human Rights in 1950. Modelled on the United Nations 'Declaration of Human Rights', this convention set out to define those civil and natural freedoms which should belong by right to the citizens of Europe. The Convention was signed by all member states and enforced by the European Court of Human Rights in Strasbourg, to which citizens of all Council of Europe members have the right to appeal, as an independent legal forum superior to the national courts of the member states. The Council of Europe should not be confused with the European Council, which is essentially the major legislative institution of the European Union. In the same way, the European Court of Human Rights in Strasbourg should not be confused with the European Court of Justice in Luxembourg, the latter being concerned with constitutional and institutional matters relating to the European Union.

The position adopted by the British government towards the Council of Europe was equivocal. The Labour government of 1945–51 was too preoccupied with implementing Labour's domestic programme to concern themselves with Europe. As has been said, Ernest Bevin was fiercely anti-federalist and in his policy towards Europe favoured a series of bilateral agreements, like the 1947 Treaty of Dunkirk, in which Britain formalised relations with Europe one country at a time. He responded to a suggestion for strengthening the Council of Europe in a statement splendidly mixing mythologies: 'open that Pandora's Box and you'll find it full of Trojan Horses'. The Conservative Opposition in Britain was highly critical of Labour's attitude to Europe but government policy remained one of limited co-operation with Europe. In summary, Britain's aims at this time were to draw Europe into a wider Atlantic Community, as in NATO, and keep organisations like the Council of Europe purely intergovernmental and to reject any moves towards supranationalism.

The Schuman Declaration and the Monnet Plan

The OEEC and the Council of Europe were moves towards greater European co-operation but both stopped short of the integration that was thought desirable by the European Movement. Jean Monnet, the most prominent supporter of the Movement and at that time Director of the French Reconstruction Plan, summed up the position in 1949: 'A start would have to be made by doing something both more practical and more ambitious. National sovereignty would have to be tackled more boldly and on a narrower front'.[7] His plan of action was based on a 'sectoral strategy', by which the federalists would tackle one economic sector at a time, until the various sectors meshed together into an integrated whole. The first sector to be tackled was heavy industry, and rationalised economic recovery in France and Germany by the formation of a common market in basic industrial materials: specifically in the creation of a European Coal and Steel Community. In explicit terms this was an economic agreement in the interests of member countries, but Monnet made it clear throughout that economic integration was merely the 'narrower front' he had spoken of and that the implicit purpose was ultimately to be political integration.

Monnet's ideas were taken up by another Euro-enthusiast, Robert Schuman, French Foreign Minister since 1948. On 9 May 1950, Schuman announced the plan for a Coal and Steel Community in what is known as the Schuman Declaration: 'The pooling of coal and steel production will immediate provide ... common bases for economic development as a first step in the federation of Europe ... The solidarity thus achieved will make it plain that any war between France and Germany becomes not only unthinkable but naturally impossible'. At that point the proposed community consisted only of France and West Germany, but Schuman made it clear that any other country was welcome, although France and Germany would go ahead whether or not anyone else cared to join them. Both he and Monnet also made it abundantly clear that the economic benefits of the community were only marginal to the main purpose of the agreement, that purpose being the first stage of political union.

It was possibly because of this blatantly supranational objective that Britain so decisively rejected the ECSC when an invitation to join the negotiations was extended in 1950. But there were also practical reasons for the Labour government's rejection of the proposal. In 1950 nationalisation of the British coal and steel industries had only just been completed. The public ownership of the coal and steel industries had been the most important plank of Labour Party policy since the party's foundation: a Labour government which had finally brought that policy to fruition was not going to give up what it had gained by handing over these two key industries to international regulation.

The Treaty of Paris establishing the ECSC was signed in April 1951 by the representatives of six countries – France, West Germany, the Benelux countries and Italy. The Community set up its headquarters in Luxembourg and Jean Monnet was appointed its first President.

- The principal body of the ECSC was the High Authority, a committee of nine experts appointed by the member countries, with at least one representative from each of those countries. This, the model for the Commission of the EU, was the first attempt at a truly supranational institution; members of the High Authority were encouraged to think of themselves as 'European' rather than national, an to be 'completely independent in the performance of their duties'.
- To counter-balance the High Authority there was the Council of Ministers, with one minister representing each member country. The Council of Ministers was intergovernmental, in contrast to the supranational nature of the High Authority. The Council was backed particularly by the Benelux countries who feared a Franco–German domination of the Authority. Over the years the functionalist wishes of the national governments not to lose too much control over their own coal and

steel industries strengthened the intergovernmental Council of Ministers at the expense of the supranational High Authority.

- The ECSC had a Consultative Assembly, appointed rather than elected, with members chosen by the national parliaments. The Assembly had few powers beyond the right to censure the High Authority, and was largely an advisory body.
- There was also a Court of Justice, made up of seven independent judges, to sort out disputes between member states or community institutions.

Both Assembly and Court of Justice became institutions of the EEC and Euratom in 1957.

The European Defence Community

The inclusion of West Germany in the European Coal and Steel Community was indicative of the extent to which Germany had recovered from the war and was achieving parity with other countries, signalling the readiness of Germany to take part in the European process. There was one area in particular which West Germany wished to enter as an equal, and this was the field of defence. As the realities of the Cold War sank in, so did the realisation that, with the internal division of Germany into East and West, West Germany was in the front line of any East–West confrontation. It was only natural therefore that West Germany would wish to play a part in defending its own territory. The United States was also keen to see European countries, including West Germany, play a fuller part in defending themselves.

For many Europeans, particularly the French, the subject of German rearmament was an emotive and controversial issue. One of the main spurs towards European integration in the immediate post-war period was a determination that Germany must never again threaten and dominate Europe. Nevertheless, there was a general recognition that German rearmament would ultimately be inevitable and there was a search for a formula which would allow

West Germany to rearm within fairly strict constraints.

The person who finally came up with the necessary mechanism was the French Prime Minister René Pleven, drawing on a speech Winston Churchill made in Strasbourg in August 1950. Churchill's speech was reported, somewhat cynically, by the English MP Bob Boothby, who said that Churchill had 'proposed the creation of a United European Army under a single Minister of Defence. I think he felt that he himself might be that Minister of Defence'.[8] In October 1950 Pleven proposed a European Defence Community, which would control a European Army to which any one country's contribution would be restricted to just one battalion, so that no single country could dominate an army under united European control. Within that framework of shared responsibility West Germany's rearmament would be acceptable to European public opinion. When the Conservatives under Churchill won the election in 1951 there was hope that, with it having been his idea in the first place, Britain would be an active participant in this European Army. Indeed, in November 1951 the Home Secretary, Robert Maxwell-Fyffe, told the Council of Europe that the UK accepted the concept of an EDC, albeit with re-negotiation. However, even as he was making this speech, the Foreign Secretary, Anthony Eden, was saying in Rome that Britain would not join the EDC 'on any terms whatsoever'. Nevertheless, by the end of 1951, the six countries of the ECSC had agreed to set up a Defence Community with much the same structure as the ECSC – it would have a Commission, Council of Ministers, Assembly and Court of Justice. In May 1952 the occupying powers signed the German Contractual Convention with the West German government, restoring German sovereignty in all areas bar that of defence. In the same month Germany, with the five other ECSC members, signed a draft European Defence Community Treaty in Paris.

The EDC did not progress beyond that first draft agreement because of remaining doubts about rearming Germany and unease about Britain's failure to participate. The Gaullists in France were bitterly opposed to any loss of control over France's own armed forces, claiming that the EDC was part of an American plot to make Europe totally dependent on the United States. In August 1954 the treaty failed to be ratified by the French National Assembly.

In October 1954, full sovereignty was restored to West Germany, permitting re-armament and opening the way to NATO membership. In order to replace the failed EDC, and at the suggestion of Anthony Eden, the UK, France and Benelux countries resurrected the Treaty of Brussels, admitting Italy and West Germany to the terms of the treaty and forming the Western European Union. The WEU had the Council of Europe as its Assembly and NATO as its defence framework. At the time it seemed a major step in the process of European integration but, on the whole, the WEU has had little importance. Or, rather, not until the late 1980s, when it was joined by Spain and Portugal and became the voice of European Defence Policy in areas where NATO could not be involved. The WEU, for example, was used to formulate the European strategy *vis-à-vis* the Persian Gulf during the Iran–Iraq War, since NATO could not have a role outside the European theatre. In 1994, former Soviet bloc countries such as Poland and Hungary, seeking to join some military alliance in the face of resurgent Russian nationalism, and refused full NATO membership, were offered WEU membership as a compromise solution. The Maastricht Treaty on European Union envisaged a growing role for the EU in determining policy on defence and foreign affairs and within that role the WEU came to be seen as the military arm of the European Union.

The Treaty of Rome

The failure of the EDC taught the federalists that it was unwise to press for integration on every issue, particularly in such a politically sensitive area as defence. It was better to return to the sectoral strategy of Monnet and Schuman, which proposed that the best way towards political union would be through a lengthy process of economic integration. In 1955, therefore, the Benelux countries suggested to their ECSC partners that they might well explore the possibility of extending the sort of economic co-operation that had created the Benelux Customs Union in 1948.

The Messina Conference, bringing together the foreign ministers of the six ECSC members, was convened in June 1955. It was
this conference that finally put into words just what it was that
Monnet, Schuman and their fellow-federalists had been aiming
for, in the communiqué known as the Messina Resolution:

The governments of Belgium, France, the Federal Republic of Germany,
Italy, Luxembourg and the Netherlands consider that the moment has
arrived to initiate a new phase on the path of constructing Europe. They
believe that this has to be done principally in the economic sphere and
regard it as necessary to continue the creation of a united Europe through
an expansion of joint institutions, the gradual fusion of national
economies, the creation of a common market, and the gradual co-ordination of social policies. Such a policy seems to them indispensable if
Europe is to maintain her position in the world, regain her influence, and
achieve a steady increase in the living standards of her population.[9]

On the basis of this resolution, a working-party committee was
set up, chaired by the Belgian, Paul-Henri Spaak. Other countries
besides the six became involved in the talks, including Britain,
but they withdrew when they found that the intentions of the
main participants went beyond a mere common market. But, as
Spaak himself said to the Council of Europe in 1964, 'Those who
drew up the Treaty of Rome ... thought of it as a stage on the
way to political union'. The project conceived at Messina was
always going to be more than a Common Market, even though
that was the label best understood by the public. The Spaak
Committee reported back to the foreign ministers in April 1956
and they in their turn began deep and far-ranging negotiations to
put the committee's ideas into practice.

Britain took no part in the Messina deliberations. Towards the
end of 1956, the new Prime Minister, Harold Macmillan, made it
clear that Britain was still primarily concerned with Commonwealth trade links. At a NATO Council meeting in December
1956 the Foreign Secretary, Selwyn Lloyd, made what might be
called a functionalist counter-proposal in what was known as the
'Grand Design'. Under this proposal there would be a rationali-

sation of the various European institutions that had emerged; the
two main proposals were:

- A single European assembly to oversee all institutions
- A Free Trade Area to cover the whole of Western Europe.

The proposals were too vague to be seriously discussed,
although the suggestion hung around for some years until it was
finally killed off at a meeting between Chancellor Adenauer of
West Germany and President de Gaulle of France in 1958.
Britain, together with Portugal, Norway, Sweden, Denmark, Austria and Switzerland, did build on Lloyd's suggestion to create the
European Free Trade Area (EFTA) in November 1959. This was
simply a low-tariff common market with no political or integrationist implications.

The Messina negotiations were complicated by special national
interests, such as French requirements for an agricultural policy,
but determination on the part of the negotiators produced the
necessary compromises and achieved success within a year. The
negotiations resulted in two treaties, which were placed before the
six prime ministers at a meeting in Paris during February 1957.
The two treaties, having received approval in Paris, went on to
be signed in Rome on 25 March 1957. The first, and most important, Treaty of Rome established the European Economic Community (EEC) – sometimes known as the Common Market –
while the second Treaty of Rome set up the European Atomic
Energy Community (Euratom). Only in France and Italy did the
ratification of the treaties meet any parliamentary opposition,
largely from the Communist Party. Once ratified by all members
the Treaties of Rome came into force on 1 January 1958.

The institutions of the EEC were essentially those created for
the ECSC.

- In the case of the Assembly and Court of Justice they were
  exactly that – the institutions of the ECSC which now, in
  addition, became the Assembly and Court of the EEC and
  Euratom.
- The executive of the EEC was the Commission, which had

two commissioners each for France, Italy and West Germany, one commissioner each for the Benelux countries.

- The Council of Ministers formed the legislature of the EEC and was normally made up of the six foreign ministers, although these could be replaced by the relevant ministers when any specific topic, such as agriculture, trade, etc., was discussed.
- The Assembly was not elected, the members being nominated, usually from the membership of the national parliaments. The Assembly had very little power, bar a certain degree of budgetary control. The first person to be elected President of the European Assembly was Robert Schuman.

EEC – the first phase

The EEC on its foundation set itself four main targets, designated as the first phase in the process of integration, and agreed that these targets would be achieved by 1970. The targets were:

1 The removal of all internal tariffs and restrictions on trade, so as to form a common market.
2 The creation of a Common External Tariff, so that imports from outside the Community pay the same tariff of duty, no matter which was the importing country.
3 Competition legislation to outlaw practices which presented free competition between member states.
4 Free movement of goods, persons, capital and services.

All four targets were achieved by 1 June 1968, nearly two years ahead of schedule. In the mean time the three communities established by the Treaties of Rome and Paris – the EEC, the ECSC and Euratom – began to come together. In April 1965 the members signed what is known as 'the Merger Treaty', which established a single Commission and a single Council for all three communities (they already shared a common Assembly and Court of Justice). The Merger Treaty took effect in June 1967, when the amalgamation of the three communities became known as the European Community (EC).

The early 1960s, however, were a difficult period in the politics of the EEC, thanks to the rise to power in France of Charles de Gaulle, who sought to establish a French hegemony over the institutions of the Communities. The French President exploited to the full the intergovernmental nature of the Council of Ministers, where a unanimous vote of all six members was required for approval of new structural measures, thus giving a single adverse vote the power of a veto. De Gaulle repeatedly used that veto to force through measures that were entirely in the interests of France and to block any measure that he felt was against those interests, including a complete block on the enlargement of the Community. De Gaulle's most notable use of the veto was twice to refuse Britain entry into the EEC.

Britain – the first application

Britain, together with Austria, Denmark, Norway, Portugal, Sweden and Switzerland, signed the agreement setting up the European Free Trade Area in Stockholm during November 1959, the agreement coming into force in April 1960. Europe was thereby divided into two rival trading camps or, to use the language of the press at the time, Europe was 'at sixes and sevens'. Britain claimed to admire the 'economic and commercial freedom' of EFTA as against the 'political strait-jacket' of the EEC. And yet, within a year, Macmillan was to change his mind and apply for British membership of the EEC.

Many factors changed the attitude of the British government; the most important are listed below:

1 The Suez crisis in 1956 led to a realisation that the days of Britain as an imperial world power were over. At the time the newspapers and others were accustomed to write as though Britain had suffered a crisis of identity and 'needed to find a new world role'. For many people the feeling was that that role might well be within Europe.
2 There was also a realisation that while the late 1950s and early 1960s were boom years in Britain, growth was even healthier

elsewhere. There was a sense of failure in the UK economy when, in comparison, EEC members had almost doubled their standard of living over a ten-year period.

3   British politicians watched the EEC creating a series of polit-
    ical and economic institutions, which could be used for the
    future direction of the Community, while building a very
    secure boundary fence against outsiders. There was a feeling
    that one day it would become necessary to join the European
    Community and, when that day came, Britain would have to
    face a Europe that had been formed without any British input
    whatsoever.

4   Britain had assumed that the so-called 'special relationship'
    between the UK and USA would ensure that, of the rival
    trade areas in Europe, the Americans would favour EFTA
    with its British connections. In 1961 President Kennedy pri-
    vately informed Macmillan that he felt confused and annoyed
    by Europe's being 'at sixes and sevens', and that if they did
    not sort themselves out, the US would be forced to choose
    between them; if that happened, the USA would choose the
    more important EEC.

In July 1961 Prime Minister Macmillan announced that Britain had applied for membership of the EEC. Three other countries applied at the same time: the Republic of Ireland, because the Irish currency was then inextricably linked with sterling; and Norway and Denmark because of their dependence on British trade, especially Denmark, for whom Britain was the principal market for its bacon and diary products. In November 1961 Edward Heath was appointed as negotiator and talks on British entry began in earnest.

The British decision was widely welcomed. For the smaller countries of the EEC Britain was seen as a useful counterweight to what was becoming the overweening influence of a Franco–German axis; as well as being an agent of democracy that might temper the potentially authoritarian Council and Commis-sion. The United States, in the person of President Kennedy, saw an enlarged and strengthened Europe as one better able to look after itself without American assistance.

The sticking point in the British negotiating position was the protection of trade with the Commonwealth and former Empire. There were those who saw this as a British plot aimed at wrecking the new agricultural policy of the EEC and returning to a much looser Free Trade Area, rather than the more integrationist Common Market. This was certainly the publicly expressed view of de Gaulle, who claimed to believe that Britain only applied to join the Community in order to wreck it. In his memoirs, published in 1970, de Gaulle said 'Having failed, from the outside, to prevent the birth of the Community, they [the British] now plan to paralyse it from within'.[10]

Ironically, if there were anyone intent on wrecking the Community from within for selfishly national reasons, it was probably de Gaulle himself. De Gaulle's fear was that Britain would be too powerful a partner for him to control. There were also the smaller European nations, like Denmark and Ireland, who would follow Britain into Europe: de Gaulle could manipulate a Community of six nations, he was less sure of controlling nine. Above all else, however, there was the French President's distrust of all things American: to him Britain was a Trojan Horse, a mere pawn in the USA's plan to gain control of European affairs.

In December 1962 de Gaulle told Macmillan that he intended to veto Britain's application unless Britain broke with the American alliance. Instead Macmillan took the opposite path: he flew to a meeting with Kennedy in the Bahamas and, in the Nassau Agreement, secured an increased stake for Britain in NATO's nuclear programme by America's offer of the Polaris submarine-based missile. Macmillan returned from Nassau in triumph, having renewed the 'special relationship', well able to shrug off the press conference of 14 January 1963 at which de Gaulle formally confirmed his veto.

The Common Agricultural Policy

Britain's rejection by the French President as done without consultation with his European partners and, naturally enough, they

were angered and insulted by de Gaulle's attitude. It was the
beginning of considerable turmoil in the European Community,
as French policies undid all the work that had gone into integration within a supranational framework. The main objective of
French policy was the realisation of a Common Agricultural
Policy (CAP). The principles underlying the CAP were laid down
in 1960:

1   Free trade within the Community in all agricultural products
2   Common guaranteed prices for most commodities
3   Protection by heavy levies on all imported agricultural prod-
    ucts
4   Purchase by the Community of all commodity surpluses.

It was points 2 and 4 in combination that led to the CAP
coming to stand for all that was wrong with the Community. The
fact that the Community would pay guaranteed prices, and would
itself buy in any surplus produce that the farmers could not sell,
would not have mattered if the Community had also laid down
limits on production. But the French held out for there to be no
such limits. It was an open invitation for farmers to make money
by producing far more than could be sold on the open market, in
the certain knowledge that the Community would buy any that
was left over, at the full market rate. It is this which produced
the great surplus stores of produce, known as the 'butter moun-
tain', the 'wine lake' and so on. It also led to two-thirds of the
Community budget being spent on the CAP, and in the 1980s, it
almost resulted in bankruptcy.

The smaller countries within the Community tried to argue the
case over the CAP, but the policy was overwhelmingly favourable
to French farmers and it had the full and unequivocal support of
de Gaulle. Whenever negotiations became bogged down he
instructed the French ministers to walk out of Council meetings
until they got what they wanted. Since French withdrawal
affected other policies as well as the CAP this was something that
had to be avoided. In the light of these threats, the CAP was
agreed in January 1962.

De Gaulle's tactics in forcing through the CAP and his veto on

British membership alienated other members of the EEC; they did not like the way he did things without consulting his supposed partners. Moreover, they found it hypocritical that he should have condemned Britain as 'not being truly European' and then proved himself to be more anti-federal than anyone. He was committed to reducing the influence of all supranational institutions within the Community and stated forcefully that he did no want an integrated Europe, but rather a loose association of nation states, an *'Europe des Patries'*. The General's position had much in common with that later adopted by Mrs Thatcher.

In 1965 France proposed to sell its surplus wheat directly to Russia and without reference to the terms of the CAP. France was reprimanded by the Commission for this breach and the then President of the Commission, Hallstein, proposed that the agricultural budget should be taken out of the hands of the Council of Ministers and given to the joint control of the Commission and European Parliament. The threat of transferring powers from the intergovernmental Council to the supranational Commission and Parliament was anathema to de Gaulle. He announced his 'policy of the empty chair', by which France withdrew from the Council of Ministers. Since the constitution of the Community demanded unanimous decisions by all six Council members, French withdrawal effectively closed Europe down. As Aidan Crawley said, 'Europe had come to a full stop'.[11]

The deadlock lasted from July 1965 to January 1966. In the Luxembourg Compromise that ended the dispute France was forced to recognise the importance of corporate decisions. But the same compromise also gave member states the right to exercise the veto if national interests were threatened by restoring the need for unanimity in many votes of the Council of Ministers. In all, the de Gaulle years strengthened the hands of the functionalists against the federalists and provided a substantial transfer of power from supranational to intergovernmental institutions.

Britain – the second application

In Britain a Labour government replaced the Conservatives in the election of 1964. Traditionally the Labour Party was hostile, or at best disinterested, in Europe. The Attlee government, advised by Bevin, had avoided any European commitment that would have included Britain in the process of integration. Under Gaitskell, Attlee's successor and leader of the party until his death in 1963, the opinion had been expressed that for a Labour government to join Europe would be like 'turning one's back on a thousand years of history'. However, while the grassroots of the party remained hostile, the leadership and parliamentary party began to change their minds during the period between 1964 and 1967. Partly this was a result of the so-called 'realities of office', but there were certain major factors affecting Prime Minister Harold Wilson's judgement:

1   As more and more former colonies gained their independence they went their own way economically; trade with the Commonwealth was rapidly declining.
2   The economies of Europe, especially West Germany, were booming, while Britain's growth was weak. Trade between Britain and the European Community was at a near standstill because of Britain's exclusion from the internal market.
3   The special relationship with the United States was somewhat damaged by America's involvement in Vietnam.
4   Harold Wilson had won two elections on slogans involving a 'technological revolution'. But research and development work in major technological industries such as aerospace was so expensive that it needed international joint funding. Projects such as Concorde were undertaken in association with the French. For closer co-operation it helped if all countries in a technological link-up were fellow-members of the Community.

In 1967 the Wilson government re-opened negotiations for Community membership. On this occasion de Gaulle acted after just five months. As before, he did not consult his partners in the Community, nor did he go through the correct channels. He simply held a press conference at which he announced '... it would be impossible to bring the Great Britain of today into the

Common Market as it stands'. It was not a total rejection as it had been in 1963. The other five members of the Community let their displeasure at de Gaulle's actions be known and it was made clear to Britain (and to Denmark, Ireland and Norway) that their application would be left in place, with the implicit understanding that the application could not proceed while de Gaulle remained in power. And the days of the General were numbered: shaken by the disturbances of May 1968, de Gaulle resigned in 1969. In 1970 the new French President, Georges Pompidou, met the newly-elected Prime Minister, Edward Heath, and a rather broad hint was dropped that France would no longer oppose British membership.

Edward Heath was probably the only British prime minister who truly believed in the European ideal. Under his guidance and his chosen negotiator, Geoffrey Rippon, the negotiations went smoothly and remarkably quickly. Britain was able to sign the Treaty of Accession in Brussels on 1 January 1972. Britain's fellow-applicants were also accepted, but all three announced that they would consult the people by holding referendums on the subject. In Ireland, voting in May 1972, 82 per cent of those voting voted 'yes'; in Denmark, voting in October 1972, 63 per cent in favour. In Norway, however, there was a bitter political argument about the terms for membership and in the referendum in September 1972, 46 per cent voted 'yes', against 54 per cent who voted 'no'. Norway withdrew from membership. The situation was repeated almost exactly in November 1994 when all arrangements for membership having been made, Norwegians voted in their referendum and again rejected membership, this time by 52 to 48 per cent.

Accession and after

There could hardly have been a worse time for Britain to join the European Community. The oil crisis of 1973 quadrupled the price of oil, producing a world recession which seriously slowed down economic growth in Europe. Britain had joined the EC to profit from the massive economic growth experienced by EC members during the 1960s, only to find that there was no growth to share because the oil crisis had made the European economies as flat as anywhere else. Without the cushion of economic growth the less attractive aspects of membership, such as the CAP, were all too evident and arguments in favour of British membership were that much harder to sustain. Europe had entered a period in which the integration process was slowing down, in a typical bureaucratic muddle that has been nicknamed 'Eurosclerosis'.

In 1974 Labour very narrowly defeated the Conservatives in the two elections of that year. Since their rejection by de Gaulle in 1967 Labour had reverted to declaring their all-out opposition to Europe, and the 1974 elections were fought by Labour with a more or less explicit commitment to withdraw from the EC. Once elected, however, Wilson found that it would be very difficult to break with Europe, and once again faced with the 'realities of office', he did not want to do so. In order to avoid too blatant a volte-face, Wilson announced that Labour was not opposed to Europe on principle, but only to the unsatisfactory terms obtained by Ted Heath. Wilson proposed that the terms should be re-negotiated and that the government would then do what Heath should have done in 1972: he revised terms would be put to the electorate in a referendum. The government would accept the verdict of the people, whatever it might be.

Negotiations were in the hands of Wilson's deputy, James Callaghan, who, in due course, came back from Brussels with what were claimed to be vastly improved terms, although to the objective eye the changes were merely cosmetic. The referendum was held in June 1975, despite what were held to be dubious manoeuvres, which will be discussed later, it produced a positive result for the government. In a low turn-out of only 64 per cent, 66 per cent voted in favour of Britain's membership of the EC.

Summary – developments up to 1979

The late 1970s saw something approaching stagnation as far as moves towards European integration were concerned. Some time was taken up with the British re-negotiation and there were the first tentative moves to create a European Monetary System. It was a time of serious criticism of some EC mechanisms, particularly the faults of the Common Agricultural Policy and the failure to create a Common Fisheries Policy. Yet the twentieth anniversary of the Treaty of Rome could be marked with a sense of solid achievement. Out of the vague aspirations towards the European Idea that marked the immediate post-war period sufficient strands had emerged to show that European co-operation and integration had become a permanent feature of international relations. Initiatives such as NATO and the OEEC ensured that at least in the fields of defence and the economy, some surrender of national sovereignty to ensure mutual benefits was seen as both necessary and possible. The Council of Europe, with its important European Convention on Human Rights, also required states to surrender some aspects of sovereignty for a greater good.

Thanks to the sectoral strategy developed by Monnet and Schuman the growth of the European Community had been an evolutionary rather than a revolutionary process. The softly-softly approach to integration and enlargement avoided the disruption of major change and created a Community strong enough to survive such strains as the position adopted by France under de Gaulle. In the 1970s, the EC emerged as 'a geographically significant, economically powerful and politically durable unit.'[12]

The nature of the Community was changing, as was inevitable with enlargement. In 1973 the Six had become Nine with the addition of the UK, Ireland and Denmark. With the late 1970s came the prospect of increasing to twelve, with the applications of first Greece and then Spain and Portugal. Each enlargement altered the balance between federalists and functionalists, with, generally speaking, the larger states – particularly France and Great Britain – in favour of intergovernmental, functionalist perspectives, while the smaller states, such as the Benelux countries, tended to look more favourably on the supranational, federalist viewpoint.

The stance adopted by the United Kingdom in this developmental period was anomalous and often contradictory. Despite the original impetus given to European integration by Churchill's

Zurich speech and the commitment of a few enthusiasts such as
Edward Heath, the British proved to be very reluctant Europeans.
The implications of that would be seen in full after 1979.

Notes

1 Churchill's Zurich speech, quoted in M. Gilbert, *Never Despair –
Winston S. Churchill 1945–1965*, Heinemann, London 1988, pp. 265–6.

2 Letter from Leo Amery to Churchill, quoted in Gilbert, p. 267.

3 Letter from Coudenhove-Kalergi to Churchill, quoted in Gilbert,
p. 267.

4 Leader in *The Times*, 20 September 1946, quoted in Gilbert, p.
266.

5 Speech of 28 November 1949, quoted in Gilbert, p. 496.

6 Article 1 of the Statute of the Council of Europe, London 1949.

7 J. Monnet, *Memoirs*, Collins, London 1978.

8 Boothby quoted in A. Thompson, *The Day before Yesterday*,
Granada, London 1971, p. 88.

9 Text of the Messina Resolution, quoted in Neill Nugent, *The Government and Politics of the European Community*, Macmillan, London
1991.

10 General C. de Gaulle, *Memoirs d'Espoir*, vol. 1: *Le renouveau,
1958–62*, Plon, Paris 1970.

11 A. Crawley, *De Gaulle*, Collins, London 1969, p. 443.

12 G. N. Minshull, *The New Europe – Into the 1990s*, 4th edn.,
Hodder & Stoughton, London 1990.

The road to Maastricht and beyond

Three events made 1979 a significant landmark in the development of the European Union:

1 The European Monetary System (EMS) came into operation, as negotiated over the previous year by Helmut Schmidt of Germany and Valéry Giscard-d'Estaing of France, as a first step in the process leading towards monetary union, an aspiration of the EC since its foundation.
2 There were the first direct elections to the European Parliament, which it was hoped would lead to a democratisation of the Community's institutions, although that hope was not to be fully borne out by events.
3 The British general election of that year produced a Conservative government under Mrs Thatcher, an event of immense consequence, particularly as it affected the stance of both Britain and the Conservative Party towards Europe.

The European Community, as it existed in 1979, was the antithesis of everything advocated by Margaret Thatcher. Strangely enough, the former Labour politician Roy Jenkins, then President of the Commission, at first believed that Mrs Thatcher would be more amenable on the question of Europe than the previous prime minister – Jenkins' former colleague, Jim Callaghan. Like many politicians at that time Jenkins had misread Mrs Thatcher. Although she had declared often enough that she was opposed to compromise and that she would stand by her chosen policies with total commitment, no one really believed her. Everyone had heard politicians claim a stance while campaigning for office, but it was usually a stance that they proved ready to abandon when faced with the reality of office. Mrs Thatcher had been in office for three years before the realisation dawned that she meant exactly what she said:

- she despised committees
- she refused compromise or the consensus view
- she would not do any deal which in any way detracted from her own demands
- her stance in any argument was that she was right and everyone else was wrong.

This was so contrary to the way in which the Community's institutions operated, that Britain's European partners were first shocked, then repelled and ultimately alienated. Mrs Thatcher may have had right on her side and she may have been fairly successful in her aims but there is little doubt that her behaviour in European Council meetings led to Britain's growing isolation in Europe. Long before she adopted her anti-European stance in the late 80s, Mrs Thatcher had created a fundamental change in the relationship between Britain and the European Community. Roy Jenkins summed up Mrs Thatcher's attitude and its effects in describing her stance at her first European Council in Dublin in November 1979:

Towards the end Mrs Thatcher got the discussions bogged down by being too demanding. Her mistake ... arose out of her having only one of the three qualities of a great advocate. She has the nerve and determination to win but she does not have a good understanding of the case against her ... her reiterated cry of 'It's my money. I want it back' strikes an insistently jarring note. She lacks also the third quality ... of not boring the judge and jury ... She only understood four out of the fourteen or so points on the British side and repeated each of them twenty-seven times during the evening.[1]

The British Budgetary Question

The question of Britain's contributions to the European budget arose at the Dublin Council and was to dominate discussions in the Council, often to the neglect of other issues, for five years, to the despair of Jenkins and the Commission. With the Community's fondness for initials, the issue became known as the BBQ, which, according to Jenkins, meant 'the British Budgetary Question', but was more usually referred to as 'the Bloody British Question'. The problem with the budget arose from the fact that Britain, despite the country's economic difficulties, was making very large net contributions to Community funds, quite as much as was being paid by Germany. This was due to the nature of Britain's agriculture, smaller and far more efficient than much of the rest of Europe and about twice as efficient as France. This meant that payments to Britain out of the CAP fund were comparatively low: the efficient farmers of Britain were subsidising the inefficient farmers of France. Under Community rules Britain, who for historic reasons imported far more food from outside the Community than did the others, had to pay a much higher import levy that they did.

Soon after her election Mrs Thatcher instructed an under-secretary at the Treasury, Peter Middleton, to discover the exact size of Britain's contribution to the European budget, and to estimate on that basis just how much Britain ought to be paying. As a result of these investigations, Mrs Thatcher was able to present her first European Council with the exact amount by which she wanted the British budgetary contribution to be reduced – a reduction of £1,000 million. The Community offered a reduction of £350 million, which the Prime Minister rejected out of hand.

It was at this point that Mrs Thatcher shocked both her European colleagues and her own advisers. Repeated demands for what she called 'her money' made it clear that the sum she wanted was not negotiable and she would do no deals. As Christopher Tugendhat, the British Commissioner, reported, she accused other European states of the outright theft of British money.[2] Foreign Office advisers were horrified, because they knew the rules of the European game. Under normal circumstances the negotiations would improve on that £350 million by some deal on oil, or fishing rights, or the price of lamb. However, there was to be no deal and even experienced negotiators were lost in what, for them, was an unprecedented situation. Among Britain's partners there were those who were originally sympathetic but who were subsequently alienated by her behaviour. As Jenkins said, 'on the merits Mrs Thatcher had right broadly on her side although she showed little sense of proportion, some of her favourite arguments were invalid and her tactical sense was as weak as her courage was strong'. Mrs Thatcher continued to demand her money throughout dinner and after. Giscard ignored her; Schmidt pretended that he was asleep and Jørgensen, the Danish Prime Minister, shouted insults. The complete breakdown of the Council was only prevented by postponing a decision on the BBQ until the next year.

That Dublin meeting set the tone for Britain's relationship with Europe as it would be throughout the Thatcher years. Her behaviour was deplored by the other Community members and at one point led the French Prime Minister, Jacques Chirac, to call for Britain's expulsion from the Community. Attitudes towards Mrs Thatcher rubbed off onto Britons in general. Even the Europhile Roy Jenkins found that his colleagues in the Commission were treating him and Christopher Tugendhat as potentially hostile.

Over the winter of 1979–80 the Commission worked for a resolution of the BBQ. The answer they came up with was that Britain should get a rebate on budgetary contributions to the value of one billion ecus (£700 million). Efforts were then made, on the one hand to persuade other members to agree to this, and on the other to persuade Mrs Thatcher to accept what she insisted on regarding as only two-thirds of what was rightfully hers. At the Luxembourg Council, in April 1980, all seemed more promising. Mrs Thatcher was far less strident, Schmidt duly made the agreed offer to Britain and Giscard added that they were willing to increase that rebate to 2,400 million ecus over two years. Everyone confidently expected that this would settle the matter but, at five in the afternoon, after a full day's discussion, she rejected the offer outright. She wanted a permanent agreement, not one for two years, and she wanted her demands paid in full; 'We must look after British interests', she said.[3]

Matters were then left in the hands of the Council of Ministers and the Foreign Office. Mrs Thatcher herself had nothing more to do with the negotiations, which were entrusted to Lord Carrington, supported by Sir Ian Gilmour. The negotiations in Brussels were long and hard, culminating in an eighteen-hour session that continued through the night of 29–30 May 1980. Ironically, the agreement, when it came, was almost identical to that rejected by Mrs Thatcher in Luxembourg. When Carrington and Gilmour took the news to the Prime Minister at Chequers they were shouted at for three and a half hours. Gilmour describes her as 'incandescent' and believes she would have rejected the agreed terms had he not leaked the story to the press, so that she was faced with the *fait accompli* of tabloid headlines praising her 'success' in extracting such good terms from Europe.[4]

Slow progress

It is not quite true that the European Community failed to progress while the British budgetary issue remained unresolved, yet progress in the first half of the 1980s was far more tentative than during the second half of the decade. Some enlargement took place when Greece became the tenth member of the Community on 1 January 1981, while progress continued on applications from Spain and Portugal. The commitment of the EC to the Third World was strengthened by the second Lomé Convention between the EC and fifty-eight African, Caribbean and Pacific (ACP) countries, who were largely former colonies of Britain or France.

Despite the Community's differences with Britain, the other nine proved supportive in 1982 during the Falklands conflict, members of the EC applying economic sanctions and a trade embargo against Argentina. Another area of disagreement between Britain and her partners was settled in 1983 when a

Common Fisheries Policy was agreed, establishing a Community-wide 200-mile zone, inside which members have national priority areas within twelve miles of their own shores. The CFP also acts in the interests of conservation by setting allowable catches that are divided into national quotas.

Other than these developments and the continuing demands by Britain for resolution of the budget issue, the preoccupation of the Community was the desire for a closer union. The European Council meeting in Stuttgart in June 1983 issued a declaration on European Union, and in the following February the European Parliament approved a draft treaty for creating a European Union. Aware that any movement towards union would be preceded by a strengthening of the EEC common market from which they would be disbarred, the countries of the EFTA agreed a free-trade area between themselves and the EC in January 1984. However, while the BBQ continued to hog the Community agenda such moves towards union remained little more than pious hopes.

The major movement towards union in those years was the European Monetary System (EMS), which was working towards a convergence between the economies of the EC members with the ultimate goal of economic and monetary union. The most important element of the EMS was the Exchange Rate Mechanism (ERM), by which EMS members undertook to keep their currencies pegged within fairly narrow bands of fluctuation, with only a limited degree of divergence allowed before intervention to maintain parities was invoked. Britain had been offered membership of the ERM in 1981 but had rejected it, saying only that the UK would join 'when the time was ripe'. The issue of ERM membership remained alive for many years but the arguments surrounding it belong more to the relationship between Europe and the Conservative Party and, as such, will be dealt with more fully in a later chapter.

BBQ – the issue resolved

The immediate problem of Britain's over-payment was resolved by the agreement of May 1980, but the cause of the problem would not go away. The deal agreed in 1980 meant that Britain got a rebate on British contributions to the EC budget, but that did not alter the fact that Britain was paying too much in the first place. What Mrs Thatcher wanted was to change the ground rules so that the problem, and the need for a rebate, no longer existed. 'I am tired of this being described as a British problem, the problems are Europe-wide,' she said to a dinner given for MEPs in Strasbourg. 'I want an agreement but I don't want to paper over the cracks. I want to get rid of the cracks. I want to rebuild the foundations.'[5]

Beginning a new round of negotiations in 1983, Mrs Thatcher was helped by the fact that her two main opponents had changed. The new West German Chancellor, Helmut Kohl, and the new French President, François Mitterand, did not have the skill, experience or sense of close partnership that typified the Schmidt–Giscard axis of 1979–81. Even so, it was a long process, dominating no fewer than four European Council meetings in a twelve-month period. A complication was that talks on the BBQ were linked with talks to resolve the growing demands of the CAP and a potential budget deficit for the EEC, which virtually threatened the Community with bankruptcy. Britain made it clear that no agreement on any other issue such as the CAP would be allowed until the BBQ had been settled to Britain's satisfaction.

At Stuttgart, in June 1983, the European Council passed a vague resolution on European Union but nothing else. At Athens in December there was not even a final communiqué, the first time that this had happened. In March 1984, at a European Council meeting held in Brussels, despite the presidency being held by France, there was hope of an agreed settlement, because French and British officials working together had put together a workable formula that would both reduce the British contribution and increase funds for the Community. In the event, the Germans put forward an impossible alternative, the Irish walked out, and Mrs Thatcher resumed her hectoring stance. The Council ended without agreement and in mutual recriminations. Britain threatened to withhold all payments from the Community until the problem was resolved. Chirac, the French Prime Minister, wanted the EC to expel Britain. This was unlikely to happen but people were beginning to talk about a 'two-speed' Europe, in which those countries prepared to progress would go ahead without those like Britain who were lagging behind.

The Fontainebleau Summit of June 1984 began as though it would also fail but, as has often been the case in crisis meetings of the Council, there was an eleventh-hour agreement. Under this agreement Britain would receive a permanent rebate worth 66 per cent of the difference between what Britain paid into the Community and the amount Britain got back from the Community. The same agreement increased Community resources by raising the levy on VAT from 1 per cent to 1.4 per cent. The matter was finally settled after five years and Britain could be said to have 'won', but it was at some quite considerable cost. The insistent demands made by Mrs Thatcher and her domineering and insulting style in dealing with her supposed partners had at times turned Britain into an outsider, almost a pariah, in European circles.

Reform of the CAP

The CAP had been recognised as a potential problem for some time, but by the mid-1980s, the problem had become a crisis. The problems of over-production and the subsidies paid to small and inefficient peasant farmers were made more extreme by the accession of Mediterranean countries – Greece in 1981, Spain and Portugal at the start of 1986. There was also the fact that more efficient, scientific farming, especially in the use of chemical fertilisers, was creating environmental difficulties. The Common Agricultural Policy was in need of reform for reasons quite separate from the need of Britain not to pay a disproportionate amount towards its support. By the time Spain and Portugal joined the Community in January 1986, the CAP would be costing the EC more than 70 per cent of its total budget, while the figures projected into the future were predicting bankruptcy within a decade.

The first proposals for reform came in 1983 from Dalsager, the Agriculture Commissioner. But it was his successor, Andriessen, who set things in motion in 1985 with a Commission Green Paper, *Perspectives for the Common Agricultural Policy*. The main thrust of this initiative was recognition that limits would have to be placed on production, together with an understanding that farmers had a part to play in the conservation of the environment and rural resources. In December 1986 the Council of Agriculture Ministers, guided by the Commissions documents and influenced by Britain's presidency of the Community, produced a package of measures that included some production quota limits, amounting to something in the region of a 6 per cent cut in milk production, and also some cuts in guaranteed prices, as with a 13 per cent cut in the guaranteed price of beef.

The agricultural negotiations became involved with the movement towards the Single Market. The reforms suggested in 1986 were discussed at both the European Councils of 1987, but it was a specially convened summit in March 1988 in Brussels which finally approved a five-year package for reform, the terms of which had been agreed in February. The main provision of this 1988 agreement was to limit farm expenditure to 74 per cent of the EC's growth in gross domestic product (GDP). Production was to be cut by as much as 15 per cent, with farmers compensated for 'set-aside' land. These reforms were again restructured in 1992–93 by the new Commissioner, Ray MacSharry of Ireland, in order to help with negotiations on the Uruguay round of the GATT talks. The reforms, together with the MacSharry proposals, were based on compensatory payments paid on land withdrawn from agricultural use, with extra payments for converting the set-aside land to other uses, such as leisure activities. The obvious aim was to reduce the massive food surpluses that were being produced, but a readier guide to the degree of success comes from the reduction in the amount of money spent on CAP subsidies out of the Community budget. In 1988 more than 66 per cent of Community expenditure was being spent on the CAP, but this had been reduced to 55 per cent by 1992, while expenditure on the CAP in 1993 was reputed to be down to 49.5 per cent.[6]

The Single European Act

'In the course of the eighties the EC emerged from a period of stagnation into one of dynamism. This relaunching of Europe was largely based on the attempt to complete the Single Internal Market.'[7] Negotiations over the British budget and reform of the CAP had been the clearing away of dead wood, and the Community was now ready to move on to complete what had been an aim since the signing of the Treaty of Rome – the creation of a single internal market within the Community. Statements in favour of the idea had been issued by the Council, Commission or European Parliament at regular intervals since 1970, but after 1983, with CAP reform under way, progress towards the Single Market was rapid, particularly after 1985 when Jacques Delors became President of the Commission.

The Commission's White Paper on the single European Market was presented to the Council of Ministers in June 1985 by the British Commissioner, Lord Cockfield. A Single European Act, proposing the creation of a single market by the end of 1992, was drawn up at the December European Council in Luxembourg. During the following year the proposed act was ratified by the various national parliaments, the British Act being steered through Westminster, quite without difficulty, by Sir Geoffrey Howe, who had been in charge of the European Communities Accession Act of 1972. The Single European Act (SEA) came into force in July 1987, with the single market due to become operative as of 1 January 1993.

The Single Market is essentially based on what are known as the 'four freedoms' – the freedom of movement for goods, people, capital and services. The aspects which most affected the general public were relaxations on duty-free purchases, a reduction in administrative costs for the movement of goods and minimal passport controls. But the SEA was concerned with more than just the single market. In what was essentially a tidying-up operation, the SEA produced fundamental changes in the constitution and operation of the Community and represented the most far-reaching move towards integration since 1957.

The SEA included many changes to the European Parliament, increasing its role in the legislative process and requiring EP assent for such things as enlargement of the Community. It also increased the legislative and decision-making powers of the Council of Ministers, extending the ability of the Council to make decisions by a qualified majority vote. For the first time since they began in 1975, the twice-yearly European Council summit meetings were given legal recognition. All these measures, as yet, were bureaucratic in nature because they were not incorporated by Treaty, and it was for that purpose that the Community moved on to consider a Treaty for European Union.

One can only assume that Mrs Thatcher accepted the Single European Act so readily because she was so delighted to be within reach of her two main aims in Europe – the reform of the CAP and the formation of a single internal market – that she ignored the supranational nature of that to which she was agreeing. Writing about Britain's acceptance of the SEA, Michael Heseltine was to say that Mrs Thatcher was responsible for 'the biggest transfer of sovereignty undertaken in any period of our history'.[8] In 1991 Lady Thatcher (as she had become) was to claim that she did not understand the SEA when she signed it, and that she would not have signed it if she had understood.

The Delors Presidency and the Bruges Speech

In 1985, a French Socialist and ardent European, Jacques Delors, became President of the Commission, a post which he was to hold for a record ten years. It was an appointment that was to have a considerable effect, not only on the speed with which the EC began to move towards union, but on the relationship with and attitude to Europe of the British political parties. There are many who would criticise Delors because, as Nugent says, he has

the requirement of a forceful personality, but he has also displayed traits and acted in ways which, many observers have suggested, have had the effect of undermining the team spirit of his Commission: he has indicated clear policy preferences and interests of his own; he has made important policy pronouncements before fully consulting with his colleagues in the Commission; and he has sometimes appeared to give more weight to personal advisers than to Commissioners.[9]

A committed social democrat, Delors was dedicated to the social and welfare dimension in the Community and was to produce the Community Charter of the Fundamental Social Rights of Workers, or the Social Charter, in 1989. Early in his presidency Delors visited Britain as a guest of the TUC and addressed the Labour Party at a time when, under Neil Kinnock, it was moderating its policy. The Labour Party and the TUC, thwarted as they were by the Conservative government's attitude towards them, found a meeting of minds with Delors, and Labour consequently adopted a Euro-enthusiast attitude. On the other hand, given that Delors was a socialist, intellectual, French and a man, 'it is difficult to think of a collection of attributes less calculated to appeal to Mrs Thatcher'.[10] It is ironic, therefore, that Delors was only appointed because France's first choice as President of the Commission, Claude Cheysson, had been eliminated by Mrs Thatcher's use of the veto in the European Council.

Jacques Delors soon made it evident that he was a Euro-enthusiast and a federalist. In particular he made it abundantly clear that he favoured political and monetary union for Europe, with a very strong social dimension. Nothing could be more opposed to Mrs Thatcher's view of Europe, and everything Delors said confirmed her belief that the EC was imposing socialism on Britain 'through the back door'. In June 1988 Jacques Delors was entrusted with the task of studying how the Community could move towards Economic and Monetary Union (EMU). The move infuriated Mrs Thatcher, and in September 1988, during a speech to the College of Europe in Bruges, she vented her anger on the integrationist tendency in Europe, saying that she had spent nine years rolling back the frontiers of the state in Britain and would not now allow that work to be overturned by Europe.

The Bruges speech marked a decisive turning-point in Britain's relationship with Europe. Mrs Thatcher's own attitude changed from a reluctant acceptance of Europe while it was advancing towards the single market to outright hostility, and opposition to any restraint on the independence of the component nation-states. The greatest impact of the Bruges Speech was, of course, on the Conservative Party and that will be considered in more detail in Chapter 8. At the time Mrs Thatcher faced a renewed momentum towards European union with a spirit of determined resistance. Alan Watkins claims, perhaps cynically, that Mrs Thatcher, sensing her growing unpopularity, had seized on an anti-European stance as a populist measure that would restore her to favour with the electorate.

The Delors Plan

In April 1989 the committee chaired by Jacques Delors, which had been examining the way forward to economic and monetary union, produced its report, sometimes known as the Delors Plan. This envisaged a three-stage progression towards EMU:

Stage One Increased co-ordination of economic policies, with all EC members within the ERM.
Stage Two The foundation of a European Central Bank free of political control, using the US Federal Reserve Bank as its model.
Stage Three Introduction of a single European currency.

The European Council meeting of June 1989 in Madrid was due to consider the Delors proposals. Mrs Thatcher was to attend that meeting, determined not to accept the proposals for monetary union: 'The Delors proposals would not command the support of the British Cabinet'.[11] Nevertheless, she was accompanied to Madrid by two cabinet members who did wish to accept the Delors plan: the Foreign Secretary, Geoffrey Howe, and the Chancellor of the Exchequer, Nigel Lawson. Lawson had been in favour of British membership of the ERM for some years, and although he was continually denied permission to join, he had unofficially been shadowing the German mark, attempting to maintain the value of the pound at around three Deutschmarks.

In Madrid both men combined against the Prime Minister, threatening to resign if she did not agree to the Delors Plan and accept Stage One of EMU. Furious at what she regarded as betrayal by her ministers, Mrs Thatcher was forced to sign the agreement, although she did manage to lay down four fairly stringent preconditions before Britain could join the ERM:

1 There must be completion of the internal market arrangements
2 Abolition of all exchange controls
3 A free market in financial services
4 There must be a strengthening of competition policy.

After her return from Madrid Mrs Thatcher had her revenge for what she saw as a humiliating climb-down. In the following month Geoffrey Howe as demoted from the post of Foreign Secretary and replaced by Mrs Thatcher's protégé, John Major. In October Nigel Lawson felt that his position too was being undermined and he resigned, again to be replaced by John Major. And it was John Major, on 5 October 1990, who finally took Britain into the ERM, albeit at what many people felt was the dangerously high rate of DM 2.95 to the pound.

From the fall of Mrs Thatcher to Maastricht

Two European Councils after Madrid advanced progress towards union. At Strasbourg in December 1989, the Council accepted Delors' Social Charter and agreed to set up an intergovernmental conference (IGC) on EMU; these decisions were confirmed at Dublin in April and June 1990. On these occasions Britain was the only country opposed and was voted down by eleven votes to one.

In October 1990, the Italians, who held the presidency, called a special European Council in Rome to prepare for the official Council meeting of December. Mrs Thatcher had been highly critical of the way in which Italy was conducting the presidency and now the Italians had their revenge by calling a vote on Delors Stage Two, despite warnings from both Delors and Kohl not to isolate the British. Inevitably Britain again found herself alone against the other eleven. Mrs Thatcher was furious, particularly at the decision to aim for a single currency before the year 1999.

In her statement to the House of Commons about Rome Mrs Thatcher began by adopting a reasoned attitude. She was still opposed to a single currency but she was quite prepared to consider a common currency based on the hard ecu. The breaking-point came when Neil Kinnock mentioned the different view of the Delors proposals taken by Sir Leon Brittan, now a British Commissioner but once a close political ally of Mrs Thatcher. At that the Prime Minister exploded:

Yes, the Commission wants to increase its powers. Yes, it is a non-elected body and I do not want the Commission to increase its powers at the expense of the House, so of course we differ. The President of the Commission, Mr Delors, said at a press conference the other day that he wanted the European Parliament to be the democratic body of the Community. He wanted the Commission to be the Executive and the Council of Ministers to be the Senate. No. No. No.[12]

It was this speech that led to the resignation of Sir Geoffrey Howe, followed by Howe's highly critical resignation speech, which proved instrumental in the downfall of Mrs Thatcher. The speech essentially concerned the relationship between Europe and the Conservative Party and will be returned to in Chapter 8. At the Rome European Council in December 1990 two IGCs were instituted, one on EMU and the other on Political Union. In the year that followed the new Prime Minister, John Major, managed to stifle debate on Europe in Britain, concentrating on achieving an outcome of the IGC which would satisfy British attitudes to Europe.

The IGCs convened in Rome on 15 December 1990 effectively determined amendments that needed to be made to the treaties establishing the European Communities, with a view to achieving economic and political union. The proposals, as amended by Britain and others, were agreed by the European Council at Maastricht in the Netherlands on 11 December 1991. The IGCs reconvened in February 1992 to draw up the actual treaty that would embody what had been agreed, and it is this treaty, known as the Treaty on European Union, that was presented in its final form at Maastricht on 7 February 1992. The Treaty would come into force on 1 January 1994, at which point the Communities covered by the treaty would become known as the European Union. The Treaty's principal aim, as set out in Article A is to mark 'a new stage in the process of creating an ever closer union among the peoples of Europe.'[13]

There are three 'pillars' forming the union, two of which are new IGCs set up to examine defence and security in one and policing and immigration policy in the other; these are both areas not previously dealt with by any of the treaties setting up the Communities. The main 'pillar' is the amendment of the Treaty of Rome in order to assimilate the provisions of the Single European Act, and to apply more democratic procedures to ameliorate some of the more bureaucratic impositions used to establish the SEA. Within the last category are moves to extend the ability of the Council of Ministers to act on the basis of qualified majority voting; to grant increased powers to the European Parliament; and to enhance the powers of the European Court of Auditors. The institutional changes will be considered in more detail in the next chapter.

For Britain there were two proposals in the Treaty to which it could not agree and John Major negotiated at length for it to be amended, as a result of which two protocols were added to the Treaty. One protocol removes the need for Britain to move towards economic and monetary union, although the facility for a change of mind remains open. The other protocol concerns social policy requiring members to work towards improvements in employment, living and working conditions, together with the proper use and development of human resources. This protocol is binding upon eleven members of the Community but the United Kingdom is specifically excluded.

The forward momentum of first the Single European Act and then the Treaty for European Union had been so swift and relatively trouble-free that there were those who labelled the mood of the time 'europhoria'. Yet, almost immediately after agreement at

Maastricht, things began to go wrong. Lady Thatcher and the right wing of the Conservative Party sympathetic to the former prime minister campaigned vigorously for the British people to be allowed to vote on Maastricht in a referendum, but such an idea was ruled out by John Major. Two other member countries – Denmark and Ireland – were constitutionally required to hold referendums prior to ratification. On 2 June 1992 the whole ratification process received a major reversal when Denmark rejected the Maastricht proposals by a margin of 40,000 votes. Two weeks later Ireland voted very positively, with 68 per cent of those voting saying 'yes'. But the damage had been done. When Britain took over the presidency on 1 July the Community was faced with the need to re-negotiate Danish terms for the Treaty before it could be submitted to another referendum. Moreover, the British government had to carry out its presidential duties while being threatened by a sizeable number of its own backbenchers, who promised to make British ratification as difficult as possible.

In mid-September economic problems with the Exchange Rate Mechanism began, which are discussed below. Further political problems arose when France also decided to hold a referendum, and it seemed very possible that the French would follow the Danes in rejecting Maastricht. In the end, when the French referendum was held on 20 September, the vote was for acceptance, but by the small majority of 51 to 49 per cent. One commentator wrote 'Public disquiet about the Treaty, expressed in the EC's "Eurobarometer" opinion polls, and in the Danish and French referendums, lends support to the claim that European integration is an élite-led process, viewed with indifference or hostility by the peoples of Europe'.[14]

During the British presidency, in the second half of 1992 there were two European Council meetings. The first of these, in Birmingham on 16 October, was an emergency meeting intended to resolve the Danish crisis and also to push the concept of subsidiarity, which was supposed to allay the fears of Britain's Eurosceptics. As it happens, the problems of the ERM dominated the Birmingham Council and it was not until Edinburgh on 11–12

December that the Maastricht Treaty could be addressed. In the event, Major got most of what he wanted: Denmark was granted an opt-out on EMU similar to that obtained by Britain, certain concessions were made on the defence aspect of the EU, and other adjustments were made, which it was hoped would make it possible for Denmark to accept Maastricht in a second referendum scheduled for May 1993. Major also got his way on subsidiarity, which was intended to remove any suggestions of federalism or centralism in Maastricht. By subsidiarity it was intended that proposals by the centre in Brussels should be implemented according to the decisions of national or regional government, and also that no major policy decision should be made in Brussels if it were more properly the concern of national or regional government. Article A of the Treaty now reads 'creating an ever-closer union among the peoples of Europe, *in which decisions are taken as closely as possible to the citizen*'.

The terms arranged for Denmark at Edinburgh proved successful, in that the second referendum accepted the Maastricht Treaty by 56.8 to 43.2 per cent. Britain, in the mean time, had resumed its debate of the Maastricht Treaty in Parliament. The debate was not strictly necessary for ratification and was much more about internal Conservative policies than about Europe. Nevertheless, the process took up 204 hours of debate, 163 of these in one 23-day Committee of the Whole House; it also involved seventy divisions, one of which was lost by the government, and another of which became a vote of confidence in the government. The UK did not ratify the Treaty until 2 August 1993, but Britain was not the last to do so: constitutional problems in reunited Germany meant that it could not ratify until 12 October 1993. Nevertheless, despite the problems, the Treaty became operational as planned on 1 January 1994, the European Community thereby becoming the European Union.

German reunification and the undermining of EMU

Since its inception in 1979 the EMS and the associated ERM had had some measure of success in maintaining parity between currencies, largely as a result of the strength of the Deutschmark and the controlling hand of the Bundesbank. When EMU and the goal of economic and monetary union was established the condition of membership was 'convergence', by which the economies of at least seven members would come together to a stable parity of currencies and compatible levels of economic activity. In the mean time the various members would try to keep their exchange parities, rates of inflation and levels of growth within a narrow band of divergence, correcting any drift by use of fiscal measures such as the interest rate. The strength of the German economy meant that the point of reference for the EMS had been the Deutschmark and the key interest rate that set by the Bundesbank.

In 1989 the Soviet bloc collapsed. Almost overnight the Berlin Wall came down, the Communist government of East Germany fell and moves began to reunify Germany. In 1990 this process was achieved by absorbing the provinces of the old German Democratic Republic as *Länder* of the Federal Republic of Germany. Despite the strength of the West German economy there were major problems associated with absorbing East Germany, with its decaying industrial infrastructure and a worthless currency. Existing problems were made worse by Chancellor Kohl's insistence that the exchange rate between east and west versions of the mark should be on a one-for-one basis. The vast sums of money expended in this currency exchange, together with all the other financial aid travelling from west to east, had the effect of throwing the German economy into crisis. This was very important in that Germany could no longer afford to take a leading role in maintaining the EMS without thought to the domestic repercussions of doing so.

Many countries in the EC had slumped into recession during the late 1980s, and their currencies had sharply fallen in value compared with the Deutschmark. This was particularly true for Britain, where John Major's late entry into the ERM had set the value of the pound far too high in relation to the D-Mark. During the summer of 1992 the weaker currencies within the ERM – the pound, the Italian lira and the Spanish peseta – came under heavy pressure from currency speculators. One response to currency speculation would have been to devalue, but national pride and the constraints of ERM membership made this difficult. The mechanisms of the ERM demanded that the central banks of EC members should intervene by buying the currencies under threat, while the threatened economies should encourage inward invest- ment by raising interest rates. Countries in recession, however, cannot afford to raise interest rates indefinitely. On the other hand, the rigid anti-inflationary measures introduced by Germany after reunification meant that the Bundesbank could not provide support beyond a certain point and interest rates could not be reduced.

In September 1992, fears about the Maastricht process arising from the Danish and French referendums rated uncertainty in the money markets and there was a massive movement out of weaker currencies into the Deutschmark. Over the weekend of 13–14 September Italy devalued the lira by 6 per cent and pressure increased on the pound and French franc.

On 16 September (Black Wednesday) desperate measures raised the British interest rate twice in the same morning, taking it to 15 per cent. In the afternoon the British government bowed to the inevitable, cut interest rates and withdrew from the ERM. On the same day Italy also 'temporarily suspended' its ERM membership.

For Britain, as the value of the pound fell rapidly to find its true level, the crisis was over. There was talk of returning to the ERM when conditions were better, but unofficially, most people said that they could not envisage conditions becoming right in the foreseeable future. Meanwhile, intense pressure switched to the French franc but this was partially eased by the 'yes' vote in the French referendum in Maastricht, and by far heavier support from Germany than the Bundesbank had been ready to give to Britain. France remained within the ERM, as did Spain, Portu- gal and Ireland, all of whose currencies came under pressure during that autumn, forcing devaluations on the peseta, escudo and punt. And the speculation continued into 1993, with further devaluations for Spain and Portugal during the spring.

- In May 1993 an EC committee rejected British claims that the EMS was flawed, and the Community repeated its faith in the ERM and the timetable for movement towards economic union.
- In July, the speculators returned in force and the Belgian, Danish and French currencies hit the bottom limit of their ERM bands. The Bundesbank refused to make more than a token cut in German interest rates and the ERM went into crisis.
- On 1 August 1993 an emergency meeting of EC finance ministers agreed that ERM constraints should be relaxed, and the bands within which currencies can fluctuate were widened to 15 per cent. The meeting announced that this had saved the EMS and preserved the timetable of the Delors Plan.

Most finance ministers, however, at least privately, were ready to concede that the ERM had collapsed, that the EMS was characterised by divergence rather than convergence and that the timetable for ultimate economic union was now meaningless. The most likely outcome is a 'two-tier' Europe, with a central Europe of six or seven states forming an economic union with a single currency, and an association of peripheral members outside the economic union.[15]

Enlargement

A phrase popularly used to describe the integration process since the mid-1980s has been 'deepening and widening'. The progress toward economic and political union is part of the deepening, but the widening is generally taken to mean enlargement through more countries joining the Union. By the mid-1990s that process of enlargement seemed to be accelerating, with an increasing number of countries applying to join, carrying the potential membership to around twenty-four by the turn of the century; a different situation from the early years, when it took thirty years for membership to increase from six to twelve.

The first enlargement of the EC by Britain, Ireland and Denmark was delayed by President de Gaulle. The second and third enlargements of the 1980s, by Greece, Spain and Portugal, were originally delayed by the fact that all three countries were somewhat less than democratic when they first became eligible for membership in the 1970s; Greece being ruled by a military junta and the other two having fascist dictators. There is no formal rule which says that members of the EU have to be democracies, but it seems to be assumed that a country would have to have a structure of democratic institutions before the other members of the Union could feel able to accept that country's accession. This does beg the question as to what would happen if one of the existing members suddenly ceased to be a democracy. As it happens, the main cause of delay in processing the Greek, Spanish and Portuguese applications was less to do with democracy than because all three countries had a weaker economic base than the existing members, and a lot of very complex and difficult negotiation proved necessary, particularly over the implications for the CAP of countries with a Mediterranean agricultural base.

After the accession of Spain and Portugal in 1986 the movement toward enlargement gathered additional momentum, until there were three groups of would-be members.

- The first group consisted of Turkey, who applied in 1987, and the two Mediterranean islands of Malta and Cyprus, who applied in 1990. In December 1989, the Commission advised the Council of Ministers to reject the Turkish application, partly out of some doubts over human rights violations but mostly because it was felt that Turkey needed much more economic development before the application could be given serious consideration. The applications of Cyprus and Malta remained on the table but were elbowed to one side by other developments.

- The second group of aspirants to membership were former members of the Soviet bloc, most of whom have negotiated 'Europe Agreements' with the EU giving them favourable trade terms. The countries most enthusiastic about membership are the so-called Visegrad states of the Czech Republic,

Hungary and Poland. All three have been promised eventual membership but have been told that they are unlikely to enter into serious negotiation before the end of the century. However, on 3 March 1994, Hungary announced that it hoped to begin negotiations for membership in 1997, expecting to achieve membership by the year 2000. The move by Hungary was followed a few days later by Poland, although the Czech Republic admitted it was not yet ready to go so far. The statements of intent by Hungary and Poland were followed by actual formal applications within the month. Finally, in October 1994, the sixteen foreign ministers of the EU, including four candidate countries, agreed privileged treatment for the Czech Republic, Hungary, Poland, Slovakia, Bulgaria and Romania, with Slovenia due to join them shortly. These six applicant states will be allowed access to key ministerial meetings and they will meet the EU heads of government once a year. The aim is to prepare the six for membership by the turn of the century.

● The third group of applicants, which seemed to achieve its end with surprising speed, consisted of former EFTA countries. Concerned by the movement towards the Single European Market, five EFTA countries applied initially for associate status and ultimately for membership. They were helped in their decision by the end of the Cold War, having previously been wary of membership because they felt it would imperil their neutral status. The applicants were Austria, Finland, Norway, Sweden and Switzerland. The proposal was that the single market would be extended to take in these five countries to form a European Economic Area (EEA), and that thereafter the applications would be processed.

Britain was very keen on the idea of enlargement and Mr Major pursued the matter at all European Council meeting for three years. The points in favour as far as Britain was concerned were:

1 The enlargement of the Union would dilute the federalist tendency in the Union, and would therefore weaken the position

of the more ardent integrationists.

2   All five countries are wealthy with strong economies. They
    would therefore be net contributors to the Community
    budget, easing the strain for the existing net contributors and
    helping to allay many of the Community's budgetary prob-
    lems. It was estimated that the net contribution from the new
    entrants would exceed £1 billion a year, which would assist
    the Community considerably in its aim to become self-financ-
    ing.

In December 1992 Switzerland held a referendum in which
membership of both the EEA and the EU was rejected; the Swiss
application was then withdrawn. Despite this, Austria, Sweden
and Finland opened negotiations on 1 February 1993, with
Norway following on 5 April. The negotiation process was rapid,
and agreement on Finnish and Swedish entry was reached by 28
February 1994. The Austrian application was held up for another
day over the right to restrict heavy lorry traffic through the Alps,
and negotiations with Norway extended for a further week
because of a dispute over fishing rights with Spain. Nevertheless,
all was settled by the end of the first week in March, and the
timetable for accession of the four countries seemed fixed for 1
January 1995. All that remained, it appeared, was for the new
members to be approved by the European Parliament prior to
each of them holding a referendum for their nationals. At which
point Britain, with some backing by Spain, imperilled the whole
proceedings by demanding that there should be no change to the
blocking majority affecting votes in the Council of Ministers.

This dispute, which went on for three weeks as Britain refused
to compromise, threatened to hold up enlargement because unless
the position could be resolved quickly, the question of accession
could not come before the European Parliament before it was dissolved for the June elections, and the four countries' entry would
be delayed beyond the start of 1995. In the eyes of many people,
of course, this argument was another stage in the internal Conservative Party argument over Europe, and was less about a point
of principle in Europe than about appearing to hold a strong

negotiating position in the eyes of party critics at home on the eve of the European elections. As it was, Britain found the position adopted by the government untenable, concessions were made at the eleventh hour and a compromise agreed. Nevertheless, the dispute soured relations between the Major government and its European partners and the incident was felt to be yet another adverse point in Britain's relationship with Europe.

Once the dispute over voting rights had been settled the process of approving the accession of the four applicant countries could proceed, and this it did with little difficulty. However, even after all the formalities had been concluded, the applicant countries still had to seek the approval of their own citizens. Referendums in Austria, Finland and Sweden during the autumn approved the accession agreements, although by very small majorities in the latter two cases. Then, on 28 November, the people of Norway voted against membership, for the second time. Norway joined Switzerland, Liechtenstein and Iceland in being the only Western European countries not to belong to the EU, retaining membership of the European Economic Area, but without any power to influence the decisions of that body.

Settlement of the voting rights dispute coincided with the application by Hungary and Poland, but it was made clear that discussions on further enlargement would not take place before the review of Maastricht due in 1996. That is true not only for Hungary, Poland and any other Eastern European applicant, but also for the long-standing applications of Malta and Cyprus.

Corfu and after

The European Council meeting to mark the end of the Greek Presidency was held on the island of Corfu in June 1994. On the agenda was the official welcome to Austria, Finland, Norway and Sweden, but the main business was the election of a new President of the Commission to succeed Jacques Delors. Britain had its own candidate in the person of Sir Leon Brittan, but it was inevitable that he would not be chosen. The tradition within the EC is that the presidency of the Commission is held alternately by someone coming from a large member country and someone from a small country, by someone on the left and someone on the right. Since 1984 the Commission had been headed by Jacques Delors, a French Socialist. It therefore followed that the new President should be a Christian Democrat from one of the Benelux countries.

The most obvious candidates when the Council assembled in Corfu were Ruud Lubbers, the Dutch Prime Minister, and Jean-Luc Dehaene, Prime Minister of Belgium. Unfortunately, Mr Lubbers had seriously upset Chancellor Kohl in a dispute between Germany and the Netherlands, and Kohl was determined that the Dutchman would not get the job. In a Franco-German summit in Mulhouse during early June Chancellor Kohl and President Mitterand had decided that the post should be given to Mr Dehaene. Several of the EC members, particularly the Dutch, Italians and the Spanish, were unhappy with this evidence of Franco-German manipulation and were prepared to vote against Dehaene on the first ballot. Ultimately, however, they knew that they would accept the majority choice for the sake of unity within the Council.

Not so Mr Major. Supported by Douglas Hurd, he stated bluntly that if he could not have Leon Brittan he might settle for Ruud Lubbers, but he would never accept Jean-Luc Dehaene and he would be prepared to use the British veto to prevent the Belgian from becoming President. The British stressed that there was nothing personal in their rejection of Mr Dehaene, although he was represented as too enthusiastic a federalist. The objection, according to Douglas Hurd, was to the way in which Kohl and Mitterand had done a secret deal that the rest were supposed to accept without question. In the last resort Britain would use the national veto to prevent Mr Dehaene's accession. The other eleven members interpreted Britain's stance as being due to Mr Major's need to look tough and resolute in the eyes of the Euro-sceptics in his own party at home. However, they assumed that once he had proved his virility by waving the big stick of the veto, Major would back down and accept Dehaene. Instead, the British Prime Minister stuck to his threat and duly employed the veto.

It was a significant moment in Britain's relations with the Community. If, as Lady Thatcher suggested, the European Council is rather like a cosy gentleman's club, John Major had just broken club rules. It was not considered the behaviour of a gentleman to use the ultimate weapon of the veto and to plunge the Community into crisis, not for the good of the Community or even the good of Britain, but to appease the dissenters within the Conservative Party.

When the Germans took over the Presidency in June 1994 their first act was to call an emergency Council meeting for the second week in July. Intensive meetings and discussions over the two weeks that followed ensured that when the ministers met in Brussels, it was to rubber-stamp a previously determined choice in Jacques Santer, Prime Minister of Luxembourg. John Major was quick to hail the new Commission President as the perfect choice. But it was soon pointed out that ideologically, and in his dedication to European integration, Mr Santer was almost indistinguishable from Mr Dehaene. The only difference was that Santer did not have the forcefulness, energy, charisma and efficiency of the Belgian. The last Luxembourgeois to hold the presidency of the Commission, Gaston Thorn, who was President from 1981 to 1985, had been a nonentity whose period in office had coincided with the condition known as Euro-sclerosis. The more cynical political commentators saw the appointment as an intergovernmental ploy by the Council to emasculate the federalist Commission in the run-up to the 1996 conference.

The aftermath of Corfu was not yet complete, however. On 20 July 1994 the European Parliament, newly elected in June, chose to exercise the right granted to the Parliament by the Maastricht Treaty, and voted as to whether to accept the nominee for the Commission Presidency. The British Labour Group of MEPs voted to reject Mr Santer on the grounds that he had been appointed by the Council of Ministers, without the consultation of Parliament written into the TEU. The Labour Group's lead was followed by the Socialist Group as a whole.

The Socialist Group is the largest party grouping in the European Parliament and there was talk of their being joined by the

Liberals and the Greens. It looked as if there was a real danger that Mr Santer might be rejected. The Parliament's rejection would not be binding, but it was hard to see how Mr Santer would have been able to carry on with any credibility once he had been rejected. As it was, Santer was accepted by a mere 22 votes and the crisis was over. But the chain of events that began in Corfu made three important points:

- John Major's use of the veto restored his standing with the Conservative Party at home but immeasurably weakened Britain's standing in Europe.
- After the Delors era the Council of Ministers appeared ready and willing to see the Commission weakened and marginalised.
- The European Parliament now has real powers for the first time, and intends to use them.

Summary

The fifteen-year period from 1979 to 1994 saw immense changes in Europe. The Single Market was achieved in full and considerable progress was made towards economic and political union. The economic troubles of 1992–93 were serious set-backs to the progress of monetary union, but the troubles also accentuated the interdependence of European economies and made it unlikely that any member could contemplate withdrawal; the economic problems that could be faced by those outside the Union were emphasised by the number of countries applying for membership. Further impetus towards integration is the inclusion in the Maastricht Treaty of foreign affairs, defence and security, previously excluded from Community concern.

The position of Britain in Europe has become that of the leading and most intransigent anti-federalist. In many ways Britain has inherited the position adopted by Gaullist France in the 60s, and has attracted the same sort of resentment and odium as was directed towards de Gaulle at that time. The confrontational style adopted by Mrs Thatcher and continued by her successor had had some successes, as over the BBQ reform of the CAP and gaining concessions over Maastricht. The same style, however, had also had the effect of annoying and alienating Britain's European partners, even natural anti-federal allies such as France or Denmark. Britain has repeatedly found itself in a one against eleven minority, which has called into question John Major's seriousness in claiming that he wished Britain to be 'at the heart of Europe'. Although it has to be said that these clashes over Europe are often more a result of the Conservative government's relations with its own backbenchers than with any consistent policy over European integration, nevertheless the result is the same. In the threat of the veto over voting rights in March 1994 and the actual use of the veto over the President of the Commission in June 1994, John Major showed himself ready to alienate his partners in Europe and plunge the EU into crisis in order to appease his Euro-sceptic backbenchers.

Notes

1 R. Jenkins (Lord Jenkins of Hillhead), *European Diary 1977–1981*, Collins, London, 1989.

2 C. Tugendhat, *Making Sense of Europe*, London 1986.

3 Reported in Hugo Young, *One of Us*, Macmillan, London 1989, p. 189.

4 Carrington and Gilmour relate the story in a BBC television programme, *Thatcher, the Downing Street Years* (part one), shown in autumn 1993.

5 A conversation of March 1984, quoted in Young, Ch. 17.

6 Figures based on those given in V. Keegan and M. Kettle (eds.), *The New Europe*, Fourth Estate, London 1993.

7 D. Wincott, 'The Conservative Party and Europe', *Politics Review*, April 1992, p. 12.

8 Michael Heseltine in *The Independent*, 10 October 1989.

9 Neill Nugent, *The Government and Politics of the European Community*, Macmillan, London 1991, pp. 70–1.

10 Alan Watkins, *A Conservative Coup*, Duckworth, London 1992.

11 Margaret Thatcher, *The Times*, 27 June 1989.

12   Margaret Thatcher, *Hansard*, 30 October 1990.

13   The full text of the Treaty is published in English by the Office for Official Publications of the European Communities, Luxembourg 1992.

14   Philip Lynch, 'Europe's Post-Maastricht Muddle', *Politics Review*, November 1993, p. 2.

15   Lynch, 'Europe's Post-Maastricht Muddle', p. 2.

3

The institutions of the European Union post-Maastricht

The organs of the European Community – Assembly, Council, Commission and Court of Justice, together with the advisory Economic and Social Committee – were formally established by the Treaty of Rome in 1957, although the basic structure – that devised for the ECSC in 1951 – was already in place. Outwardly, these institutions changed little over thirty years of existence, despite the translation of the Assembly into the European Parliament, but behind their apparently unchanging façade, their nature and functions were subject to a continuous and fundamental process of change. One of the tasks of the Treaty for European Union was to redefine the institutions of the EU in the light of these changes and to formalise the resulting amendments by incorporation in the Treaty. Even so, the Intergovernmental Conference that reported at Maastricht was not able to complete a full review and it was accepted that the institutions, like other aspects of the TEU, will be re-examined fully by the IGC to be convened in 1996.

There are two main constitutional problems as regards the restructuring of the Union's institutions. One is the so-called 'democratic deficit' of those institutions and the other is the vexed question of the rights belonging to individual member nation-states.

It is accepted that most of the bodies involved in the policy- and decision-making processes of the EU are not directly accountable to the people of the Union. Until 1979 the Assembly was appointed rather than elected, and even after the introduction of direct elections, the European Parliament was left with very few powers to control the unelected Commission, and even less power to control the Council of Ministers. As Nugent says, "It is the case that Community decision-makers are less directly accountable than are national decision-makers'.[1] Constitutionalists would argue that the Council of Ministers is ultimately accountable in that it is composed of elected ministers of the member countries, and ministers are therefore answerable to the electorate of their own countries for their actions in Europe. Furthermore, countries such as Britain argue against giving too much power to the European Parliament because by doing so the sovereignty of national parliaments is undermined. The democratic deficit is yet another issue between the federalists and functionalists.

Another issue also relates to the supranational versus intergovernmental perspectives. This concerns the comparative powers of member states when those states are of disparate sizes and populations. Within the EU, Germany has a population of 80 million, while Luxembourg has 400,000. If each state were to have equal voting rights then it might legitimately be asked what right Luxembourg has to an influence equal to that of a country 200 times its size. On the other hand, to give the member countries an influence weighted for their comparative size would mean that the larger states could trample over the wishes of the smaller countries, even if those countries were to act in concert.

The solution arrived at by the Federalists drawing up the American constitution was to create two houses of Congress, in which one, the House of Representatives, represents the population through constituencies of roughly equal size; the second, the Senate, represents states' rights by having equal representation (two senators) for each state of the union. There are those in Europe who would like to replicate this system by granting full legislative powers to the European Parliament and Council of Ministers, with the supranational EP taking the role of the House of Representatives and the intergovernmental Council of Ministers acting as Senate.

This has not yet proved possible because the anti-federalists –

represented most vociferously by Mrs Thatcher – are so opposed. As a result, the institutional changes included in the TEU give additional powers and legitimacy to the European Parliament but not sufficiently to remove the democratic deficit nor yet to make the EP a true legislative body. The federalists will, however, return to the attack in the IGC of 1996 and any survey of the EU's institutions must be read with the federalist/functionalist division in mind.

A: The Commission

The College of Commissioners
The Commission is the executive arm of the European Union. As such it is sometimes perceived as the 'government' of the Community, while others see it as the 'civil service'. In fact, it is neither, being both more and less than either. For example, in policy-making decisions the Commission differs from a civil service in that it is the body which formulates statements of policy but, unlike a government, the Commission is powerless to control the vote on acceptance or rejection of that policy.

There are twenty commissioners representing all fifteen member countries, the five largest – France, Germany, Italy, Spain and the UK – having two commissioners each and all the rest having just one. The number of commissioners, having started as nine in 1957, is growing all the time and this remains a problem that will have to be addressed with some urgency in 1996. As long ago as 1977 Roy Jenkins was complaining that there were more commissioners than there were suitable portfolios for them, and that was when there were only thirteen commissioners in all.[2] In 1994, the distribution of portfolios among the twenty-one commissioners, then proposed, ran into trouble when the British Commissioner, Sir Leon Brittan, objected, almost to the point of resignation, when his very large trade relations portfolio, about the largest portfolio then existing, was stripped of its Eastern European dimension in order to make for a more egalitarian distribution. Commentators were saying that serious consideration would have to be given to the question of whether the larger member states should continue to have two commissioners each and whether the smaller states would not have to share the posts of commissioners between them.

Since January 1995 commissioners have been appointed to serve for five years; prior to that the period had been for four years. In theory, and according to the Treaty of Rome, appointment to the Commission is a collective decision of all member governments, but in fact the appointments are usually as the result of nominations by the individual countries. Those member states which have one commissioner normally appoint a member or supporter of the government or majority party. Those states which have two commissioners have their individual arrangements; the normal practice for Britain has been to nominate one commissioner each for the Conservative and Labour Parties.

The Commission is a supranational body and anyone appointed to the Commission is supposed to forget their national origins and serve only the Community. Indeed, newly-appointed commissioners must make an undertaking that they shall 'neither seek nor take instructions from any government or from any other body'. Furthermore, 'Each Member State undertakes to respect this principle and not to seek to influence the members of the Commission'.[3] While it is only natural for commissioners to maintain their links with former colleagues in the home country and to remain sympathetic to their own national interests, the Commission cannot function efficiently if its members are too blatantly nationalistic in their attitude. On the whole, commissioners are Community-minded, often to the despair of the governments that appointed them. As Brittan says, 'I may be a British Conservative but I do not agree with the Conservative government on many European questions'.[4]

Each commissioner is given a portfolio, which is to say that they are placed in charge of some function of the Commission's work. In that respect they are rather like government ministers, although with greater freedom. As Brittan says, 'Commissioners do have somewhat greater personal political autonomy than a cabinet minister – you do not have to clear things with the top'.[5] To assist them in their work, commissioners have a small group of aides or advisers known as a *cabinet*. The word here is used in its French sense and would be better translated into English as 'private office'. The members of a commissioner's *cabinet* are usually civil servants seconded either from the commissioner's own national civil service, or from another part of the Community's bureaucracy. Members of the *cabinet* are often fellow-nationals of the commissioner, although convention expects at least one to be from another member state.

The President of the Commission
The governments of the Member States shall nominate by common accord, after consulting the European Parliament, the person they intend to appoint as President of the Commission.[6]

Before the TEU came into effect the rules concerning the nomination of the President stated that the President should be chosen from the ranks of the existing commissioners. This, however, was never a practical possibility. The office of President is so important that the member governments need to spend a long time making their choice, and it would be impossible to wait until the entire new Commission was in place before beginning that selection process. As it is, the process of lobbying and negotiation begins well over a year in advance of appointment and, traditionally, the nominee is announced at the June European Council before the January appointment. An unwritten convention has grown up over the years under which the office of President is held alternately by a large country and a small country, and alternately by a representative of the right and of the left. Under that convention the obvious successor to Jacques Delors, a French socialist, was a right-of-centre politician from a small country.

Under normal circumstances negotiations for the appointment of a new President go on for anything up to a year and the situation is tacitly agreed between the member states before the European Council meets to appoint the new President. Twice the preliminary agreement has not been reached and the chosen candidate has been vetoed by one country – Britain. In 1984 the

French candidate, Claude Cheysson, was vetoed by Mrs Thatcher, and in 1994 the Belgian Jean-Luc Dehaene was vetoed by John Major.

Although the post's gubernatorial powers are limited, the President of the Commission is the nearest thing the EU has to a head of government. Probably the true head is the President of the European Council, but since that is a transferable post which circulates on a six-monthly rota, the President of the Commission is a more clearly identifiable figure-head for the Community as a whole.

The President of the Commission chairs the weekly meetings of the College of Commissioners and co-ordinates the work of the various commissioners. This is an even more arduous task than it might appear, since the commissioners are not like cabinet ministers and their priority interests and ideological positions are often at variance with those of the President. Commissioners tend to be autonomous and ready to fight to preserve that autonomy. The President of the Commission has to work very hard to maintain a cohesive programme of action from such a disparate team.

Probably the most important, and most difficult, task undertaken by the President is the allocation of portfolios at the start of a new Commission. It is in this process that the President is most in need of the skills of negotiation and political judgment. There is always a shortage of portfolios, or at least a shortage of important portfolios, compared with the number of commissioners available. Ambitious commissioners will always look for the important tasks, such as external relations or regional policy. Even keener are those commissioners who have been reappointed for a second term and who are naturally looking for promotion. Add to this the complication of national interests and jealousies. One of the fascinations of Roy Jenkins' *Diary European* is the picture he paints of the months of negotiation involved in fixing jobs for the Commission members.

The bureaucracy

Around two-thirds of the administrative staff of the EU are employed by the Commission. Despite public perception of a massive bureaucracy, the actual size of the Commission's staff – approximately 15,000[7] – is remarkably small, being no larger than the average government ministry in one of the member states. One factor that swells the numbers required is the question of translation and interpretation. Although within the Commission the working languages are French and English, there are larger meetings for which interpreters are required and, of course, all documents of record must be issued in all the official languages of the Union. Almost 3,000 staff are involved in translation work. A survey undertaken in 1994 by the pressure group promoting Esperanto as a universal language for the Community, found that the EU generates more than three million words a day, at a cost in translation and interpretation services of £1.2 billion a year.

Staff of the Commission are permanently employed and, for the most part, are appointed on merit. In the case of senior or specialised staff, that merit is judged by means of highly competitive open examination. There is a career structure and most promotions are internal, but the ever-present question of national jealousies prevents the organisation being truly meritocratic. Something in the nature of a national quota system does exist, at least for those senior administrators who can initiate legislation, and it is still not unknown for outsiders to be seconded from their national civil services into the service of the Commission in order to preserve the balance of nationalities.

The Commission administration is divided into twenty-three policy responsibilities, similar to government ministries, each headed by a Director-General. These Directorates-General are not known by their area of responsibility but by a roman numeral preceded by DG for Directorate-General, hence DGVI for agriculture, DGXVI for regional policy, and so on. The normal hierarchical structure divides the Directorates-General into directorates and the directorates into divisions. The pattern is not uniform, however, because the size of the Directorates-General varies so much: DGIX, for example, which deals with budgetary matters, has a staff of more than 2,500, while DGXXII, dealing with structural policy, has a staff of less than 60. Some of the smaller Directorates-General have directorates but no divisions, while others have divisions but no directorate. Each Director-General is answerable to a Commissioner but there is not a precise match between the areas of responsibility given to the Directorates-General and the portfolios given to Commissioners.

The Commission is the archetypal multi-organisation, with each directorate-general anxious to preserve its own territory. This produces a chronic lack of co-ordination, and plenty of jurisdictional fights. The style and attitude of directorates an vary enormously and can change over time according to the nationality and personality of the director-general.[8]

Apart from the Directorates-General there is a sizeable section of Commission staff which is organised into specialised and service units, such as the translation services mentioned above.

The tasks and duties of the Commission

- The most important duty carried out by the Commission is the drafting of policy documents for discussion and decision by the Council of Ministers, the remit of the Commission being to initiate and formulate policy that will promote the aims for which the European Communities were founded. The Commission is not the only source of policy to be presented to the Council, but the majority of issues discussed by the Council can only be accepted if they have been framed by the Commission.
- The Commission has an executive role after policy decisions have been made through the issue of regulations, directives and instructions by which Community decisions are executed in the member states. The Commission issues something like 5,000 of these legislative instruments each year, although most of these are dealing with very minor matters such as price levels for a single commodity in the CAP.
- The Commission is responsible for preparing the Community Budget and for the management of Community finances, including the various funds such as the regional fund, the Social Fund and the CAP.
- The Commission must monitor the actions of member states in obeying and carrying out Community law. In the event of

non-compliance or deliberate law-breaking it is up to the Commission to demand obedience or, if the offence continues, to prosecute the country or organisation through the European Court of Justice.

• Commissioners and senior Commission staff must attend the meetings of the European Parliament and its committees. Commissioners must answer questions from MEPs as well as attending, and even participating in, debates which are within the ambit of the commissioner's portfolio. The President must make an annual report to the Parliament.

• The Commission is represented and participates in the work of various international bodies such as the United Nations, the General Agreement on Tariffs and Trade, the Council of Europe and the OECD.

• The Commission deals on behalf of the EU with diplomatic relations with non-member countries. Just as a country would receive ambassadors from foreign countries, the Commission deals with diplomatic missions from over 125 foreign countries accredited to the EU. On the other side of the same coin, the Commission itself maintains diplomatic relations with nearly 100 non-member states.

• The Commission acts as the first check on new applications for membership of the EU. On receipt of such an application the Commission is asked to conduct an enquiry into all the implications of that application. Negotiations only begin with the Commission's approval.

B: The Council

The Council shall consist of a representative of each Member State at ministerial level, authorised to commit the government of that Member State.[9]

The Council of Ministers is the decision-making body of the European Community, which has to give its approval before any important legislation can be adopted. However, to use the term Council of Ministers as though there were only one specific institution of that name would be misleading. There are, in fact, several Councils, because the type of minister present varies according to the subject-matter of the meeting – transport ministers will meet to discuss transport policy, energy ministers to discuss energy, and so on. If there is such a thing as a definitive Council of Ministers it is the General Council, which is made up of foreign ministers from the member countries. This Council of Foreign Ministers is not concerned with foreign affairs, but deals instead with general issues relating to policy matters. Another important Council is the Ecofin Council, made up of the economic and finance ministers and obviously dealing with matters such as the EMS. The other Councils – transport, energy, etc. – are known generically as Technical Councils.

There are between eighty and ninety Council meetings each year (eighty-seven in 1989, eighty-two in 1992, for example), of which the meetings of agriculture ministers are by far the most frequent, closely followed by the foreign ministers in General Councils and economic ministers in Ecofin Councils. The General Council, the Ecofin Council and the Agricultural Ministers' Council will meet at least monthly, but some of the minor technical councils may not meet more than once or twice a year. Meetings very seldom last more than one day: even if the meeting extends over two days it is usually from lunch-time to lunch-time. However, advisory groups and working parties continue to operate between meetings and some groups of ministers, especially the foreign and finance ministers, will meet informally outside Brussels, perhaps within the context of a social weekend.

Leadership of the Council is vested in the Presidency of the European Union, a position which rotates among member states, each holding the responsibility for a period of six months. During their tenure ministers of the country holding the Presidency will call Council meetings, decide the agenda, introduce initiatives and take the chair for all Council meetings. The presidency changes hands in the same order as the members are seated in Council meetings, and this is by alphabetical order, according to how the country's name is spelt in its own language – the rota therefore begins Belgie/Belgique, Danmark, Deutschland, Ελλασ, España, and so on. Britain comes last, as the United Kingdom.

Policy issues are not evenly distributed throughout the year – agricultural matters tend to be concentrated in the first half, for example. So that all countries should get a fair turn at dealing with all matters during their presidencies the rota changes after each complete cycle, each pair of countries which shared a year's presidencies reversing their alphabetical order. Thus the round which ended in 1992, with Portugal having the presidency in the first half of the year and the United Kingdom in the second half, began 1993 not with Belgium again but with Denmark, Belgium taking over in July. In 1994 Greece took the first half of the year, followed by Germany.

The Secretariat and COREPER

There is a vast bureaucratic input into Council meetings from a number of sources, including the administrative staff of the Council, known as the General Secretariat. There are about 2,000 members of the Secretariat, whose duties are to service the Council in preparing for meetings, keeping records and giving advice; indeed providing all the services that might be looked for in civil servants, although there are some services that are peculiar to the European situation, such as the need to translate working documents into the various official languages. Since the responsibility for arranging meetings and agendas lies with the Presidency, the Secretariat will work closely with the national officials of the state holding the Presidency, the numbers of such national officials seconded to Brussels always increasing substantially during the six months of the Presidency. The size of the supporting secretariat turns Council meetings into very large affairs. Roy Jenkins wrote of the room in which the Council of Ministers met as reminding him of a crowded aircraft hangar.

Of considerable importance in the policy- and decision-making processes of the Community is the body known as COREPER, which stands for Committee of Permanent Representatives. These representatives are the diplomatic missions sent by the member states as a form of embassy to the Community. While civil servants seconded to the Commission to assist the commissioners must forget their national loyalties, and civil servants accompanying ministers to Council meetings are transient, the senior diplomat sent to Brussels as Permanent Representative ensures the continuous representation of national interests at all times. The Permanent Representative has a large staff, including a delegation of up to forty officials, most drawn from Foreign Office staff but with other policy areas also represented.

The permanent representatives used to meet informally but they were recognised as an official organ of the European Community in the Merger Treaty of 1965, and a definition of COREPER's duties was written into the Treaty and its subsequent amendments: 'A committee consisting of the Permanent Representatives of the Member States shall be responsible for preparing the work of the Council and for carrying out the tasks assigned to it by the Council'.[10] The Committee is, therefore, not only a vital part of the legislative process but it is the principal channel of communication between the institutions of the Community and national governments. There are in fact two COREPER groupings, of which COREPER 2 is the senior, dealing with the General Council and Ecofin as well as having an input into the European Council, and dealing with the more delicate or more controversial issues to come before the Council. COREPER 1 is headed by the Deputy Permanent Representatives and deals with the various Technical Councils and more routine matters. The Council of Agricultural Ministers does not use COREPER but has its own Special Committee on Agriculture (SCA).

The Troika

This is a function of the Council that has been in existence for some time but which has recently come to have wider applications. Originally the Troika began because a six-month presidency was too short for initiatives to be carried to a conclusion within that term. In order to provide continuity co-operation grew between the current Presidency and those immediately preceding and following it. Later this trio was employed as a sort of trouble-shooting team if Council matters were deadlocked in a dispute between member states. The ultimate use of the Troika is as an international mediation team, as in 1991 when the foreign ministers of Holland, Luxembourg and Portugal led missions to Zagreb and Belgrade in order to mediate over the break-up of the former Yugoslavia.

The Troika as an institution is still not officially recognised by treaty, but it is obviously an arm of the Council that could have important uses and it will come under examination during the constitutional review of 1996.

Voting in the Council
There are three ways in which the Council of Ministers can vote to take a decision – by unanimous vote, by simple majority or by qualified majority. Originally, decisions of the Council tended to be unanimous, which in effect gave a dissenting state the veto, as was exploited by de Gaulle in the 1960s. The Luxembourg Compromise of 1966 reduced the need for unanimity and extended the number of issues that could be settled by qualified majority. Since then there has been a steady extension of qualified majority voting (QMV), most significantly in the Single European Act.

Unanimity is still required for all new policies or amendments to major policy issues, or where the Council wishes to agree or amend a policy against the wishes of the Commission. In addition, since 1966 the member states have insisted on retaining the right to veto a decision that one or more members could clearly claim to be against their national interests. The veto, however, is regarded as something of a nuclear deterrent, held in reserve but never used. No one was surprised at Corfu when John Major threatened to use his veto to block Dehaene, but they were astounded, and even horrified, when he actually did use it.

Simple majority voting is not allowed on policy or legislative proposals; its use is mainly for procedural reasons. QMV is the most contentious of the voting methods, since it is directly related to the question of states' rights and the comparative strengths of small and large states within the Community. Under QMV the member states are given so many votes each, with a very approximate regard for their comparative size. From the start it was agreed that for a decision to be passed it would require in the region of 70 per cent of the votes, representing something like 60 per cent of the population of the Community. The votes are distributed in such a way that the large countries acting together cannot outvote the smaller states, while it would need the combination of two major countries and at least one more to block the decision-making process.

The votes given to the member states increased with each enlargement of the Community, and the required majority was adjusted to the 70 per cent mark each time. No one felt that the matter was in dispute until the enlargement of 1995. At that point there were seventy-six votes available to the Council distributed among member states as follows:

10 votes each	France, Germany, Italy, United Kingdom
8 votes	Spain
5 votes each	Belgium, Netherlands, Greece, Portugal
3 votes each	Denmark, Ireland
2 votes	Luxembourg

The number of votes required to pass a decision was fifty-four and the number required to block a motion was therefore twenty-three. Under enlargement it was proposed to give four votes each to Sweden and Austria and three votes each to Finland and Norway. This took the total number of votes to ninety, and in order to retain the blocking minority at 30 per cent of the total it was proposed to raise the necessary number of votes to twenty-seven.

Two countries objected to the proposal. Spain complained that Mediterranean countries felt threatened by the entry of four northern countries. To raise the threshold to twenty-seven was to reduce the Mediterranean countries' ability to look after their own interests, since the three countries concerned – Spain, Italy and Greece – could only raise twenty-three votes between them. The other country to object was Britain, with the claim that this was yet another example of the way in which Community institutions were biased towards the small states at the expense of the larger countries. The argument over this point produced a crisis which, for a time, threatened progress on enlargement, but finally a compromise was struck which made concessions to the British and Spanish positions but moved the blocking minority to twenty-seven, a position not greatly changed by Norway's later defection. The crisis did, however, make it very clear that a closely scrutiny of the relationship between voting rights and the size of the member state is a priority for the constitutional review of 1996. Ironically, in the light of this controversy, majority voting is very seldom used by the Council of Ministers even in areas where QMV is expected. The Council prefers to give the appearance of unanimity by continuing discussion overnight or other successive meetings until a compromise on a consensus decision is reached.

The European Council

With a membership made up of the heads of government from all member states, together with the President of the Commission, and with all the media attention that surrounds its biennial summit meetings, the public could be forgiven if they believe that the European Council is the most important institution of the Community. It is therefore ironic to realise that the European Council only received official recognition in the Single European Act of 1987, and still does not form part of the legal framework of the EU. The European Council cannot legislate unless it transforms itself for the purpose into an extraordinary meeting of the Council of Ministers, and decisions of the European Council are not subject to the jurisdiction of the Court of Justice.

Throughout the 1960s the heads of government of the member states of the Common Market met from time to time in what were largely unofficial and informal summits. In the early 1970s, however, after the first enlargement, a feeling grew that there was a lack of leadership in the Community: the institutions of the Community coped well enough with detailed policy but there was no focus of authority to give a more general direction and purpose to the development of the EC. It was the Franco-German partnership of Giscard d'Estaing and Schmidt who proposed, at the Paris Summit in 1974, that the occasional summit meetings should be formally institutionalised to serve this purpose.

The European Council therefore came into being as the result of a communiqué issued at the Paris Summit. The details were left vague and indeed the Council has tended to evolve on a pragmatic basis. During the 1970s the European Council was most concerned with general discussions of economic problems. In the early 1980s, with issues such as the British Budgetary Question and reform of the CAP providing problems, the European Council tended to take over the crucial preliminaries in the decision-making process, before referring back to the Council of Ministers. In the late 1980s and early 1990s the European Council became much more bound up in the issues of political and monetary union. Since the establishment of the European Union the European Council has been recognised as the body co-ordinating and integrating the three pillars of the EU.

It very soon became established that the European Council meets at least twice a year, usually being held in the final month of a member state's Presidency and hosted by the country holding the Presidency. The meetings of the European Council have therefore come to represent a public statement on the performance of the presiding country during its half-year tenure. And, since most member states now strive to satisfy some objective during their Presidency, the European Council meetings can be seen as a judgment on the achievement of those objectives. During the UK's Presidency in the second half of 1992 it was Britain's stated aim to amend the TEU to accommodate the preferences of countries such as the United Kingdom and Denmark; this was accomplished at the Edinburgh Summit with the strengthening of opt-out clauses and the doctrine of subsidiarity.

If an additional problem arises during a Presidency a special European Council may be called. In that second half of 1992, for example, a special Council was called in Birmingham during October, in order to do some work on the Danish question prior to Edinburgh. At first the actual meetings were always held in the capital of the country holding the Presidency, and if any special meeting was called, that was held in Brussels. Increasingly the host country tends to place the summit meeting in some other city, as was the case with Edinburgh or Maastricht. And, increasingly, special meetings are held in the presiding country rather than Brussels, as with Birmingham in 1992. These meetings are seen as a public relations exercise, with a lavish and successful European Summit being seen as a prestige symbol for the host country. Considerable time and money is spent on the two days of the Council, which can be critical for some of the smaller countries called on to host these meetings. The Edinburgh Summit in 1992, for example, cost the British government £9 million.[11]

Meetings of the European Council are much smaller than those of the Council of Ministers. Those attending are the heads of government for all member states (head of state for France, where the president rather than the prime minister leads the delegation), together with the foreign minister of each country. The President and Vice-President of the Commission also attend. Apart from these the national delegations can bring their own officials and advisers with them, but only one at a time can attend the meetings. Records are kept by members of the Council and Commission secretariats, together with officials of the presiding country. This secretariat is, however, restricted to a total of six. Other than interpreters these are the only persons permitted to attend the negotiating sessions.

Much of the work of a European Council takes place outside the meeting room. Some of that work takes the form of informal head-to-head meetings between individual leaders in what are sometimes called 'fireside chats'. Most of the work, however, is accomplished by the officials of the presiding country working alongside officials from the various national delegations. There is always far too much on the agenda for the participants to debate at length. In the months preceding the Council teams of officials will have drawn up papers which they feel will be agreed by the members of the Council. If they are successful it is only the finer points of detail that need to be discussed in the meeting. Then, following the afternoon and evening meetings of the first day, the officials can incorporate any changes made to the original draft in order to have a final communiqué ready for the lunch-time close on the second day.

C: The European Parliament

Until 1979 the European Parliament (EP) was composed of delegates nominated by their national governments in the same proportions as the various parties were represented in their national parliaments, many members having a 'dual mandate' membership of both European and national parliaments. The European Council of 1974, held in Paris, decided to implement the provision for direct elections that had been written into the Treaty of Rome, and this was put into effect from 1979. What did not happen at that time was any strengthening of the powers of the EP. Its powers have increased since then, most notably under the provisions of the SEA and TEU, but throughout its life the Parliament has been restricted by the member states through the Council of Ministers and European Council, for fear that a strengthening of the EP would be at the expense of national parliaments.

The EP has had three locations:

- the Assembly Chamber for plenary sessions in Strasbourg
- the committees structure in Brussels
- the administrative machinery in Luxembourg.

There used to be an Assembly Chamber in Luxembourg (it was the Assembly of the ECSC), but this was abandoned when the size of the EP doubled on the introduction of direct elections. The Strasbourg Chamber became too small in 1994, with the addition of forty-nine MEPs to allow for German reunification and with a further seventy-eight due in 1995, after enlargement. Many MEPs wanted to transfer plenary sessions to Brussels where there are ample facilities in the new parliament buildings, thus ending the MEPs' nomadic existence. However, 'this possibility is being blocked by the French government which intends to force through the construction of a new parliament building in Strasbourg for the benefit of *la Gloire*'.[12] Although almost all MEPs wanted to centre their activities in Brussels, the new parliament building in Strasbourg had the support of the French government, which refused to ratify the addition of extra members for German reunification in time for the 1994 elections, unless the EP agreed to continue meeting in the new Strasbourg buildings.

An MEP spends one week of every month in plenary session and between one and two weeks in every month on committee work. The rest of the time is spent working with the political group they belong to, travelling with an EP delegation on a fact-finding mission, or consulting with EP officials in Luxembourg. British MEPs also do a certain amount of constituency work, although with European constituencies nine times the size of a Westminster constituency, such links are not strong. MEPs from other countries do not face this problem since they are elected on a national or regional list without constituency ties. In the Assembly Chamber there are debates, commissioners deliver reports, there is a Question Time and the plenary session votes quite often, using electronic means to do so. Yet there seems to be little interest in the debates: the perpetual language problem means that speeches are deprived of oratory or humour, leaving debates that are uniformly dull and boring. The important work is done in the committees. Each MEP is assigned either to one of the nineteen standing committees or to an *ad hoc* specialised committee. These have an important input into the legislative process since Committee members draft reports on proposed legislation and put forward amendments, about a third of which, it is estimated, find their way into Community law.

The EP works closely with the Commission on proposed legislation but finds the Council less sympathetic. About 75 per cent of EP amendments are accepted by the Commission, whereas less than 20 per cent get past the Council into final legislation. This is part of the EP's 'democratic deficit', in that the Council are not legally obliged to listen to what the EP has to say. In January 1994 the EP voted to remove David Owen from his position as the EU's negotiator on Bosnia, but the decision was simply ignored by the Council of Ministers.

Powers possessed by the EP include the right to vote on the accession of new member states, and the right to be consulted by the Council of Ministers on the granting of associate status. On matters relating to the single market the EP can reject or amend

Council decisions, and such EP acts can only be overturned either by a unanimous vote of the Council if a proposal is rejected, or by qualified majority to overturn an amendment. Possibly the most important power is the ability to reject the EC Budget in its entirety, or to amend any part of the Budget that does not relate to a provision required by Treaty. The EP can therefore use the threat of delays in the Budget to extract concessions from the Commission or Council. The Commission must report to the EP every month, and the EP has the ultimate weapon of being able to dismiss the entire Commission (although it cannot dismiss individual commissioners) on a two-thirds majority. The TEU also gave the EP the right to pass a vote of confidence or non-confidence in an incoming Commission.

Another major innovation of the TEU is the right granted to the EP to appoint an ombudsman, who can investigate complaints of maladministration. This is part of a general policy which is increasing the EP's ability to scrutinise the working of the other EU institutions. Also, in Article 189b, paragraph 4, the Treaty establishes a Conciliation Committee with a membership drawn from both the EP and the Council, and with members of the Commission having a watching brief, so as to reconcile the views of EP and Council.

The democratic deficit of the European Parliament is being reduced by an increased willingness of the EP to challenge decisions of the Council. The most spectacular use of its new powers was the decision of the newly-elected Parliament of 1994 to challenge the appointment of Jacques Santer as President of the Commission, which for a time threatened to throw the Community into a renewed constitutional crisis.

However, the largest contributor to the democratic deficit is the apathy or disinterest of the public. The people not only do not seem to be interested in the workings of the EP but they are universally ignorant as to the function and identity of MEPs, and with the exception of those countries such as Belgium where voting is compulsory, their turn-out in European elections is pitifully small, while the issues on which people vote have more to do with national than with European factors. We shall return to the subject of European elections, parties and voting behaviour in Part Three.

D: The European Court of Justice

This court, based in Luxembourg, is not to be confused with the European Court of Human Rights, which meets in Strasbourg. The latter has nothing to do with the EU, even though all member states of the EU have signed the European Convention of Human Rights. The Court of Justice is exclusively concerned with the administration of Community Law.

The Court is made up of one judge for each member state, plus one additional judge. By the constitution of the Court, as laid down in the treaties, the judges should be chosen by agreement between the member states, but in fact each member state nominates its own judge and it is only the additional judge who needs to be appointed by mutual agreement. The judges are appointed for six years at a time but continuity is assured by a staggered replacement over a three-year cycle. The judges choose one of their members to act as President of the Court, with a three-year term of office. The presiding judge administers the work of the Court, in particular assigning cases to specific panels of judges and appointing the individual judge-rapporteurs who will be in charge of those panels.

In charge of collecting evidence and documentation for presentation to the judges, together with their own conclusions and legal judgments, are six advocates-general. Since there are less advocates-general than there are member states, their appointment is far more a case of mutual agreement than it is for the judges, but they tend to come from the larger states.

Cases can be brought before the Court by the institutions of the Community or by member states. Possibly the most frequent are cases brought by the Commission against member states for non-compliance with Community directives or regulations. Cases can, however, be brought by individuals or organisations who feel that their national governments are penalising them in breach of Community Law. For example, a man of 63 recently claimed that the UK was in breach of Community agreements on sexual equality because a man has to be 65 to get a state pension whereas a woman receives hers at 60. Many cases are referred to the European Court after they have failed on appeal in the national courts. Actual court actions, however, only form part of the Court's duties. About half the work arises from requests by member states for clarification or interpretation of some aspect of Community Law.

Only the most important cases, involving the Community institutions or member states, are heard before a full plenary Court, for which the quorum is seven judges. Most cases are heard in chambers before a panel of three judges in most cases, or five judges for more complex matters. There are five areas of competence for the Court:

1   Rulings on the Treaties which form the basis of the Community – Treaty of Paris (1951), the two Treaties of Rome (1957), the SEA (1986) and the TEU (1992).
2   Regulation of any international agreements made by the EC as a Community.
3   Any problems arising from EC regulations, which are those instructions which automatically become part of a member state's national law.
4   Any problems arising from EC directives, which are those instructions which become part of a member state's national law after ratification by the state's legislature.
5   Rulings on decisions made by the Commission.

Because of the pressure of business as the Community has grown, a second court was introduced in 1989 as a result of the Single European Act. This is the Court of First Instance, which deals with more routine matters. It has three areas of competence:

• Cases arising from the ECSC Treaty
• Cases involving breaches of competition rules
• Disputes between the Community and its staff.

The Court of First Instance has twelve judges as members. Cases are not heard before a plenary court but before one of five chambers, each with a panel of three or five judges. This court does not have advocates-general: one of the judges will act in the capacity of advocate if one is required.

For the individual or small business, the problem is that the Court of Justice is far too expensive for the average person (legal aid is not available) and the process is far too slow (the average time for a case in the Court, from application to judgment, is five years).

E: The Court of Auditors

The Court of Auditors is one of the most important of the institutions set up to scrutinise the conduct of Community institutions. As a single body it has only existed since 1977 and it has been less than powerful in the past. However, its powers were strengthened in the TEU in order to enhance the principle of accountability for Community institutions.

Each member state nominates one member for the Court, such nominees having to be suitably qualified as auditors, and usually being members of an official audit body in their own country. The nominees have then to be approved by the Council of Ministers and the EP. Appointment is for six years, after which the appointment can be renewed. From among their number the Court elects one member to serve as President of the Court for three years.

The duties of the Court of Auditors are related to the auditing of the Community's annual budget and the validation of the Commission's efficiency at administering the budget. There are groups within the Court of Auditors dealing with specific budgetary questions such as the CAP or the Regional Fund. Since the revisions under the TEU the Court has extended its activities away from merely concern over financial rectitude, and is more involved in questions of policy effectiveness.

Like the Commission, the Court of Auditors is very strongly supranational and its members and staff, like members and staff of the Commission, must sign an undertaking on appointment that they will not favour one member state in preference to another.

F: Special Interest Advisory Committees

The Economic and Social Committee (ESC)
This committee was written into the Treaty of Rome because it was felt that the Assembly, as a forerunner to the EP, would not be fairly representative of the sectional interests of the Community. The committee which has resulted bears faint echoes of the corporate state but has two main functions within the EC:

- as a forum within which special interests can co-operate in the exchange of views and ideas
- as a body that has a minor but integral place in the policy and decision-making process.

Originally the ESC was regarded on almost equal terms with the Assembly as a consultative body for the Council and Commission, but whereas the Assembly has gone on through direct elections to become the European Parliament, the ESC has retained a purely consultative role with no sanctions to ensure that its opinions are accepted.

Members are appointed to the ESC by their national governments through the Council of Ministers. Membership is roughly proportional to the size of the member state and falls into one of three categories:

Employers, of which about half represent industry, the other half being commercial bodies or services in the public sector
Employees, which basically means representatives of trade unions
Other interests, of which about half represent protectionist groups in areas of importance to the Community such as agriculture and transport, the other half representing special interest groups such as those concerned with the environment or consumer affairs.

The members of the ESC elect a president and two vice-presidents, as well as an executive committee known variously as the Bureau or Praesidium. The ESC will meet in plenary session on about eight occasions each year, but most of its work is in delivering opinions to the Council and Commission and, for this purpose, the ESC is split into nine working groups with interests in Agriculture, Industry, Economic Affairs, Social Questions, Transport and Communications, External Affairs, Energy and Nuclear matters, Regional Development and Environmental and Consumer Affairs.

The Committee of the Regions (COR)

This is the newest of the Community's institutions, being established by the TEU and meeting for the first time in March 1994. It is an attempt to bridge the gap between Brussels and the citizens of the Union, although anti-federalists such as Norman Tebbit claim that it is part of a Brussels plan to undermine the nation-state.[13] It does, however, reflect the growing importance of the regions in many member countries and, indeed, for the new relationships encouraged by the cross-border regions, such as the Rhine-Meuse Region created from parts of Belgium, Germany and the Netherlands. The COR provides a body that must be consulted during the legislative process on any matter which it is felt has regional implications, such as health, education, culture and infrastructure. There are also those who feel that in the future the COR may become a directly elected body and form a second chamber in an enlarged and strengthened European Parliament.

The pattern of membership follows that for the ESC but the criteria for appointment differ between member states, dependent on the degree of devolution existing in those states. Germany already is a federal state and COR membership is represented by members of the *Länder* governments. Belgium is also virtually a federation of the Flemish and Walloon communities. Other countries, such as Italy and Spain, are highly regionalised with semi-autonomous regional administrations, and these countries will draw most of their COR members from regional governments. The more centralised states such as Britain have appointed COR members from local councils. This issue was the cause of an important defeat for the British government in the Maastricht debate because the government wished to send unelected quango representatives to COR, but the opposition parties demanded that these representatives should all be elected councillors.

The COR is a new institution which has still to find an effective role and mode of operation. For Britain its major significance lies in its potential for those regions such as Scotland or Wales which look for independence or autonomy from Westminster: 'The widening wealth gap among regions is feeding demands for more radical action to redistribute wealth and refocus EU economic priorities. The poorer regions see greater decision-making power in Brussels not as an obstacle but as a pre-condition for greater autonomy'.[14]

G: Foreign affairs, defence and internal security

The institutions described so far have all been institutions of the European Community. But the Treaty for European Union recognised the EC as only one of the three 'pillars' of the European Union. The other two 'pillars' are a common foreign and security policy and a common policy relating to justice, home affairs and internal security. The only institution common to all pillars of the EU is the European Council. For the two sectors other than the EC the TEU created new institutions, or rather it rationalised existing *ad hoc* institutions within a framework of intergovernmental co-operation.

The European Council will co-ordinate policy under the leadership of the country holding the Presidency. On foreign affairs a new Political Committee has been set up to oversee the international situation and to deliver opinions to the Council.

Common Foreign and Security Policy (CFSP)
This was established under Title V of the TEU and has the aim of encouraging co-operation between member states in the formulation of a common foreign policy, and with the ultimate aim of implementing joint action of all member states where a

common interest is recognised. Also assumed in this process of increased co-operation is the need to safeguard the external interests of the Union through a common defence policy. The defence arm of the EU is to be the WEU, to which most member states already belong.

There are, obviously, problems concerning a common defence policy, particularly as far as the neutral status of many countries is concerned, and in respect of the applications for membership of former Soviet bloc countries. The relationships between the CFSP and the WEU will be investigated in the constitutional review of 1996, and in the mean time informal links have been set up between the organs of the CFSP and the Commission and EP, which may ultimately co-ordinate policy in this area.

During 1994 the role of the WEU as the defence arm of the EU increased as relationships within NATO showed signs of increasing strain over Bosnia. Britain and France forged new defence relationships in the face of American criticisms of European handling of the situation in former Yugoslavia. There is now a military planning unit for the WEU in Brussels, and from 1995 a multinational Eurocorps will operate from a base in Strasbourg, forming the nucleus of a possible future European army.

TREVI, the Schengen Group and Europol

There is no suggestion that the EU is to set up its own police force, nor institute a common judicial and legal system. What the TEU did do under Title VI was to set up or formalise certain institutions for co-operation on matters of law and order. The main preoccupation of the TEU is the preservation of the right to free movement of citizens within the EU, and so the areas of policy covered by co-operation procedures deal with terrorism, immigration, drug traffic, political asylum and border controls.

The TREVI group has been in existence since 1975, when it was set up to exchange information on international terrorism and violence. The name is supposed to stand for Terrorism-Radicalism-Extremism-Violence-International, but is in fact a punning joke on the name of the French Justice Minister, Fontaine, who helped set up the group at a meeting in Rome close to the Fountain of Trevi. The group has functioned since then as part of the Council of Ministers, although more in the exchange of information between officials than in meetings between ministers.

The Schengen Group was formed in 1985 in the town of Schengen on the Luxembourg–German border. It arose as a reaction to the reluctance of some EC members to see the removal of internal border controls. At Schengen, France, Germany and the Benelux countries agreed to abolish border controls between their countries. In 1990 they were joined by Italy, and in 1991 by Spain and Portugal. The TEU accepted the Schengen principle as part of its home affairs policy, with the intention of extending its provisions to the whole of the EU. But some countries, most notably the United Kingdom, were reluctant to join for fear of giving assistance to the free movement of terrorists, drug traffickers and illegal immigrants.

The TEU instituted the European Police Office (Europol) initially to exchange information and ideas to control drug traffic. Since it began operation in 1992 its remit has been widened to include the exchange of criminal intelligence of all kinds. Europol has a Co-ordinating Committee of senior officials, reporting to the Council of Ministers. There are many problems concerning the development of Europol as a union-wide police body, not only questions of language and incompatible central computer systems but the basic difference in legal systems between member states.

Summary

Beyond the institutions listed above there are a number of bodies and mechanisms aimed at the goal of economic union. Since Britain has opted out of the EMS and the whole question has been in flux since the economic crises of 1992–93, it has been felt best to ignore these issues for the present and to concentrate instead on those organs of the EU which can form the basis of a constitutional framework in the IGC review of 1996.

Notes

1 Neill Nugent, *The Government and Politics of the European Community*, Macmillan, London 1991, p. 309.

2 R. Jenkins (Lord Jenkins of Hillhead), *European Diary 1977–1981*, Collins, London 1989.

3 Treaty for European Union, Title II (amendments to the Treaty of Rome), Article 157, clause 2.

4 Quoted in an article by John Palmer in *The Guardian*, 23 March 1994.

5 *Ibid.*

6 TEU, Title II, Article 158, clause 2.

7 No one source seems able to agree on the exact size of the Commission staff – figures quoted range from 13,000 to 16,000, the figure chosen depending on variable factors. The figure I give is approximate but that does not invalidate the point that, for a busy bureaucracy with wide-ranging responsibilities, the Brussels establishment is very small.

8 Sonia Mazey and Jeremy Richardson, 'Pressure Groups and the EC', *Politics Review*, September 1993, pp. 20–4.

9 TEU, Title II, Article 146.

10 TEU, Title II, Article 151, clause 1.

11 A useful insight into the organisation of European Council meetings can be gained from a BBC television documentary in the series *True Brits*, showing the workings of the Foreign Office. The first programme in the series, *The Minister*, shown on BBC2, 28 April 1994, followed the Minister of European Affairs, Tristan Garel-Jones, during Britain's tenure of the Presidency in 1992.

12 Matthew Engel, 'Parliament of Snoozers', *The Guardian*, 25 January 1994.

13 John Carvel, report on the first meeting of the COR, *The Guardian*, 7 March 1994.

14 John Palmer, 'Devolved power redraws map', *The Guardian*, 7 March 1994.

II

The impact of Europe on the
British political system

4

Sovereignty and constitutional change

In 1972, by signing the Treaty of Accession, the British Government tacitly accepted as part of British law some 43 volumes of European legislation, made up of more than 2,900 regulations and 410 directives – the sum total of legislation agreed by the Community over the twenty years since its formation. Admittedly, much of this legislation was trivial: most regulations or directives from Brussels deal with small points of detail such as intervention prices for commodities within the Common Agricultural Policy. Nevertheless, there were some major issues involved, and in any case, the triviality of certain details is unimportant compared to the basic principle that here was a solid corpus of law that became binding upon the peoples of the United Kingdom, despite that law never having been scrutinised or debated by the British Parliament. It was a massive breach of the constitutional convention which holds that Parliament is the supreme, and indeed only, law-making body in the UK.

Ironically enough, this major shift in the constitutional position was hardly notice at the time. In the early years of British membership, most complaints about Europe concerned the operational faults and absurdities of the Community. People complained that Europe was

- too bureaucratic
- too time-wasting
- too remote from the people

- too undemocratic
- and far too expensive.

That which most alienated public opinion and which attracted the lion's share of complaints, however, was the cost and irrationalities of the CAP. The CAP was seen as criminally wasteful, with three major drawbacks:

- it penalised the British taxpayer to the benefit of profligate foreigners
- it gave over-generous aid to French, and other inefficient, peasant-farmers
- it produced the so-called 'mountains' and 'lakes' of food surpluses.

Once this perception of cost and waste became fixed in peoples' minds, it has to be said that many of the criticisms levelled at the Community in those early years were value-judgements, or emotional reactions based on preconceived ideas, which often did not stand up to serious scrutiny. Such fears and criticisms concerned practical operational matters relating to the working of the Community. Very few people, including MPs, understood, let alone concerned themselves with, constitutional theory. Only the old-fashioned parliamentarians such as Enoch Powell concerned themselves at that time with constitutional matters and the issue of sovereignty, and it is only since the late 1980s that a more widespread concern has been expressed as to the extent to which membership of the EU has led to a transfer of sovereignty from Westminster to Brussels, and the extent to which the United Kingdom has ceased to be a fully sovereign and independent state.

Sovereignty

A dictionary definition of the word sovereignty is 'supreme and unrestricted power residing in an individual or group of people or body';[1] to be precise it is the legislative or judicial body that has no superior body able to override legislative or judicial decisions made for the territory over which it is sovereign. In Britain, Parliament is held to be sovereign because no other body has the right to pass and implement laws. So jealously does Parliament guard the right to be the only legislative body that other governmental or non-governmental bodies which need to pass laws, rules and regulations, such as local government or national institutions like British Rail, can only do so through the device known as delegated legislation. Through delegated legislation, Parliament grants to other bodies the facility to pass laws, but only laws specifically related to the jurisdiction of the authority concerned. In strict legal parlance they are not laws, but by-laws. As the nineteenth-century constitutional writer, A. V. Dicey, put it:

> The sovereignty of Parliament is the dominant characteristic of our political institution ... [Parliament] has, under the English constitution, the right to make or unmake any law whatever, and, further, that no person or body is recognised by the law of England as having a right to override or set aside the legislation of Parliament.[2]

Sovereignty is a difficult concept to define precisely. In Classical Greece Aristotle defined it as 'belonging to whichever group of citizens should make the final administrative decisions'. Aristotle distinguished between two kinds of sovereignty, one based on personal rule and the other on impersonal institutions: 'Rightly constituted laws should be the final sovereign'.[3] In modern political theory these two types of sovereignty are distinguished as:

Legal sovereignty which, in unitary states, is usually vested in the legislature. The source of legal sovereignty in federal or supranational states is harder to define, although the general belief for the United States is that the Constitution is sovereign.

Political sovereignty which is vested in a person or persons. At one time the sovereign was the monarch, but with democracy has come the belief that sovereignty is vested in the people. Under this form of constitution it is felt that no change can be made in the nature of the state without consulting the people through a referendum or plebiscite.

In Britain sovereignty is said to be vested in 'The Crown in Parliament'. This concept evokes the image of Parliament on the day of the State Opening, with the Queen enthroned in the House of Lords, surrounded by both her Houses of Parliament. In practice, the term 'Crown' refers not to the person of the monarch as such but to the body which now exercises the royal prerogative on behalf of the monarch: in other words, the crown equals the executive which equals the government. This highlights an anomaly in any dispute over the surrender of sovereignty. In the face of 'the ability of the Government to whip its own backbenchers through the voting lobbies to support its policies',[4] it is only fair to say that what is called by ministers 'parliamentary sovereignty' is rather more accurately 'executive' or 'governmental' sovereignty. David Judge has claimed that this is the 'contradiction at the heart of the British Constitution: of the principle of parliamentary sovereignty being used by executives to minimise their accountability'.[5]

This ambivalence and imprecision over the definition of sovereignty can lead to problems, in that those who believe they are arguing about sovereignty from a common basis can in fact be arguing about quite different things: 'Sovereignty has two meanings in UK politics, whereas it has only one in other European countries ... [therefore] ... debating sovereignty is more difficult in the UK than elsewhere in Europe because of its other reference to parliamentary sovereignty'.[6] Any government which speaks about the need to preserve sovereignty is almost certainly talking about parliamentary sovereignty, and therefore about the government's fears of a curtailment of its own powers. Those opposed to Europe, however, tend to speak in terms of national sovereignty, playing upon those chauvinistic and xenophobic tendencies that sometimes seem natural to British people.

Lady Thatcher, for example, has tended to wrap herself in the Union Flag when speaking of Europe, hinting that the freedom of Britain is at stake. 'Willing and active co-operation between independent sovereign states,' she said in her Bruges speech, 'is the best way to build a successful European Community'; in this view, to suppress nationality in favour of a centralised Europe

would be extremely damaging. Some of Lady Thatcher's supporters were even more willing to play the xenophobic card to
maintain national independence, often by playing on anti-German
prejudices that have lingered since the last war. In July 1990 there
was a furore over an interview given to Dominic Lawson, of the
Spectator magazine, by the late Nicholas Ridley, then a government minister. In the midst of other anti-European remarks
Ridley went so far as to say, 'I'm not against giving up sovereignty
in principle, but not to this lot. You might just as well give it to
Adolf Hitler'. The implication was that the surrender of British
sovereignty to the European Community was akin to the Germans using the EC to fulfil the dream of world domination that
had been pursued by Hitler and the Nazi Party in the Second
World War. The outrage that greeted Ridley's comments, particularly in Germany, led to his resignation but his words had re-
awakened the seemingly natural distrust of foreigners on the part
of the British, which led in turn to a fear of Europe as representing foreign, particularly German, domination.[7]

What the Euro-phobes tend to obscure is the position that any
surrender of sovereignty that has taken place so far is only partial
and that, quite irrespective of the European Community, all
nations in the modern world are having to surrender some aspects
of their sovereignty. The multinational nature of life in the late
twentieth century, particularly in the fields of defence, trade and
the economy, has forced most countries into a series of compromises between independence and dependency. One result is a
marked decline in the nature and status of the nation-state, and,
as the nation-state has declined, so too have the more chauvinistic aspects of national sovereignty that are so much a part of the
nationalist credo.

The nation-state

In the Middle Ages the concept of a politico-geographical entity
composed of people with a common ethnicity, religion, language
and culture was unknown. Everyone paid lip-service to a vague
concept known as Christendom, within which the Emperor rep-

resented secular power and the Pope spiritual dominion. Within that dual hegemony, loyalties and allegiances were personal, made up of the reciprocal oaths, duties and obligations of the feudal system. When the nation-state began to emerge, as early as the fourteenth century, it as largely due to a breakdown in feudal relationships through disputed allegiances. In 1320, protesting at English interference in the affairs of Scotland, the letter to the Pope known as the Declaration of Arbroath was the first known expression of a belief in the natural right of a nation to be free and independent of foreign domination.

Within a few years of the Declaration of Arbroath the dispute between France and England known as the Hundred Years War had transformed a feudal quarrel between two kings into a bitter war between two countries, each of which developed a strong sense of national identity, if only through the hostility expressed by one people towards the other. Most nation-states arose through war, or revolution, or the expulsion of an alien power. Thus England and France discovered their national identities in fighting each other, while Spain and Portugal emerged though expulsion of the Moors from the Iberian Peninsula.

Yet although the nation-states mentioned above had emerged by the fifteenth century, the widespread development of the nation-state, to the point at which it is perceived as the natural order of things, is a fairly recent development. In Europe the persistence of supranationality retained the Holy Roman Empire until 1800. But an attempt by the 1815 Congress of Vienna to recreate the old regime through the institution of an Austro-Hungarian Empire led, in reaction, to the rise of liberal nationalism. Nationalism had its nineteenth-century successes, such as the independence of Greece and the unification of Italy, in the creation of what Mazzini called 'a sovereign nation of free and equal beings'.

The heyday of the nation-state, however, undoubtedly came in the aftermath of the two world wars. After 1918 the collapse of the Austro-Hungarian, Russian and Ottoman Empires created a wealth of new nations. Even more productive was the period of decolonisation which followed the Second World War, with further to come with the collapse of the Soviet bloc in 1989.

Between 1870 and 1914 there were only about 50 sovereign states in the world, 16 of them in Europe. The figure barely fluctuated over the period. By the end of the first world war the community of nations had grown by 10 as new states emerged in Europe. When it was founded in 1920 the League of Nations had 42 members: its successor the United Nations, was established in 1945 with a membership of 51. By 1960 this figure had grown to 82; by 1973 it was 135 and in 1992 it stood at 183.[8]

The supranational institution of the European Union has therefore grown up in a period when the nation–state internationally was seen as the normal political unit. In the words of John Major, 'Europe's peoples in general retain their favour and confidence in the nation state ... I believe the nation state will remain the basic political unit for Europe. The European Union is an association of states, deriving its basic democratic legitimacy through national parliaments'.[9] Yet, at the end of the twentieth century, the nation–state is under threat from two directions: overshadowed by supranational and multinational organisations, and yet undermined by the minor nationalisms of regions, religious groups or ethnic minorities.

The state survives, but it is no longer the supreme authority within a defined territory. Increasingly, it finds itself bargaining with multinational companies strong enough to play one state off against another, and sharing power with sub-national provincial or regional authorities on the one hand and with the proto-federal institutions of the EC on the other. It has ceased to be the sole, or even the chief, custodian of the interests of its citizens.[10]

The appeal of Euro-scepticism to the adherent of the nation–state, as a defence of national sovereignty against the encroachment of an alien Europe, is therefore essentially flawed because the nation–state, instead of reaching its apotheosis in the post-war world, is in decline in the face of international reality.

The decline of the nation–state

The impression given by the opponents of European Union is

that Europe is the only threat posed to national sovereignty and that withdrawal from the EU would leave the country once more fully independent of foreign influences. This is to ignore the realities of the modern world and the extent to which Britain, in common with most other countries, has surrendered vital aspects of its sovereignty quite independently of EC membership. In the latter part of the twentieth century it is no longer possible for a country to exist in glorious isolation: in defence, economics and the development of trade the countries of the world are interdependent.

During the D-Day anniversary ceremonies in 1994 it was often stressed that the D-Day invasion of Normandy was probably the last occasion when Britain could be regarded as a major power and a military equal to the United States. Thereafter Britain, France and other European countries were dwarfed militarily, and in every other way, by the two so-called superpowers of the USA and the USSR. Defence in the post-war world was only possible through the collective security of international alliances such as NATO. Elements of national sovereignty were therefore sacrificed as part of the nation's armed forces was put under international control, and national defence policy was subordinated to strategic decisions made by a supranational body – in this case the North Atlantic Council for NATO.

If defence proved to be too difficult for individual nation-states to handle in the face of the world superpowers, then so also was international trade and commerce. Very few national economies are strong enough to survive in a world of unrestricted market forces, and indeed all nations find that it is in their interests to subordinate themselves to GATT (the General Agreement on Tariffs and Trade) and its successor emerging from the Uruguay Round.

In any country one of the hallmarks of sovereignty is the ability of that country's government, banks and financial institutions to dictate the nature of economic and fiscal policy within that government's jurisdiction. In 1976 the economic situation facing the Labour government became so grave that Britain was on the verge of what, in an individual, would have been called bankruptcy. In order to escape from its difficulties the government, in the person of the Chancellor Denis Healey, appealed to the United Nations agency, the International Monetary Fund (IMF), for help and Britain was granted a loan to extricate the country from the situation in which it found itself. But the loan came with conditions attached. One of those conditions was that the Treasury would receive a team of advisers from the IMF, who would have the power to dictate certain aspects of British economic policy. A programme of cuts in services and public expenditure followed, which represented important economic policy and legislation that was not originated by the government and which was not subject to amendment by Parliament. Healey, as Chancellor, was forced to implement these harsh economic conditions and could do nothing to soften the blow, even though many of his actions were against the socialist principles of his government. This was a major intrusion on the nation's sovereignty far more significant than any European legislation to date, in that it overrode the 600-year-old principle that the House of Commons has sole jurisdiction over the money supply.

In signing the European Convention for the Protection of Human Rights and Fundamental Freedoms in 1950, and in accepting the subsequent establishment of the European Court and Commission of Human Rights, the British government acknowledged a source of law other than Parliament and a final court of appeal other than the House of Lords. In accepting and implementing the decisions and judgments of the Court or Commission since then, the government has voluntarily surrendered the main theoretical plank which makes up parliamentary sovereignty.

In these contexts it can be said that any surrender of sovereignty that resulted from accession to the European Community is merely a continuation of a more general recognition that the modern state cannot be nationally self-sufficient, and that states are now essentially interdependent. In that light the more enthusiastic Europeans tend not to talk of surrendering sovereignty but of pooling sovereignty. In other words, the nation-state retains its separate identity in the more general sense, while sharing sovereignty with other states in certain agreed areas.

At the same time as the nation-state is diminished by the pooling of sovereignty over major policy matters there is also a sense whereby the nation-state is undermined by the growth of regional autonomy, or separatist movements, on ethnic, linguistic or religious grounds. Most European countries have powerful regions or separatist movements:

- Within Britain there are Scottish and Welsh Nationalist parties, as well as the problems of Northern Ireland.
- France has language-based separatist movements in Brittany and Languedoc.
- Belgium's division between Dutch and French speakers has turned the country into a *de facto* federal state, with separate assemblies for Flanders and Wallonia.
- In Italy the Lega Nord has won major electoral successes and now has a share in government, on a programme of federalisation for Italy through a division into North, South and Central.
- In Spain, regions such as Catalonia have become semi-autonomous, while the Basques continue to fight for independence.
- In the border areas of the Community regions are being created that cut across national frontiers. Along the Rhine and the Meuse new local areas are being set up, with their own municipalities and town halls, which ignore the orders between Belgium, Germany and the Netherlands.

In ways such as this, the monolithic power of the nation-state, whilst being vigorously defended against the external threat of a federal Europe, is crumbling and fragmenting internally.

This dual attack on the nature of the nation-state leads to many anomalies. National governments, in defending themselves against what they see as the centralising powers of Brussels, claim rights for themselves which they deny to those of their own regions that are seeking decentralisation. Thus the British government protests at regulation from a distant and remote Brussels but still insists on Westminster's domination of Scotland's affairs, even though London is equally as remote to the Scots as is Brussels. These anomalies and other difficulties with European integration arise from differences in the interpretation of the term 'federal'.

1   For the ardent adherents of the nation-state, such as the British or Danish governments, federalism is equated with a centralised super-state in Brussels, eating away at the independence of member nations.

2   The view of federalists is that the federal state is the prerequisite for decentralisation. In their view the federal structure provides an overall policy framework from which the power to take decisions may be devolved, to national governments if need be, but equally to regional or local administrations where that is more appropriate. As Lord Thomas has said:

> it seems that when John Major talks of disliking a centralised federal Europe, he must actually be saying nothing, since the essence of the word 'federal' is that it is not centralised. If a group of states wish to act in common in some ways and, at the same time, want to preserve national identity, how can you avoid having a (federal) polity ... There is thus a paradox if those who say they want to preserve national identity insist, at the same time, that they are against a federal solution in Europe. Surely only a federal structure can preserve the identity of peoples.[11]

The loss of sovereignty

By signing the Treaty of Accession in 1972, Britain accepted the Treaties of Rome and the other foundations of European Community law. Since then the UK government has signed for itself the Single European Act and the Treaty for European Union. All these agreements mean that Britain has accepted a diminution of sovereignty, in that:

• laws enacted by the Communities are directly applicable in Britain
• the UK Parliament is barred from passing laws in areas where Community law already exists or where national law would be

inconsistent with Community law
- British courts must accept and enforce decisions of the European Court of Justice.

As European law states:

> On the basis of the powers thus conferred on them, the Community institutions can enact legal instruments as a Community legislature legally independent of the Member States. Some of these instruments take effect directly as Community law in the Member States, and thus do not require any transformation into national law in order to be binding, not only on the Member States and their organs, but also on the citizen.[12]

This surrender of sovereignty is not, however, all-embracing. The Community works according to the principle of the *specific attribution of powers*. This means that the scope and parameters of Community competence are limited and vary according to different tasks. There are areas which lie outside the objectives set the Community by the founding treaties, and where Community law therefore has no relevance. In other areas Community law is directly applicable and has clear primacy over national law. In between are areas where Community decisions lay down the general aims and objectives of the law but where national governments are permitted considerable latitude as to how those decisions are applied. Above all, the argument can legitimately be advanced that sovereignty is not abandoned when Community law is made by the Council of Ministers on which all member states are strongly represented: 'The Member States have pooled certain parts of their own legislative powers in favour of these Communities and have placed them in the hands of Community institutions in which, however, they are given in return substantial rights of participation'.[13]

It must be said, however, that those Euro-sceptics who comfort themselves with the thought that the transfer of sovereignty to Europe is limited and of no great importance are embracing false comfort. It has long been established that, if there were a conflict between Community law and national law then, constitutionally, Community law has primacy. This was tested very early in the history of the EEC by a case referred to the European

Court of Justice by a magistrate in Milan in 1964. The case was brought by a former employee of the electricity generating company Edison–Volta, who claimed that his interests had been harmed by the formation of the ENEL, the Italian nationalised electricity industry. It was claimed that the Italian government's nationalisation of the electrical generating and supply industries, in 1962, had infringed EEC regulations. It therefore became a case of conflict between national and Community law and was referred to the European Court for decision. As a result of the judgment given the relationship between Community law and national law became subject to Community case law.[14]

- Member states have transferred sovereign rights to a Community created by them. They cannot reverse this process by means of unilateral measures inconsistent with the Community.
- No member state may call into question the status of Community law as a system uniformly and generally applicable throughout the Community.
- Community law, enacted in accordance with the Treaties, has priority over any conflicting law of the member states.
- Community law is not only stronger than earlier national law but has a limiting effect on laws adopted subsequently.[15]

The most obvious constitutional change consequent upon membership of the European Union is therefore a surrender of the UK's parliamentary sovereignty to the primacy of Community law. One interesting argument put forward prior to 1972 was that advanced by Harold Wilson. In reply to the accusation that membership of the EEC would diminish British sovereignty, particularly parliamentary sovereignty, he said: 'Accession to the Treaties would involve the passing of United Kingdom legislation. This would be an exercise, of course, of Parliamentary sovereignty … Community law, past and future, would derive its force as law in this country from that legislation passed by Parliament'.[16] The suggestion would seem to be that the Act of Accession, which gave entry into the British legal system for all past, present and future Community law, was little more than an advanced form of delegated legislation. In other words, Community law can be applied in Britain without detracting from British parliamentary sovereignty because the right to apply that law was originally granted by a law passed by the British Parliament. Harold Wilson was an astute politician and a past master of the sophistry of political argument, but it has to be said that to see Community law as yet more delegated legislation is simply misleading. The British Parliament cannot refuse to accept Community law, nor debate it, nor repeal it, unless Britain were to cancel the Treaty of Accession and withdraw altogether from the European Union.

So it must be accepted that the UK has surrendered both parliamentary and national sovereignty through the act of joining the European Union. That loss of sovereignty, and thereby the loss of national identity, is the main complaint about membership now brought by those hostile to the European ideal, whether they are known as Euro-sceptics or as Euro-phobes. In recent years this mantle of hostility has been taken on by the government in its attitudes and policy, and measures have been taken to counter or ameliorate the degree to which the Community can impinge upon the country's independence of action.

Defending the national identity

It was Lady Thatcher, when she was still Prime Minister, who first expressed the government's determination to defend British national independence and oppose federalism, which she stigmatised as 'centralisation'. Yet the irony is that it was Mrs Thatcher who signed the Single European Act, which, more than any other act, made a loss of sovereignty inevitable. As a prominent student of the EU stated: 'If you remove internal barriers you let illegal as well as legal substances cross Europe. If you want to police that, you have to have co-operation and this will affect the law-making authority of individual countries'.[17] When John Major succeeded Lady Thatcher as Prime Minister he made much of his commitment to Europe and of maintaining Britain's place 'at the heart of Europe'. Nevertheless, it was not long before the Major government, faced with the opposition of Euro-sceptical Tory back-benchers, was showing itself to be just as opposed to European integration as the Thatcher administration had been. From being mildly Euro-enthusiast in his views, John Major became what Hugo Young called 'a pragmatic Euro-sceptic'. In November 1992 the FCO published a pamphlet to mark Britain's Presidency of the EC. Called *Britain in Europe*, it purported to explain the European Community and the Maastricht Treaty to the general public. In fact it represented a statement of government policy:

The original Community treaties aimed at an 'ever-closer union among the peoples of Europe'. The Government are committed to closer co-operation with our Community partners. This has brought political and economic benefits. But the Government don't want, and won't have, a United States of Europe.[18]

In negotiating the Maastricht agreements and in subsequent relations with Europe the British government has moved steadily away from federalism towards a militant functionalist defence of national identities against encroachment from Brussels. Whether it is inspired by conviction or from a fear of the thirty or so Euro-sceptic Tory MPs is not certain, but it is clear that the Major administration has defended British self-interest through agreeing opt-outs in the Maastricht Treaty, the concept of subsidiarity, the retention of the national veto in the Council of Ministers and the possibility of a multi-track, multi-speed European development.

Opt-outs and variable geometry

Having agreed the terms of the Maastricht Treaty, a number of member states negotiated protocols giving them exemptions from the clauses of the Treaty. Some of these were quite minor, as with France, Spain and Portugal, who all negotiated exemptions for overseas territories such as the Canary Islands or the Azores, where those territories are unable to meet the Community's economic objectives. Spain and Portugal were also granted an exemption until 1999 from the need to meet emission targets.

A much more serious exemption was agreed for the UK over the agreement in Maastricht as to the goal of European monetary union. Protocol 11 of the TEU states, 'The United Kingdom shall not be obliged or committed to move to the third stage of economic and monetary union without a separate decision to do so by its government and Parliament'. Most importantly for the argument over sovereignty, this opt-out preserves the independence of the Bank of England in its freedom from moves to establish a European Central Bank. On the other hand it might be argued that the opt-out prevents the UK from having any say in the development and nature of the European Central Bank, and of the form taken by an economic union that Britain may well have to join in the future.

The main constitutional issue involved in economic and monetary union is that of economic sovereignty – loss of which would mean the government, the Governor of the Bank of England and the Chancellor of the Exchequer having to surrender control of the British economy to central European institutions. For the public, however, a much more relevant issue, because it is an emotional one, is the question of whether a common currency would mean having to give up the pound and penny. In their pamphlet the government were reassuring in this: 'Britain is not committed to joining a move to a single currency. If we choose we can stay out indefinitely'.

The same exemption from the need to follow the other member states into economic union was granted to Denmark, on the grounds that Denmark could only enter into negotiations over economic union if required to do so by a referendum of the Danish people. Denmark also won opt-outs over the defence element within the TEU and over certain aspects of EU citizenship. It is to be noted that neither the UK nor Denmark see these opt-outs over economic union and the common currency as necessarily permanent: both countries retain the right to rejoin the process at a time which suits them best. The two countries are exercising their sovereignty in that any future pooling of that sovereignty will be done at the wish of the member country and at a speed set by the member country.

A more significant gesture of national independence for Britain is the implementation of the so-called Social Chapter, the programme for social protection in the workplace and elsewhere, which was accepted by all the other member countries. The UK Government claimed that the Social Chapter, particularly in its provisions for a minimum wage and legislation on maximum working hours, was potentially harmful to the competitiveness of British industry. As such, the British negotiators at Maastricht did not so much opt-out of the agreement on social policy, as never opt-in in the first place. In the final treaty the Agreement on Social Policy is described as 'Concluded between the Member States of the European Community with the exception of the United Kingdom of Great Britain and Northern Ireland'.

This approach – of only signing the parts of a treaty with which you agree – opens up the possibility known in Community jargon as *variable geometry*. This was an option originally devised for future member states in Eastern Europe, who might never become members if they had to wait until they had parity of economic strength and stability with the countries of Western Europe. As a result, member states would progress towards integration at a speed suitable for each individual state. According to Philip Lynch:

The 'variable geometry' approach envisages European integration as a Chinese meal at which some diners take large portions of each dish but are left still wanting more, while the more sceptical steer clear of those bits they cannot stomach. This option may prove an attractive proposition for a British government eager to claim economic benefits without paying for them through further losses of national autonomy. But inherent in this is the danger of being relegated to Europe's 'second division'.[19]

This was the pattern John Major appeared to advocate during the 1994 European elections campaign, when he claimed that the best way forward for Britain might lie in a multi-track, multi-speed Europe. Those members who wanted it could proceed towards integration without involving those members less sympathetic to a federalist approach. And yet, when the French and Germans put forward just such a plan for a centre-core, fast-track

integrated Europe consisting basically of France, Germany and
the Benelux countries, coupled with a peripheral, slow-lane status
for the rest, John Major was the first to condemn it and made a
major speech in the Netherlands to denounce the idea.[20]

Subsidiarity

The concept of subsidiarity was developed, much at the wish of
John Major's negotiating team, in order to counter British fears
of what was seen as the committed pro-federalism of the Maastricht agreement. In Britain, unlike the rest of Europe, federalism
was equated with centralism, giving rise to fears of a powerful
federal administration in Brussels imposing its will on the
member states, with no regard being paid to the wishes of national
parliaments. What was developed at Maastricht was the doctrine
of subsidiarity, originally defined in the Treaty itself as 'decisions
are taken as closely as possible to the citizen':

In areas which do not fall within its exclusive competence, the Community should take action, in accordance with the principle of subsidiarity,
only in so far as the proposed action cannot sufficiently be achieved by
the Member States and can therefore, by reason of the scale or effects of
the proposed action, be better achieved by the Community. Any action
of the Community shall not go beyond what is necessary to achieve the
objectives of this Treaty.[21]

This, the definition of subsidiarity at the time the Treaty was
signed in February 1992, was felt by the British government to
be inadequately stressed. Britain therefore used its Presidency in
the second half of 1992 to strengthen and refine the principle,
much of the Birmingham and Edinburgh Summits being given
over to the matter. The communiqué issued at the conclusion of
the Edinburgh meeting stated in clarification that 'the Community [is] to act only when member states cannot achieve the
desired goal themselves'. The intention therefore has been to
ensure that an important role remains for national governments
in the legislative process. Any proposed legislation in Brussels
must now be first scrutinised for its subsidiarity, and if action

would be best dealt with by national governments then the proposal must be passed down to the most appropriate authority.

It is here that the proponents of subsidiarity have made a rod for their own backs. Simply because a proposal is thought to be inappropriate for Community action does not necessarily mean that action by national governments is any more appropriate. It could well be the case that regional or local action might be even more suitable. Certainly, the Scottish National Party has adopted the concept of subsidiarity with enthusiasm, with its slogan of 'Scotland in Europe', meaning that in matters of importance to Scotland, there need be no intervening English body between Brussels and a Scottish Assembly or Council. The anomaly is that although the Westminster government has advocated subsidiarity to prevent centralisation in Brussels, that government is very ardently centralist in its management of the affairs of the United Kingdom. The British government may find that in safeguarding the principle of national sovereignty they have sacrificed the union of the United Kingdom.

The veto

The use of opt-outs and the doctrine of subsidiarity are useful weapons for national governments in their fight to retain sovereignty, but their ultimate weapon, as proved by de Gaulle in the 1960s, or John Major at the Corfu Summit in 1994, is in the use of the national veto in the Council of Ministers. The original plan or decision-making in the Council of Ministers was that there should be unanimity or the proposal would fail, thus effectively giving each member state a veto and the ability to block decisions even when they were approved by all other members. In the 1960s de Gaulle's use of the veto not only blocked British accession on two occasions, but effectively stymied progress by the Community in any direction that did not suit French interests.

The reaction to de Gaulle's use of the veto was to move towards extending the number of areas that could be decided by majority voting instead of by unanimous decision. Because the smaller member countries were concerned that a simple majority voting system would disadvantage them in any confrontation with the larger countries, a qualified majority voting system (QMV) was introduced. This gave differential numbers of votes to the countries, roughly dependent on size, and required a coalition of around 30 per cent of the total number of votes in order to block a proposal. The figures were so arranged that it would take a coalition of at least three member states to prevent a decision from going through. It was on this basis that the use of QMV was steadily extended, in both the SEA and TEU, to the extent that decisions requiring unanimity, and therefore subject to veto, were increasingly confined to major constitutional matters involving changes to the original treaties. Qualified majority voting was becoming accepted as the norm until the proposed enlargement of January 1995, when the issue of voting and the veto became a sticking-point of principle for a Conservative government attempting to appear firm so as to allay the fears of Euro-sceptics on its own back-benches.

In 1994, when the crisis over voting rights erupted, the total number of votes assigned to the twelve members of the Council of Ministers was seventy-six, distributed roughly according to size. The four largest member states had ten votes each, while the smallest, Luxembourg, had two votes. The then blocking minority was twenty-three, about 30 per cent of the total. As from 1995, however, it was proposed to enlarge the Community by admitting four more countries to membership, these four countries being given weighted votes in the Council of Ministers in accordance with the rule of thumb previously applying: Austria and Sweden getting four votes each, and Finland and Norway three each. Still applying the rules of precedent, it was proposed that the blocking majority should be raised to twenty-seven, so as to remain at 30 per cent of the new total of ninety.

Britain at once objected, claiming that the change would weaken the position of the large countries within the Community. The argument which followed threatened to overthrow the timetable for entry of the new applicants, even though Britain was very much in favour of the Scandinavian countries' accession. However, the position of the Conservative Party in Britain seemed to be that the veto in Council, as something that prevented other countries from telling Britain what it could or could not do, was the last safeguard of national sovereignty. Ultimately, Britain had to agree to a compromise in which the blocking minority rose to twenty-seven, but member countries retained a strengthened right to apply the veto if they could show that otherwise their national interests were threatened. In the European election campaign which followed, the Conservative Party made it clear that their first priority in Europe was now to be the defence of the national veto, and they would be looking for it to be strengthened in the IGC consultations of 1996, as well as reassigning the voting figures to reflect more closely the relative population sizes of Community members.

Only a short period later, in June 1994, Britain emphasised the importance of the veto by being the one country at the Corfu European Council to block the appointment of Jean-Luc Dehaene, Prime Minister of Belgium, as President of the Commission in succession to Jacques Delors. This was the second time that the UK had used its veto to block the appointment of a President of the Commission: in 1984 Mrs Thatcher blocked the nomination of Claude Cheysson. On that occasion the nomination passed to Jacques Delors – perhaps a warning to John Major that the veto can be a double-edged weapon and does not always produce the intended result.

Accountability

Euro-sceptics, in their criticism of Europe, often use the terms 'unelected' and 'undemocratic' in talking about the institutions of the Community. Britain needs to defend its parliamentary sovereignty, they suggest, because at least the British Parliament can claim to speak for the British people since the British electorate elected that Parliament. For whom can the European Commission claim to speak when its members are appointed rather than elected, and to whom is the Commission accountable?

There is, however, an anomaly in the situation when national parliamentarians criticise the Community for its lack of democratic institutions – the so-called 'democratic deficit'. There are three simple solutions to accusations of non-accountability:

1   Strengthen the powers of the European Parliament
2   Make more European institutions, and their officials, answerable to the European Parliament
3   Open up even more European legislation to scrutiny by MEPs.

The anomaly arises, however, because proposals to democratise the Community through strengthening the European Parliament are bitterly opposed by national parliaments, on the grounds that:

● To increase the democratic nature of the European Parliament would be to legitimise its activities, whereas now its actions can be contemptuously dismissed as being 'unrepresentative'
● To legitimise the European Parliament is to strengthen it in relation to national parliaments, to the extent that national parliaments could become irrelevant in time.

So we end up with the ironic situation that the very ministers who criticise the Community for being 'undemocratic' are the same people who, as members of the Council of Ministers, refuse to legislate for democracy within the Community.

The ultimate in accountability, however, is the referendum, much used in parts of the Community where it is, indeed, required by constitutional law. The referendum is primarily used in those states where sovereignty is said to be vested in the people and where the constitution will often state that if major constitutional changes are to be made then this can only be done with the approval of the people as shown in a referendum. There are those in Britain, for example the Liberal Democrats, who believe that changes in the British Constitution, including those brought about by EU membership, should similarly be subject to referendum. Most of those who advocate referendums are, however, those who hold very strong opinions, which the government will not accept but which their advocates believe have the support of the public. Referendums, therefore, are a way to appeal to public support over the heads of government.[22]

British parliamentarians have always been opposed to referendums, which are seen as something unknown in British history, antipathetic to representative democracy and therefore liable to undermine the British Constitution. In opposing calls for a referendum the principle of parliamentary sovereignty is evoked, as it was in reply to calls for a referendum on Maastricht such as the Irish, Danish and French had held. In the government pamphlet *Britain in Europe*, already mentioned, it says:

The British system is a parliamentary democracy: the Government are accountable to Parliament and Parliament is accountable to the electorate. The House of Commons approved the British negotiating stance before Maastricht and the results afterwards. Parliament will have a thorough and detailed discussion of the Bill ... The Government believe that this is the right way to proceed in a parliamentary democracy.[23]

The reasons advanced for this position were expressed by the Foreign Secretary, Douglas Hurd, in the Commons debate on whether to hold a referendum on Maastricht:

As Parliament is sovereign it is clear that it could decide to hold a referendum, which it could either accept or reject. It could certainly choose, as it has before, to ask for advice from those who sent us here. But I return to the fact that we owe our constituents our judgment, and if we decline to exercise that judgment we are to some extent damaging the authority of Parliament.[24]

The expression 'as it has before' referred to the previous occasion on which the government had resorted to a referendum – indeed, the one and only instance of a national referendum for the whole of the UK. This was the referendum of June 1975, in which Harold Wilson's Labour government asked the British people to endorse the 're-negotiated' terms for continuation of British membership of the EC. On that occasion the British people voted for membership two-to-one, although on a turn-out of 64 per cent, that meant that only 43 per cent of the electorate had voted in favour, as against 22 per cent of the electorate opposed to membership.

There were special circumstances associated with the 1975 referendum. It only took place because Harold Wilson was determined to keep Britain in Europe, despite having fought the two elections of 1974 with Labour committed to British withdrawal. Wilson only kept his party with him by promising to consult the people of Britain before reversing party policy. There is also the point that it is a psychological quirk of referendums that people are more likely to vote for the status quo than for change, and prefer to vote 'yes' rather than 'no'. At the time of the 1975 referendum Britain was already a member of the EC, and the question posed to the electorate was so phrased that continuation of membership received the 'yes' while withdrawal demanded the 'no'.

In 1993, at the height of the Maastricht debate, the issue of a referendum was brought up again by rebel Euro-sceptics in the Conservative Party. Ironically, the champion of a referendum was Lady Thatcher, once the most scathing critic of referendums. The Euro-sceptics basically said that they would withdraw their opposition to the ratification of Maastricht if the government promised to lay the issue before the electorate in a referendum before enacting the Maastricht Treaty. Naturally, the Euro-sceptics wanted a referendum because they believed that the electorate shared their scepticism about Europe, but they acquired allies who were not opposed to Europe but were in favour of referendums, most notably the majority of the Liberal Democrats. However, a motion that a referendum must be held before the Act could take effect was defeated in the Commons on 8 March 1993 by 363 votes to 124. A similar motion in the House of Lords on 14 July 1993, for which Lady Thatcher and her friends pulled out all the stops, was defeated by 445 votes to 176, the highest number of peers voting in any division of the twentieth century.[25]

The issue of a referendum will not go away. Dissident voices in the Conservative Party are calling for a referendum to be held before Britain accepts the idea of a single currency. There are even those who suggest that any constitutional changes arising from the 1996 Inter-governmental Conference would have to be endorsed by referendum before acceptance of the changes by Britain. Conservative advocates of this attempted to get the commitment to referendums written into the Party manifesto for the

1994 European elections. They failed, but the idea remains alive and has some cross-party backing, certainly from the Liberal Democrats.

Collective responsibility

The referendum of 1975 was not the only breach of constitutional convention permitted by the Wilson government in the European cause. One of the oldest and most sacrosanct of conventions used to be that of collective responsibility, the premise of which is that all members of a government are collectively responsible for government policy. In Cabinet and elsewhere ministers might argue all they like about government proposals but once the Cabinet has reached agreement, and the proposal becomes official policy, even dissenting ministers must support that policy. If they feel unable to do so they must resign from the government.

In 1975, when Harold Wilson was proposing the referendum on Europe and it was decided that official government policy was to campaign for a 'yes' vote, the Prime Minister was faced with the serious prospect of about a third of his government being so opposed in principle to European membership that they could not in conscience keep silent under the rules of collective responsibility. At the same time, Wilson could not afford to lose so many prominent members of his government if they obeyed the logic of the doctrine and resigned. On the basis that it was only a convention and not a statutory part of a written constitution, Wilson simply suspended the rules and stated that the doctrine of collective responsibility was inoperative for the duration of the referendum campaign. This enabled politicians such as Peter Shore and Tony Benn to campaign vigorously against government policy while remaining members of the Wilson government.

The suspension of the doctrine of collective responsibility was a pragmatic device to meet a specific dilemma, intended to be temporary. Once the referendum was over and the outcome decided, the rules of collective responsibility were reasserted. The rules were briefly suspended again in 1977, on the question of direct elections to the European Parliament, but were rapidly reinstated when the decision had been made. However, the significance of conventions within an unwritten constitution is that if they are ignored once, they can be ignored again if it is seen as expedient so to do. In theory all members of a government are bound by collective responsibility, but in fact, if a minister is in conflict with government policy over an issue of principle, particularly over European issues, then that minister no longer feels so bound to silence as was once the case. In the post-Maastricht period, government ministers of the Euro-sceptical tendency, the most notable being Michael Portillo, felt free to make anti-European statements in despite of government policy.

Summary

There have been minor changes to the British Constitution as a result of EC membership, such as the use of the referendum and the abandonment of collective responsibility. But the major change has been the fundamental loss of sovereignty caused by British acceptance, through the Treaty of Accession, of the primacy of Community law. Despite rearguard actions by the Euro-sceptics over issues such as the national veto, opting-out and variable geometry, the sovereignty of parliament has been diminished. However, it has to be considered how much that loss of sovereignty has to do with British membership of the European Union, or rather, how far it is part of the inevitable interrelatedness of modern economic life and the decline in the status of the nation-state. It is also a moot point as to whether some of the attitudes towards Europe adopted by John Major's government – as was the case with Margaret Thatcher and Harold Wilson before him – are a result of a coherent policy decision, or whether they are adopted to appease the critics of Europe in his own party.

Notes

1 'Will sovereignty suffer?', *Education Guardian*, 17 May 1994.
2 A. V. Dicey, quoted by Andrew Adonis in *Parliament Today*, Manchester University Press, Manchester 1993, p. 8.
3 Aristotle, *Politics*, Clarendon Press, Oxford 1946.

4 Duncan Watts, *Reluctant Europeans*, PAVIC Publications, Sheffield 1994, p. 114.

5 D. Judge, *The Parliamentary State*, Sage, London 1993.

6 D. Wincott, 'The Conservative Party and Europe', *Politics Review*, April 1992, pp. 14–16.

7 The Thatcher Bruges Speech and Nicholas Ridley's comments are quoted by Alan Watkins, *A Conservative Coup*, Duckworth, London 1992.

8 Peter Alter, 'A Giant Leap into the Unknown', in V. Keegan and M. Kettle (eds.), *The New Europe*, Fourth Estate, London 1993, pp. 19–25.

9 John Major in 'William and Mary Lecture', at the University of Leiden, Holland, 7 September 1994.

10 David Marquand, 'Heart of the Matter', in V. Keegan and M. Kettle (eds.), *The New Europe*, Fourth Estate, London 1993, pp. 16–18.

11 Hugh, Lord Thomas of Swynnerton, in a lecture calling for a written constitution for the EU, delivered to the Menendez Pelayo Summer School, Santander, 3 July 1994.

12 All the quotations referring to Community law are taken from a publication of the European Commission, *The ABC of Community Law*, 3rd edn., European Documentation Series, Luxembourg 1991.

13 *Ibid.*

14 Case 6/64 *Costa v ENEL* [1964] ECR 585 (Primacy of Community law).

15 *The ABC of Community Law*.

16 Harold Wilson's words quoted by Watts in *Reluctant Europeans*, p. 112.

17 Professor Juliet Lodge, of the Centre for European Studies, University of Hull, quoted in 'Party divisions over unity', *Education Guardian*, 7 June 1994.

18 Foreign and Commonwealth Office, *Britain in Europe, the European Community and Your Future*, HMSO Publications, London 1992.

19 Philip Lynch, 'Europe's Post-Maastricht Muddle', *Politics Review*, November 1993, p. 5.

20 Major in the 'William and Mary Lecture', September 1994.

21 TEU, Title II (Amendments to the Treaty of Rome), article 3b.

22 Quite irrelevant to the subject but just a word about the plural form of the word 'referendum'. Many people seem to treat the word as though it were a Latin noun of neuter gender, with the singular form '-um' becoming '-a' in the plural. However, the word is not a noun; it is the gerund form of the verb and as such does not naturally have a plural form in Latin. In English, therefore, it is equally acceptable for the plural to be 'referendums', and this is the form I have used.

23 *Britain in Europe, the European Community and Your Future.*

24 Douglas Hurd, in *Hansard*, 21 April 1993.

25 David McKie, *The Guardian Political Almanac 1993/4*, Fourth Estate, London, 1993.

5

Policy and the decision-making process

There are two categories of law in the European Union:

Primary legislation, which involves the body of law established by the founding treaties of the Communities, together with all later amendments and protocols attached to those treaties.

Secondary legislation, which encompasses all laws passed by the institutions of the Communities in order to fulfil the aims and purposes of the treaties.

It is important to recognise that all this law is applicable to the United Kingdom, and that the United Kingdom has its part to play in the formulation and implementation of that law.

Primary legislation

Community law in this respect is provided by the three treaties, with the various annexes and protocols attached to them, and their later additions and amendments: these are the founding acts ... Because the law contained in the treaties was created directly by the Member States themselves, it is known as primary Community legislation. This founding charter is mainly confined to setting out the objectives of the Community, establishing its mechanisms and setting up institutions with the task of filling out the constitutional skeleton and conferring on them legislative and administrative powers to do so.[1]

Primary law is therefore largely constitutional law and deals with relations between member states, institutions and each other. On

the other hand, primary law is the basis on which the European
Court of Justice makes its judgments and, as in any legal system,
the decisions made by judges and the precedents set by them
form the basis for case law. And case law can apply to individual
citizens, firms and organisations.

We spoke in the last chapter of how case law established the
primacy of Community law over national law. Even more important are the judgments that rule on what is called 'direct applicability', which means that the rules laid down in the foundation
treaties are applicable not only to the member states and institutions of the Community, but directly impose obligations and
confer rights on the citizens of the member countries, without
those rules having to be adopted and amended by national law.

The first important judgment was made in 1963 and concerned
Article 12 of the Treaty of Rome, which limited the ability of
states belonging to the Common Market to impose or raise customs duties on goods circulating within the Common Market. A
Dutch transport firm, Van Gend and Loos, were importers of
chemical products from West Germany, and in 1962 they went
to court in the Netherlands protesting that Dutch customs had
increased customs duties on the goods they handled, in clear
breach of Article 12 of the EEC Treaty. At that time it was
believed that laws contained in the treaty applied only to states
and institutions and could apply to firms and individuals only if
they were adopted by national law. Now the Dutch court was
being asked to rule that the Treaty of Rome conferred rights on
individuals within the member states. Feeling that it was not
competent to rule on Community law, the Dutch court referred
the case to the Court of Justice. Naturally, as was suggested in
the last chapter, any such decision had major implications for
national sovereignty and many member states made representa-
tions to the Court, even the Advocate-General of the Court being
opposed. Nevertheless, judgment was given in favour of the firm,
the judges stating, 'Community law not only imposes obligations
on individuals but is also intended to confer upon them rights'.[2]
This judgment was taken as the criterion for direct applicability
and the case law thus established set a precedent for all subse-

quent cases of this nature. In this way, other articles of the Treaty were tested for their direct applicability.

In May 1973 a young Dutch woman, Miss Van Duyn, was engaged as a secretary by the Church of Scientology in the UK. The Church of Scientology was regarded by the authorities as a highly dubious cult, under investigation for practices by which young people were 'converted' and encouraged to join a community which took all their assets and forbade them to have any contact with family or friends. As a result the Church had been declared 'socially harmful' by the British government, which was trying to shut it down. Consequent upon her known association with an undesirable organisation, Miss Van Duyn was in effect declared *persona non grata*, barred from entry to the UK and refused a work permit. She immediately appealed to the British High Court on the grounds that Article 48 of the EEC Treaty guaranteed freedom of movement for all workers within the Community. The High Court referred the matter to the European Court of Justice and received the judgment that 'Article 48 has direct effect and hence confers on individuals rights that are enforceable before the courts of a Member State'.[3]

The importance of primary law in the EU is, therefore, that

1 Primary law, as established in the Treaties, has primacy over national law and, in these matters, the European Court of Justice has primacy over national courts.
2 Its provisions are as binding on the citizens of member states as they are upon the states themselves.
3 The foundation laws of the Community are to be enforced by the national courts of the member states in exactly the same way as they apply national law.

One result of these decisions by the European Court of Justice has been to create a new role for national courts such as Britain's. In the past British judges have enforced and interpreted the laws of the UK: it has never been within their remit to question the validity of those laws. Now it is very much the duty of a UK judge to overrule UK law if it conflicts with Community law. Quite early in Britain's membership, in 1974, a senior British judge wrote that Britain was now 'part of a legal system which not only confers a right but imposes a duty on the Court in certain circumstances to invalidate legislation'.[4]

Secondary legislation

By 'secondary legislation' is meant all those legal instruments devised and issued by the Community in order to administer the policies laid down by the Community and to achieve the aims and objectives of the Community, as established under primary legislation. Decisions made by the institutions of the Community are passed to national governments for acceptance and implementation. There are five different classes of legal instrument issued to national governments:

Regulations Once issued, regulations become immediately effective as law within the member states without the need for any national legislation to endorse them. For the UK the European Communities Act of 1972 gives authority for all subsequent EC regulations to have the same effect as UK domestic law approved by Parliament. Although regulations become law in the form that was agreed in Brussels, sometimes additional legislation is required in the member countries to make them more effective.

Directives These are not as complete and detailed as regulations, but consist more of policy objectives. The results to be achieved are communicated to national governments and those objectives are binding on the governments. But the form and method in or by which those results are achieved is left to the discretion of the national governments.

Decisions Unlike regulations and directives, decisions are not directed to all member states but are specifically directed at one country, although it may equally be a firm, organisation or individual. Because these decisions are so specific they are often administrative rather than legislative acts.

Recommendations and Opinions These are little more than suggestions or tentative proposals put out by the Council or Commission, and are not binding on the member states in any way.

Strictly speaking they are not part of Community law but they are included here under secondary legislation because they may be taken into consideration by the Court of Justice in making a judgment.

In any one year more than 12,000 legal instruments are issued. Two-thirds of these are non-political, being purely routine administration, dealing with matters such as price levels in the CAP. Of those instruments that can be considered legislative, 4,000 are regulations, 500 are decisions and 100 are directives. Again, the majority of these are Commission legislation, which is in effect delegated legislation, enacted under powers delegated by the Council. This Commission legislation is largely made up of administrative detail arising from legislation already agreed by the Council. When these merely routine matters are deducted from the total number of instruments issued during the course of a year, the instruments that are issued by the Council under the full legislative procedure consist of about 400 regulations, 170 decisions and 80 directives.

The policy, decision-making and legislative process

As has already been shown, much of the administrative or regulatory legislation coming from Brussels takes the form of Commission regulations or decisions. In these cases the legislation is drafted by the relevant Directorate-General, with the assistance of an advisory or management committee. With these routine measures there is little need for scrutiny or decisions by ministers, commissioners or national officials.

However, when it is felt that the regulations or directives to be issued are important or likely to set a precedent or establish principles, they are thought to need examination through the full legislative process for which the Council is ultimately responsible. There has traditionally been a legislative process that was described some time ago as 'a dialogue between the Council, representing national cabinets, and the Commission ... acting ... in the "interests" of the Community as a whole'.[5] Under this procedure the European Parliament acts in no more than an advisory capacity. It is known as the *consultation*, or *single reading, procedure*.

With the arrival of the Single European Act in 1987, followed by the Treaty for European Union, not to mention a growing awareness of the 'democratic deficit', the need was felt for a greater involvement by the European Parliament in the legislative process. For a range of important measures specifically relating to matters arising from the implementation of the SEA, a three-way process involving Commission, Council and Parliament has evolved. This is known as the *co-operation*, or *two readings, procedure*.

A: The consultation procedure

1 **Initiation** New policy initiatives are being put forward regularly and originate from a wide variety of sources; a suggestion may arise in the Commission, the Council of Ministers or in the European Parliament, or it may be the proposal of a member state, either through the Council or through the state's permanent representatives. It may also come from an outside body, such as a pressure group. Whatever the source a measure can only progress when it is adopted by the Commission, which is the only body with the power to draft legislation. Once a proposal is adopted by the Commission – a decision made at the highest level within the relevant Directorate-General – that same DG is set to work in framing the first draft proposal.

2 **Consultation** The first draft is treated rather like a Green Paper in the British system. It is circulated to experts, national governments, committees of the EP, the ESC and the Committee of the Regions, even pressure or interest groups if they are involved. The views of these various bodies may or may not be considered when the draft is framed into a formal proposal. This proposal is passed by the DG to the *cabinet* of the responsible Commissioner, from there to the *chefs des cabinets* and then, ultimately, to the College of Commissioners.

The Commissioners may accept, reject or amend the proposal, or they could just as easily refer it back to the DG for re-drafting. The consultation process is very long-winded and it can take twelve months for the measure to move from draft to formal proposals.

3 **Scrutiny** The formal proposal is passed to the Council of Ministers. It is also sent to the European Parliament, the ESC and, if relevant, the COR for their Opinions. As has been said, the EP has no legislative role here, its Opinion being purely advisory, which the Council is free to accept or reject as it chooses. The EP does, however, have the means to delay legislation if it wishes, since the measure cannot proceed until the Parliament has given its Opinion. If it wishes to delay matters until, for example, some change or amendment is made to the proposal, the EP can refuse to give its Opinion until such time as it gets its way over the amendment, or at least until such an amendment has been considered. Nevertheless, however effective the delaying process may be as a tool of negotiation, it has to be stressed that the EP has no veto in the Consultative Procedure.

4 **The Decision** The proposal from the Commission is passed to the Council for a decision, work on the proposal often beginning in the Council before the EP or ESC have given their Opinions. Preliminary work for the Council begins with a working party of national officials and representatives from the member states, who have the task of safeguarding national interests while reaching a common agreed text for the proposal. When the working party has gone as far as it can, the text of the proposal is passed on to COREPER, who will attempt to reach final agreement. Any disagreements that COREPER cannot resolve can either be referred back to the working party for further negotiation, or it can be passed to the Ministers in Council for a political resolution.

Only the Ministers can make a legislative decision, either by unanimous agreement or by qualified majority voting. If no agreement can be reached at ministerial level the proposal can either be passed back to the Commission for the process to

begin again, or the proposal can be referred to a future meeting in the hope that differences can be eliminated in the
interim. In the event that agreement is reached in Council and
the proposal adopted by the Ministers, that is the end of the
Consultative Procedure.

B: The co-operation procedure
Brought in by implementation of the Single European Act, and
extended by the TEU, this new procedure is an extension of the
consultative procedure in an attempt to involve the European
Parliament in the legislative process. The procedure grants the
Parliament powers over legislation that previously it had only
possessed over the Budget. When the co-operation procedure is
to be used is prescribed by the relevant Treaty. The alternative
name for the co-operation procedure is the 'two readings procedure', because it involves the proposal being presented twice to
both the Parliament and the Council.

1 **First reading** The initial stages of this procedure are very
   much the same as the whole consultative procedure, including the reference to the EP for its Opinion. In this case this
   is known as the *European Parliament First Reading* and the
   Parliament is free to suggest amendments to the proposal,
   which are then forwarded to the Council after having been
   incorporated in the text of the proposal by the Commission.
   Under the *Council First Reading*, the Council of Ministers
   does not reach a decision but comes instead to a 'Common
   Position', usually by qualified majority voting, although unanimity is needed if the Council does not agree with the Commission.

2 **The European Parliament, second reading** The EP con-
   siders the Common Position of the Council over a maximum
   period of three months, although this can be extended to four
   months with the consent of the Council. At the end of this
   time they can act in one of three possible ways:

   a Parliament can approve the Council's Common Position.
   b Parliament can reject the Council's Common Position, as

long as it is by an *absolute majority of all MEPs.*

c Parliament can amend the Council's Common Position, as long as it is by an *absolute majority of all MEPs.*

There is, of course, the fourth option of choosing, or failing, to act in one of these three ways within the three-month period. Whatever the decision by the EP the matter is sent back to the Council, except where the Parliament has proposed amendments. These must go first for further consideration by the Commission.

3 **The Commission** Any amendments made to the Common Position by the EP must be considered by the Commission over a maximum period of one month, and one of two positions adopted:

a The Commission can accept some or all the amendments made by the EP and incorporate them in the text of the Common Position. It is this amendment text which is then sent to the Council.

b The Commission may not accept some or all of the EN amendments, in which case they are not incorporated in the text of the Common Position. However, the Commission must send to the Council of Ministers even those amendments it has rejected, together with the reasons for that rejection.

4 **The Council, second reading** The Council can follow a number of different courses of action depending on what has happened in the Parliament or with the Commission.

a If the Parliament has approved the Common Position, it can be passed without further discussion, and becomes a legislative act of the Community.

b If Parliament rejected the Common Position by an absolute majority it can still be accepted by the Council, provided that action is taken within three months and that the Council decisions is unanimous.

c If amendments made by the Parliament have been incorporated in the Common Position by the Commission, the Council can accept the text by qualified majority voting.

d   If amendments were not accepted by the Commission and not incorporated in the text, the Council can still override the Commission's objections and accept the amendments, but only by unanimous decision.

e   If the Council fails to act on an amended proposal forwarded by the Commission within three months of receiving that proposal from the Commission, the proposal is judged to have lapsed.

f   If the Parliament failed to take any action during its second reading the Council can choose to adopt the first agreed Common Position without any further procedures.

Transparency?

As part of the Maastricht agreement, and at several subsequent European Council meetings, the Council of Ministers of the EU proclaimed the need for greater 'transparency', by which they meant a greater openness and freedom of information. This was felt to be of particular importance for the applicant Scandinavian countries of Sweden, Norway and Finland, all three of whom prided themselves on their tradition of open government, and who had reassured their populations about their EU membership applications with the assurance that the Community was working towards greater freedom of information.

In 1994, however, the Council was challenged by the British newspaper, *The Guardian*, on the basis that the paper had requested and been refused sight of documents revealing the position taken by the foreign ministers of member states on vital legislative proposals. In May 1994, *The Guardian*, supported by some Euro-groups such as the European Trade Union Confederation (ETUC), submitted its complaint to the European Court of First Instance, accusing the Council of misusing its power by preventing 'the widest possible access to documents held by the Commission and the Council'.

In late August the Council asked the Court to reject the newspaper's complaint, saying that 'its entire decision-making process would be in jeopardy if the public had the right to know the stance of member governments in negotiating EU legislation'. In explaining their public expressions of openness, lawyers for the Council told the Court that the Council 'may have given a policy orientation towards more transparency but the basic rule of the Council remained confidentiality'.

The Council's position was immediately attacked by Euro-groups such as the ETUC, the Ecumenical Commission for Church and Society, the European Round Table and the EU Migrants Forum. Tara Mukherjee, President of the Migrants, asked what democratic justification there could be for 'ministers who deliberate in secret to produce instruments of binding legal effect, which cannot be amended by the European or national parliaments, and which are not subsequently opened up to even a modicum of public scrutiny?'[6]

Decision-making – the budget

In Britain, where the English House of Commons has had control over the money supply since the fourteenth century, decisions taken about the Community Budget are held to be very important. This was seen as especially true in the period 1979–84, when Mrs Thatcher was fighting hard to reduce Britain's budgetary contributions. Yet the Community Budget is remarkably small in comparison with the budgets of even medium-sized member states. However, the outgoings of the Community, especially on the Common Agricultural Policy, have always been very heavy and that expenditure continues to increase, despite reforms to the CAP, to the dismay of net contributors such as Britain and, even more so, Germany. Part of the eagerness for the enlargement of the Community in 1995 was that countries such as Austria and Finland would also be net contributors and would make a useful addition to swelling the hard-pressed Budget.

The Community sets a ceiling on revenue and expenditure which is expressed as a percentage of the gross domestic product (GDP) of all member states combined. For the period 1988 to 1992, during the implementation of the SEA, that ceiling as fixed at 1.2 per cent of GDP. The ceiling for 1993 to 1997, which covers the implementation of the TEU, was raised by the Delors Plan to 1.37 per cent of GDP. It is estimated that expenditure by the EC will rise from ECU 66 billion in 1992 to ECU 80 billion in 1997.[7] The rise in expenditure will be somewhat eased by reforms of the CAP, which means that the proportion of the Community Budget spent on farming will fall from 53 per cent in 1992 to 46 per cent in 1997, the first time that expenditure of the Agricultural Policy will fall below 50 per cent of the Community Budget.[8]

Revenue

Originally, the Community was financed by contributions levied on member states, but this was found to be unsatisfactory and since 1975 the Budget has been financed through what are called 'own resources'. The components of these resources have changed over the years but there are three principal forms of contributions made by member countries, as determined under the Delors budget package introduced post-Maastricht in 1992. These components of Community revenue are:

- A levy on the customs duties, agricultural dues and other premiums charged on imports from non-member countries
- A proportion of national VAT revenue as the one consumer tax common to all EC member states
- A direct charge on a country's gross national product (GNP) as the best indication of what a country can afford to pay. This charge was raised from 1.2 per cent in 1994 to 1.21 per cent in 1995.

These three components were first introduced in 1988 and the proportions of Community revenue represented then by the three were: VAT 59 per cent; customs duties, including agricultural levies: 28 per cent; GNP charge: 10 per cent (there was also about 3 per cent in miscellaneous revenue outside the three main headings). From 1993 the balance between the components was changed, with substantial reductions in the proportion represented by the VAT component, compensated for by increases in the GNP component. This change is because some of the poorer

EC countries have a high consumption rate (and therefore pay more VAT) in relation to the size of their economies.

It has to be noted that all the revenue of the Community comes from levies on the revenues of member states. The Community, unlike any form of government, has no tax-raising powers of its own but must rely on those levies which the Council of Ministers sees fit to grant, and out of which the Community must meet the expenditure commitments also fixed by the Council. It should also be noted that only the EC has a Budget, the other two pillars of the European Union created by the TEU being directly paid for by national governments.

Expenditure

The largest proportion of Community expenditure has always been devoted to the CAP, but recent reforms mean that this proportion is being reduced to below 50 per cent. This reduction, however, is balanced by a whole new range of expenditures called for under the Maastricht agreements. This new spending is divided between three main areas:

- Increased aid to the Social and Regional Development Funds, to provide help for the poorer regions of the EU and to assist convergence of economic standards prior to the ultimate goal of monetary union. After the CAP these funds are the largest recipient of EC expenditure, taking about one quarter of the Budget.
- Money spent on increasing the competitiveness of European industry to reap the full benefit of the Single Market.
- Increased foreign aid to countries outside the EU, especially to states in eastern and southern Europe that were formerly part of the Soviet bloc.

The budgetary process

Each year's Budget is different and there is therefore no typical format for the determination of the Budget, yet it is possible to detect a standard pattern for the process.

1   The financial year of the Community corresponds to the calendar year and therefore begins on 1 January. During the previous spring and summer the Commission will begin preparing its estimates for the year's expenditure. The estimates are collected and collated by the Directorate-General responsible for the Budget, DGXIX. From these estimates DGXIX draws up a draft budget before 1 September at the very latest, and this is submitted to the Council of Ministers.

2   The Council of Ministers has previously, in consultation with the EP, drawn up what is known as the 'financial perspective', which is in effect a ceiling on expenditure. Most of the Council's work at this stage is ensuring that the Commission's proposals do not exceed the spending limits fixed by the financial perspective. Within the Council the draft budget is scrutinised by the Budget Committee, often with the assistance of COREPER. The draft, with any amendments or revisions, is passed on to the Parliament. The deadline for this to happen is 5 October.

3   Some control over the Budget has always been one of the few powers possessed by the European Parliament and MEPs are very jealous of their right to examine the proposed expenditure of Council and Commission. Most of the work is done by committees, most notably the EP's Committee on Budgets, but the revised version of the draft budget is approved by a plenary session of the Parliament. Up to 500 modifications or amendments are known to have been demanded for the draft budget, and it is only skilled negotiation by the chairs of the various EP committees that will succeed in producing a satisfactory text for approval by the plenary session.

4   In the second reading by the Council, during November, the Council may modify, accept or reject EP amendments by means of qualified majority voting. The Council is bound by two conventions:

    • The Council *may* reject Parliament amendments on issues that affect compulsory expenditures (as CAP expenditure is compulsory)

- The Council *must* accept Parliament amendments on discretionary expenditure (on foreign aid, for example) as long as the required expenditure does not exceed the ceiling on total expenditure previously agreed.

5   The second reading by Parliament must take place before the end of December, by which time it is hoped that any disagreements between Parliament and Council will have been eliminated. If they have not been settled then the Parliament is within its rights to refuse to pass the Budget. This, in fact, has been done quite often. For four years in the mid-1980s – 1984–88 inclusive – the Budgets were rejected by the Parliament.

6   If the Budget has not been adopted by 1 January, either because it has been rejected by the EP or because negotiations have become long drawn-out, the EC continues to function by means of 'twelfths'. Each month the Commission is allowed to spend up to one-twelfth of the agreed expenditure for the previous year. As a result some programmes may be delayed or put on hold, so it is in the interests of all to resolve any remaining differences before they get too far into the new year.

All matters relating to the Budget are closely scrutinised by the Court of Auditors, whose work is discussed in Chapter 3.

Britain is, and always has been, a net contributor to the EC Budget in that more money is paid in through the revenue components than is received in return through social, agricultural or regional aid. Other net contributors are Germany (by almost twice the amount paid by the UK), Belgium, France and Luxembourg. However, Britain receives a disproportionately small share of the CAP payments, and since 1984 (see Chapter 2 for discussion of the British Budgetary Question), the UK has received a rebate or, in EC terminology, an 'abatement'. In 1994 Britain paid approximately £8 billion to the Community Budget, but received back £4.5 billion in EC expenditure in the UK and £2 billion in abatement, leaving a net payment of £1.5 billion.

Scrutiny by the UK Parliament

By accepting the terms of the Accession Treaty in 1972,[9] the British Parliament accepted the primacy of EC legislation within the UK, with the exception of the need for some UK legislation to supplement Regulations and implement Directives. The House of Commons seeks to overcome this breach with parliamentary sovereignty by insisting that when a proposal goes from the Commission to the Council, the British minister concerned will not approve the measure until it has been scrutinised by the relevant parliamentary committee. This reservation has been expressed in a series of resolutions by the House, most recently in a Resolution of 24 October 1990:

In the opinion of this House:–

(1) No Minister of the Crown should give agreement in the Council of Ministers to any proposal for European Community legislation –
   (a) which is still subject to scrutiny (that is, on which the Select Committee on European Legislation has not completed its scrutiny);
   or
   (b) which is awaiting consideration by the House.
(2) In this Resolution, any reference to agreement to a proposal includes, in the case of a proposal on which the Council acts in co-operation with the European Parliament, agreement to a common position.[10]

It has to be said that the scrutiny process can do nothing to prevent the implementation of Community legislation; the committees involved can only concern themselves with *prospective* legislation. Parliament can advise Ministers on the line to take in negotiation; they cannot amend or revise legislation that has been through either of the legislative procedures. However, Parliament obviously believes in the need for national scrutiny of European legislation, and Select Committees for both Houses of Parliament to investigate the scrutiny process were set up even before the UK formally became a member of the EC.

Scrutiny by the House of Lords

Ironically, the House of Lords has always been more concerned with the workings of Europe than the Commons. In recent years the tradition has grown that the Lords have the ability to deal with non-legislative matters for which the Commons does not have time in its busy legislation timetable. The Lords therefore not only have time to discuss Community policies on the floor of the House, but members of the Lords appear to be more willing to serve on European Committees than their opposite numbers in the Commons. Their interest is probably aided by the fact that, unlike the rules pertaining to parliamentary elections, members of the Lords are permitted to stand for election to the European Parliament. In the EP that was dissolved in 1994 there were four Tory peers sitting as MEPs, although the four were reduced to just Lord Plumb in the election of 1994. Also in the Lords are those who have served Europe in one capacity or another, such as Lord Jenkins, former President of the Commission.

For the actual scrutiny process, the select committee, under the chairmanship of Lord Maybray-King, investigating the procedures for the House of Lords, reported its findings in July 1973. Discussions arising from the recommendations made in the Maybray-King Report finally resulted in the establishment of the Lords' European Communities Committee on 10 April 1974. The Committee is appointed for each parliamentary session only, but its renewal has been as good as automatic in each session since then.[11]

The actual size of the Committee is not fixed, although it normally numbers about twenty. They are then divided up between five sub-committees, each of which has the power to co-opt members, so that, between permanent and co-opted members, about sixty peers are involved in the committee system. Add to these Lords with a special interest or expertise on a given subject who are invited to take part, and any Lords who are MEPs, who have an open invitation to attend, and it can be seen that there is considerable involvement by the Lords in the scrutiny of European legislation. To reflect the importance attached to this, the Chair

of the European Communities Committee is appointed to be
Principal Deputy Chairman of Committees and is paid a salary as
an official of the House of Lords.

There are five permanent sub-committees, labelled A to E:

A Finance, Trade and External Relations
B Energy, Industry and Transport
C Environment and Social Affairs
D Agriculture and Food
E Law and Institutions.

This last is very important because it reflects the former status of
the House of Lords as Supreme Court for the UK. It has the special task of considering the legal implications of Community law
on UK law. The sub-committee is chaired by a Law Lord and
has access to expert advice from a Counsel and a Legal Assistant.
Ad hoc additional sub-committees can be set up at need. In the
wake of the Maastricht Treaty, for example, sub-committees were
set up to examine the implications and problems of Monetary and
Political Union.

The sub-committees meet once a week to hear and discuss evidence, from which they draw up draft reports. The reports are
passed on to the full committee, which meets once a fortnight. If
the draft is approved it is published as a Report of the Select
Committee of the House. These reports also recommend whether
there should be a debate on the report on the floor of the House.
Both committee and sub-committees have close relations with the
EC Commission, the European Parliament and the British Permanent Representative in COREPER, with visits to Brussels,
Strasbourg and Luxembourg by the chairs, representatives and
clerks of the various sub-committees. Officials of the Commission
may also come to London to join in deliberations of the sub-committees.

Scrutiny by the Lords begins with a memorandum from the
relevant Ministry concerning the legal and political implications
of a proposal submitted to the Council of Ministers. There are a
large number of such memoranda since about 800 EC documents
are submitted to national parliaments each year. The Chair of the

Lords' Committee must sift through these memoranda and decide which are worth consideration and which are mere routine detail. About half of the proposals submitted are considered worth discussion and these are referred to the relevant sub-committee. Only about 10 per cent of these are sufficiently important to merit a Report, and only about half of the Reports are debated in the House. As is the case in the Commons, government ministers are not expected to approve measures in the Council of Ministers until it has the endorsement of the House of Lords.

Scrutiny by the House of Commons

The equivalent of the Maybray-King Committee in the Commons is the committee chaired by Sir John Foster, which reported in 1973 and which resulted in the formation of the Commons' Select, or Scrutiny, Committee on European Legislation, appointed in May 1974. The Committee has a membership of sixteen, but unlike the session by session approach of the Lords, these are elected for the term of a Parliament. Like the Lords' Committee, it receives copies of proposals made by the Commission to the Council of Ministers, together with an explanatory memorandum from the relevant government department. The Committee meets once a week to consider the various matters laid before it, producing a report together with recommendations for any further discussion or debate within the Commons.

Originally, and until 1989, the reports prepared by the Select Committee were published as White Papers every six months under the title *Developments in the European Community*. However, in 1989 the whole system of scrutinising European legislation was passed to the Procedure Committee of the Commons. The main recommendation of the Procedure Committee was that debates on European legislation should be moved from the floor of the House and into committee. The proposal was for five Standing Committees, which would differ from all the other Standing Committees in that not only would they be permanent, but they would have no power to amend legislation.

In 1990 the Commons agreed to the setting up of the Standing Committees but modified the Procedure Committee's recommendation by saying that there should be just three, each having ten members. In the event it proved too difficult to find sufficient interested MPs to staff three committees and the system initiated in January 1991 provided for two committees of thirteen members each. To these committees go all European questions that the Select Committee has decided need further discussion. There are two Standing Committees with divided responsibilities:

A   Agriculture, Fisheries, Forestry and Food; Environment and Transport
B   All other Departments.[12]

The Committees meet on a weekly basis and their programme consists of a Ministerial Statement followed by two and a half hours' debate. Any resolution reached is reported to the House by the Committee's Chair. That resolution is put before the House as a motion, which is moved in the House a few days later. This recognition by the full House is merely a formality and there is no debate allowed on the subject.

As has already been said, the only power over European legislation processed by either House of Parliament is the Resolution requiring ministers to await the scrutiny procedure before giving assent to measures coming before the Council of Ministers.

Role of the Civil Service

Unlike most other EC member states, Britain has no Ministry for European Affairs, nor, in the normal course of events, is any specific minister charged with responsibility for European matters. The tendency has been for British governments to treat European policy as a branch of foreign policy, thereby leaving the operational aspects in the hands of the Foreign and Commonwealth Office. Mrs Thatcher tried to restrict the influence of the FCO, partly because she always distrusted the 'old-school-tie' type of links between the Foreign Office and what she called the 'Tory Grandees', and partly because she detected pro-European sentiments in the terms of officials provided by the FCO for

European Councils and other meetings with EC fellow-members. During her premiership she actually did contemplate the setting up of a separate Department of State, but abandoned the idea when it was suggested to her that those Britons who formed a close relationship with Europe tended to 'go native' and a Department of European Affairs could prove to be a Trojan horse of Europeanisation in Whitehall.

The nearest thing there has been to such a ministry in Britain was during the UK Presidency in the second half of 1992. Tristan Garel-Jones, a Minister of State at the FCO, was given the special task of co-ordinating the FCO's servicing of the many committees and working parties that Britain had to administer as President of the Community. As Duncan Watts has said, the FCO has shown every sign of welcoming its work for Europe: 'Involvement in European policy has given the Foreign Office an interest in many areas of policy not usually associated with it; hence the powerful ... (role) ... of the Foreign Secretary ... (in pressing) ... for membership of the ERM'.[13]

It is not only the FCO that has acquired new duties because of EC membership. Many government departments find themselves increasingly involved with Europe, especially the departments dealing with agriculture and trade and industry. Sometimes this duty involves civil servants in advising their ministers on policies with a European dimension; at other times a civil servant is involved in supporting a minister in the Council of Ministers; at yet other times a civil servant may be seconded to Brussels. The work of the national civil services is increasingly tied up with Europe, and British civil servants can operate in the European dimension in a variety of ways.

- *Support of Minister in Council of Ministers*: When a minister attends a Council meeting, he or she is accompanied by a team of national civil servants, who act as advisers as well as providing a secretariat. This includes regular meetings within and between national delegations over a period of several weeks in order to prepare the ground for Council meetings. Council meetings are themselves so short that they rely on the national delegations having reached a provisional agreement before the actual meeting takes place.

- *European Council*: Both Prime Minister and Foreign Secretary take powerful teams of officials to support them in European summit meetings. Here again the officials concerned will probably visit Brussels regularly for contact with their opposite numbers in other member countries for preliminary negotiations.

- *European Presidency*: The ministers chairing the various Council meetings during a member state's Presidency rely very heavily on national officials to provide them with support: 'Something of a dual servicing of the Presidency is apparent in the way, at Council meetings, the President sits with officials from the Council's Secretariat on one side, and national advisers on the other'.[14]

- *The Committee of Permanent Representatives*: The permanent representatives who make up COREPER are, of course, like ambassadors to the Community and are therefore senior diplomats from the FCO. The UK Permanent Representation has a staff of about forty officials plus ancillaries. This staff is provided not only by the FCO and Diplomatic Service but also officials seconded from appropriate ministries, such as Agriculture.

- *Working Parties*: In the outline of the legislative process set out earlier in this chapter, mention is made of the working parties which work on the proposals put by the Commission to the Council of Ministers. These working parties are made up of officials and experts provided by national governments, either seconded directly or via the Permanent Representation. A member state such as Britain might have up to four members in a working party, of which there may be ten operating at any one time.

- *Other secondments*: There are a variety of other reasons for seconding national officials to Community institutions. A British Commissioner, for example, may well ask for a specific official they had known in the UK to be seconded to help them in the formation and operation of the Commissioner's *cabinet*.

In this way even the average civil servant has to treat the institutions of the Community and work – directly or indirectly – for the Community, as being as much a part of their natural environment as any Whitehall ministry. Increasingly, an important aspect of civil service operations is liaison with the bureaucracies of other member states or with the Commission.

The role of pressure and interest groups in the Community

One indication of the way in which an increased share of policy-making has moved from national governments to the EC, is the way in which pressure and interest groups are coming to focus their attention on the institutions of the Community in Brussels. The role of the Single European Act in removing the national veto from the Council of Ministers on all matters relating to the single market has meant a massive shift of influence over policy away from the Council to the Commission and, increasingly, the Parliament. 'Any British pressure group which continues to rely exclusively on lobbying Whitehall and Westminster is adopting a high-risk strategy, because on a large range of issues policies are now being determined in Brussels'.[15]

Recent years have seen a proliferation of interest groups operating in Brussels, sometimes with a permanent office and a large staff, at other times represented by a single lobbyist working on their behalf. These interest groups largely fall into one of four types:

Regional and local authorities Some of these groups, from member countries which have a federal or semi-federal constitution, have offices in Brussels which act almost like embassies for the region concerned and have official backing. Other, less powerful groups will be represented much less strongly and will sometimes work through their national delegation. The UK has tended not to be over-represented in this sphere, but some regions, such as Wales, have felt it worthwhile to maintain a promotions office in Europe. And some local organisations feel that they can negotiate better directly rather than through national bodies. Merseyside, for example, have direct contact with Europe, over the heads of the UK government, in its campaign to get Objective One funding for the area: 'According to Harry Rimmer, Labour leader of Liverpool city council, Whitehall was never keen on the Objective One campaign because the status was gained over ministers' heads with a direct appeal to Brussels'.[16]

Multinational companies and private or public corporations EC directives can have an immense influence on business activities within the Community, either directly through tariff-control, taxation or competition legislation or indirectly through employment policy or measures of consumer protection. The Ford Corporation was one of the first to seek representation in Brussels in response to worries about competitiveness in the motor industry, but many other companies have followed their example.

National interest groups National groups probably still find it easiest to deal with their own national governments and civil services. But, increasingly, these groups find that it is worthwhile to have some representation in Europe, even if they cannot afford the expense of a permanent office in Brussels. The effectiveness of contact with the European decision-making process is particularly relevant for groups whose aims are not totally sympathetic to the government of the day, such as environmental groups, trade unions and those working for the interests of women, consumers or welfare recipients: 'The EC decision-making process provides greater access to what in Britain would be considered "outsider groups", not normally influential in the inner circle of Whitehall-group contacts.'[17]

Euro-groups These are interest groups that represent sectoral interests within several, if not all, the member states of the Community. These groups are obviously most active in areas that are seen to be of most concern to the Community; for example, around 150 different Euro-groups are active in lobbying for agricultural interests. This reflects the fact that the growth of the CAP within the Community has meant that decisions on agricultural policy are increasingly taken in Brussels rather than at national level. As Nugent says, 'Pressure groups usually go where power goes.'[18]

The most important Euro-groups are the umbrella organisations representing an entire sector of interest. Among the best-known are

COPA, the Committee of Professional Agricultural Organisations
UNICE, which is the employers' organisation, the Union of Industries of the European Community
ETUC, the European Trade Union Confederation
EEB, the European Environmental Bureau
BEUC, the European Bureau of Consumers Organisations.

The umbrella groups suffer from two main disadvantages in the Brussels setting:

1   They represent such a range of interests that they can lack cohesion and fail to present a united front.
2   They are often not specific to the EU but are generally European, so that the ETUC, for example, represents over thirty trade-union bodies in twenty different European countries.

Influence of the interest groups

The extension of lobbying interests within the Community has mushroomed in recent years. There are now estimated to be more than 500 Euro-groups whose existence is officially or semi-officially recognised, over a thousand advisory committees working with the Commission, and over 3,000 full-time, professional lobbyists working in Brussels. In numbers, the lobbyists in existence probably match the numbers of Community officials involved in the policy-making process. What distinguishes the Community from most national governments is the apparent openness of Community institutions to those promoting sectional interests, and the willingness of officials to talk to any lobbyist beyond just a few favoured groups: 'The very willingness of officials to talk to groups and individual firms means that the

market for policy ideas is much more broad and fluid than in the
UK.'[19]

Interest and pressure groups are involved with the European
Parliament and committees such as the ESC and COR, but
mostly with the Commission. Pressure on the Council of Ministers is usually conducted at national level. The Commission above
all, however, has formalised its relationship with the lobby groups
by setting up recognised channels of communication.

- There are a large number of advisory committees specifically
  created so that they can brief and advise the Commission at
  the start of the policy-making process.
- The so-called 'Social Dialogue' between the Commission and
  both sides of industry, which involves regular meetings
  between the Commission, the ETUC, UNICE and CEEP
  (European Centre of Public Enterprises).
- Commissioners and Directors-General receive delegations and
  documentation from interest groups of all kinds and are in
  regular telephone communication.
- Representatives of the Commission attend meetings of the
  larger Euro-groups.
- Commission representatives will travel to member countries
  to meet national interest groups as well as national governments.
- The Commission will participate fully in conferences and
  seminars set up by interest groups to investigate policy areas.

It is not surprising therefore that interest and pressure groups
increasingly focus their attention on Brussels rather than Whitehall.

Summary

The Community has an established and complex procedure for
the determination of policy-making and legislation, in which
national representatives can take part and which involve all the
institutions of the Community. Provisions of the SEA and TEU
are leading to a reduction in the democratic deficit through

increased powers for the European Parliament in an extended legislative process. National involvement in the European process includes the scrutiny of European legislation by both Houses of Parliament and through the direction of civil servants to work in Europe. Possibly the greatest involvement of national interests is through pressure and interest groups and lobbyists of all kinds working on Brussels.

Notes

1   European Commission, *The ABC of Community Law*, 3rd edn., European Documentation Series, Luxembourg 1991.

2   Case 26/62, *Van Gend & Loos* [1963] ECR 1 (nature of Community law).

3   Case 41/74, *Van Duyn* [1974] ECR 359 (direct applicability – freedom of movement).

4   Lord Scarman, quoted in Duncan Watts, *Reluctant Europeans*, PAVIC Publications, Sheffield 1994, p. 94.

5   L. N. Lindberg and S. A. Scheingold, *Europe's Would-Be Polity*, Prentice-Hall, 1970.

6   Reported by John Carvel in *The Guardian*, 31 August 1994.

7   For some guidance as to the sort of expenditure involved, in the early 1990s the average exchange rate was 1 ECU = £0.70p.

8   European Commission, *From Single Market to European Union*, Official Publications of the European Communities, Luxembourg 1992.

9   European Communities Act 1972, Section 2 (1).

10   Factsheet no. 56, *The House of Commons and European Communities Legislation*, Public Information Office of the House of Commons, London 1991.

11   Information Sheet no. 4, *The House of Lords and the European Community*, Journal and Information Office, House of Lords, London 1993.

12   As far as European legislation is concerned, documents distributed to the two committees listed here are allocated according to the departmental responsibilities shown, even if those matters are also dealt with by the Scottish, Welsh or Northern Ireland Offices.

13   Watts, *Reluctant Europeans*, p. 100.

14   Neill Nugent, *The Government and Politics of the European Community*, Macmillan, London 1991, p. 111.

15   Sonia Mazey and Jeremy Richardson, 'Pressure Groups and the

EC', *Politics Review*, September 1993, p. 20.

16 Peter Hetherington, in *The Guardian*, 13 July 1994.

17 Mazey and Richardson, 'Pressure Groups and the EC'.

18 Nugent, *The Government and Politics of the European Community*, p. 227.

19 Mazey and Richardson, 'Pressure Groups and the EC'.

6

The impact of European legislation on British policy issues

The Europeans have gone too far. They are now threatening the British sausage. They want to standardise it – by which they mean they'll force the British people to eat salami and bratwurst and other garlic-ridden greasy foods that are totally alien to the British way of life. They've turned our pints into litres and our yards into metres, we gave up the tanner and the threepenny bit. But they cannot and will not destroy the British sausage!

Jim Hacker in Yes Prime Minister[1]

In *Party Games*, the episode of 'Yes Minister' in which he becomes Prime Minister, Jim Hacker, as Minister for Administrative Affairs, is given the task of implementing an EC Directive whereby a sausage can only be so called if it contains 75 per cent of lean pork or beef. Since the humble British banger is composed largely of fat, gristle and head-meat it would not qualify under Brussels' criteria for the name of sausage. In discussions the European Commissioner concerned admits that it is only the name that is in question but, for political reasons affecting his own career, Hacker lets it be known that Brussels is seeking to abolish the British sausage and impose such alien products as salami and wurst. The tabloid press goes berserk at this latest European idiocy threatening the British way of life. Finally Hacker lets it be known that, after long and difficult negotiations, he has wrung a valuable concession from Brussels. As long as it is clearly labelled as a 'British Sausage' the humble banger can continue as before. Jim Hacker is hero of the hour and saviour of British sovereignty.

The programmes 'Yes Minister' and 'Yes Prime Minister' were written as comedy to amuse and entertain. Yet they managed to rise above run-of-the-mill situation comedy by an uncomfortable knack of being remarkably close to the truth. The episode described above may be exaggerated until it borders on farce, but it is equally true that the reaction of the British press to perfectly legitimate European directives has been to treat them as bureaucratic nonsenses that threaten to undermine the British constitution and overthrow our way of life. And when a compromise, which has always been on offer, is found, it is announced by the government minister concerned as if it were a success for British hard-headed common sense over the lunatic excesses of Brussels bureaucrats.

It is impossible to consider the impact of EC legislation on the British political and administrative structure without also considering the tendency on the part of a largely Euro-sceptical British press to mythologise the practices and intentions of the Commission. For no other member country have the Commission felt constrained to publish a handbook de-mystifying the Euromythology created by the British media.[2]

Euro-myths

Ever since Britain's entry into the EC in 1973 it has seemed as though the British press, and in particular the tabloid press, can only present Europe in a negative light. It began with criticisms of the CAP but rapidly extended to all directives and regulations emanating from the Commission. Positive benefits stemming from British membership are generally overlooked and the British public is left with the impression that the EC does nothing but dream up ridiculous regulations that at best involve ordinary people in bureaucratic nit-picking, and at worst threaten the British way of life.

Most of these stories are untrue or, typically of myths, they contain a grain of truth upon which a ludicrously exaggerated fiction has been constructed. Other stories are the result of mis-understandings or through a report of proposed legislation being leaked before it is properly drafted by the Commission. Occasionally the stories are true but have a rational explanation if their purpose is examined. There have been too many myths perpetrated in this way to examine them all here, but the following selection is typical:

'**Get Netted. We won't play Ena Sharples, fishermen storm at Europrats**.' The story, featured in the *Daily Star*, the *People* and the *Independent* during October 1992, claimed that British fishermen, while a sea, were required by the Commission to wear hairnets. The only truth in this story is that there is an EC directive in force – which in any case only reinforces an existing UK ruling – stating that workers in food processing plants should wear a suitable head-covering, to prevent hairs from getting into the food. The EC directive merely pointed out that this rule also applies to those working on factory ships, processing fish at sea.

'**Brussels sprouts a barmy tree law**.' This story broke in the *Sunday Mirror* and was repeated by the *Observer*. According to their information the EC required Christmas trees to be perfectly symmetrical in shape and have regularly spaced needles all of the same colour. There is no EC regulation on the subject: the definition is the product of French and Danish members of a trade association – the European Christmas Tree Growers Association.

'**Brussels sprouts the curve-free cucumber**.' The *Sun*, *Daily Mirror*, *Daily Mail* and *Daily Express* all reported this story, claiming that EC regulations require all cucumbers to be straight. The EC has laid down quality standards for cucumbers but nowhere requires them to be straight. That is the work of the producers, who prefer straight cucumbers because then they can get more into the boxes in which they are marketed. Much the same sort of fuss sprang up in September 1994 over a Brussels directive on the length and curvature of bananas. The regulations laid down that bananas should not be less than five inches (fourteen centimetres) long and should not be 'abnormally' curved: the measure was to prevent producers claiming EC subsidies for inferior products. The British tabloid press had a field day with banana jokes *(... another banana skin for Europrats ... Brussels goes bananas over bananas* and so on) but, finally, it transpired that Britain already had rules about the length and curvature of imported bananas that were far more stringent than those being applied by Brussels.

'German who wants to nobble our nibbles', 'How 16-stone German put a heavy bite on the traditional British crisp', 'The great snack attack.' This was the story that got into most of the British press, claiming that Brussels had banned the use of flavourings such as 'prawn' and 'spring onion' for snacks such as crisps. The story had an added attraction for the British press in that the Commissioner supposedly responsible was an overweight German, re-named as 'Bulky Bangemann' by the tabloids, who vented all their xenophobic feelings on the story, which, of course, was untrue. Mention of artificial flavourings had been omitted from a directive, an omission that was put right as soon as it was pointed out.

A similar misunderstanding arose with directives over the use of colourings in food but, despite scare stories in the press, EC rules permit smoked haddock to be yellow, Red Leicester cheese to be red and mushy peas to be bright green.

'Carrots are fruit, sprouts Brussels.' This was made much of by the Sun and is, in fact, true, although without the implications suggested by the newspapers. Portugal, alone in the world, makes jam from carrots and enjoys a large export sale of the product. When Portugal was about to join the EC they became worried that regulations already in force within the Community requiring jam to be made only from fruit would restrict their trade. In 1979 an EC directive on jam classified carrots as fruit for the benefit of the Portuguese jam-making industry.

In 1994 the Commission set up a 'rapid-response' unit in the Information Division under a Danish director, Niels Thorgesen, to react immediately to any similar story, with the intention of nipping such stories in the bud before they can achieve mythological status. During the 1994 Conservative Party Conference Michael Portillo made an anti-European speech in which he made six accusations of Brussels' bureaucratic interference, which were immediately shown by the unit to be entirely false or considerably distorted.

Harmonisation and the Single Market

Many of the misunderstandings over EC directives arise from attempts to apply the principles of the Single Market as from 1993. The problem initially was that each member country had its own national rules on health, safety and consumer standards, but a product which satisfied all the standards in one country might still offend the regulations of another. As a result, products made in one country might not be accepted for sale in another, negating the principles of the Single Market.

In the many years of preparation for the Single Market the solution was originally seen to be the standardisation of rules, replacing national regulations with a set of rules common to the whole Community. This, of course, gave rise to many anomalies such as the Portuguese carrot jam described above, and over the years the emphasis has changed. Standardising or harmonisation has been replaced by *mutual recognition*. Whatever is legally produced in one member country is legally available for sale in any other member country. The consumer is protected by stringent rules concerning labelling and consumer information.

The consumer in the EC is protected according to five fundamental rights:

1 The protection of consumers' health and safety. This means banning the sale of products that may endanger the health or safety of the consumer.
2 Protecting the consumer's economic interests. This largely involves regulation against misleading advertising, unfair contractual agreements and unethical sales techniques, such as those used in selling time-shares.
3 Granting the right to full information about goods and ser-

vices offered. Included in this are all the directives on labelling of food stuffs, textiles and medicines. There are a range of ingredients, additives and weights and measures that are legitimised by e-numbers.

4   The right to redress. This involves the rapid and affordable settlement of complaints when a consumer feels that they have been injured or damaged by the use of certain goods or services.

5   Consumer representation in the decision-making process. This is largely due to the Consumers Consultative Council, which is a committee advising the Commission and made up of the consumer associations of the various member states together with five EC advisory bodies – the European Consumers' Organisation (BEUC), the Confederation of Family Organisations in the EC (Cofae), the EC Consumer Co-operatives (Eurocoop), the ETUC and the European Inter-regional Institute for Consumer Affairs (EIICA).[3]

Despite the flood of regulations and directives devoted to consumer affairs emanating from the Commission, most legislation on these matters is the responsibility of national governments, with Community legislation either filling in gaps left by national laws, or covering areas where the consumer in one member state has a complaint concerning another member state, as when a British consumer is the victim of dubious time-shares sales in Spain. The guide-line for Community legislation is 'As little regulation as possible, but as much as is necessary to protect consumers'.[4]

Since the EC's first consumer programme was issued in 1975 there have been EC directives requiring national action on:

● the safety of cosmetic products
● the labelling of foodstuffs
● misleading advertising and doorstep selling
● consumer credit and unfair terms in sales and service contracts
● the safety of toys
● the safety of building and gas-burning materials.

Agriculture

The impact of European agricultural policy upon the UK is measured more in terms of the controversy surrounding the policy than in its implementation. From the first days of Britain's membership the Common Agricultural Policy has epitomised just what the British people think of as being wrong with the Community.

In its conception the CAP had the worthiest of aims and objectives. Its purpose was to make the Community self-sufficient in food, while guaranteeing a good standard of living for those involved in agriculture. In the implementation of the CAP, however, some of the worthiness of purpose disappeared. Encouraged by the French, with an essentially peasant agricultural economy, the CAP provided a guaranteed intervention price for all agricultural products, without any limit being put on production.

The result was that the CAP could be claimed as both a success and a failure. By 1973 the Community, on the threshold of enlargement, became self-sufficient in cereals, beef, dairy products, poultry and vegetables. In the years that followed, despite the increase in population brought by enlargement, production increased into ever greater surpluses. By 1990 the countries of the Community were producing 20 per cent more cereals than they could consume but were continuing to pay the farmers more than the world price for all the cereal crops they could produce. The costs of the CAP increased at an even faster rate than production, since there was not only the cost of the support price to farmers but also the cost of storing the vast food surpluses.

By 1990 the cost of the CAP to the EC, in terms of the taxes and higher prices needed to pay for it, had reached around £92 billion, or £270 per head for each man, woman or child.[5] There was also the non-financial cost, both in terms of the dubious morality of laying out expenditure of that extent for the benefit of the mere 7 per cent of the EC population actually engaged in agriculture, and in the righteous indignation of the rest of the world when it saw the EC surplus production sold off at rock-bottom prices and at what amounts to a massive subsidy. The repercussions of this last point nearly destroyed agreement on the

Uruguay round of talks to replace GATT. And this is not to mention the moral indignation expressed by people at the potential waste of food in Europe when thousands are starving elsewhere in the world.

For Britain the situation was even more aggravated by the fact that the CAP was devised before Britain was a member, and the ground rules laid down bore no relation to the needs of British agriculture. Britain's farmers were both fewer in number and more efficient than, say, the French, and the feeling was that Britain was paying heavily to support inefficiency elsewhere. There was also a question of national taste. British farmers can produce large quantities of wheat, for which the farmers are paid large sums under the CAP. But British taste does not like the flour produced by British wheat, preferring hard wheat imported from Canada and elsewhere outside the Community, on which Britain has to pay the levy raised on all non-Community food imports. Figures produced by the Treasury suggest that an average family of two adults and two children in Britain pays an extra £14 a year in food bills, simply as a result of the CAP.[6]

The impact of Community agricultural policy on the UK has largely been financial, leading to the fierce arguments instigated by Mrs Thatcher to get some sort of rebate for Britain. But there have also been significant changes in the farming environment, including the destruction of hedgerows for the sake of large-field cereal production, and the bright yellow fields of rape as farmers turned to lucrative oil-seed crops.

Reform of the CAP became inevitable in the 1980s as the Community failed to agree a budget over successive years and the Community teetered on the brink of bankruptcy. In 1991 the process of reform began under the Farming Commissioner, Ray MacSharry, and switched the whole emphasis of the CAP.

The reforms are clearly needed if the Community is to break out of the vicious circle created by high prices and excessive over-production. The reform process should encourage farmers to use less intensive production methods, thereby reducing their impact on the environment and on the creation of surplus. The reforms are also the cornerstone of a strategy to put the CAP at the heart of the Community's rural development strategy.[7]

The main thrust of the reforms was to replace support payment for unlimited production by topping-up payments for farmers who restricted their production within strict quotas. At the heart of this reform is a 'set-aside' policy by which farmers withdraw 15 per cent of their land from food production, for which the farmer is then compensated. For poorer farmers such as the hill farmers of Wales, Scotland and the Pennines, the emphasis of support has moved from the CAP to the 'Leader' programme of regional aid.

The impact of the reforms on the UK environment can clearly be seen in the extent of 'set-aside' land in British farms. Although there are special payments available to support non-agricultural uses of land – by conversion to golf courses, nature reservations or afforestation, and so on – many farmers are merely allowing the set-aside land to lie fallow, growing weeds and presenting a derelict appearance. In its way the new policy is as controversial as the old, since farmers are now seen as being paid large sums of money for doing nothing. The implications of this for the future have been outlined by Professor Howard Newby, head of the Economic and Social Research Council, who points out that set-aside is likely to take 30 per cent of farmland out of agricultural use by the end of 1996. This could lead to subsidies of £4–5 billion from the EC and UK government being paid to around 30,000 landowners, merely to keep the land out of production.[8]

The economic impact of the reforms for the individual farmer has been estimated by Larry Elliott.[9] He postulates a 100-acre cereal farm with an annual yield of 3 tonnes an acre, producing, under the old CAP, a support price of £108 a tonne. The farmer would have an income of £32,400. Under the reformed CAP the farmer would have to set aside 15 per cent of his land, reducing productive land to 85 acres. A guaranteed support price of £77 a tonne would yield £19,635, to which £7,600 compensation for the set-aside would be added. The total income would now be £27,235, representing a drop in income but incentive payments would be available if the set-aside fields were turned over to leisure use, conservation or the growing of non-food products.

Regional aid

For Britain, this is the reverse side of the CAP coin. Where the UK is a net loser over agriculure, it is a major beneficiary of Europe's policy towards regions in need of regeneration and development, especially since, out of the fifty million Europeans living in run-down industrial areas, some twenty million of them live in the United Kingdom.[10]

There are significant inequalities between the economies of Europe's member countries and between different regions of the same country. Compared to the GDP of the EC as a whole, for example, the standard of living for Greece, Portugal and Ireland is, for each of the three countries, less than 75 per cent of the average. In other countries the GDP for the entire country may equal or exceed the EC average but there will be regions which fall below that 75 per cent figure. In Italy, for example, the GDP for the region around Milan is 137 per cent of the EC average, but that for Sicily is 68 per cent.[11] These differences in wealth between one member country and another, and between regions within the same country, needed to be redressed ahead of the Single Market. The structural funds of the Community were reformed in 1989 and five priority areas identified as objectives for financial aid, three of those five being purely regional in scope.

The United Kingdom as a whole has a standard of living 100.7 per cent that of the EC average, but that figure conceals a significant difference between the 121 per cent enjoyed by the South-East of England and the figure of 74 per cent for Northern Ireland. Indeed, only the South-East of England and East Anglia can claim a standard of living higher than the EC average. Large areas in the regions of the UK can therefore lay claim to support from the regional funds of the EC under one of three different types of regional aid, all of which are represented in Britain.

Objective 5b regions

Objective 5 as a whole deals with rural areas. Objective 5a is given over to the modernisation of farms and has little relevance to much of Britain, except for a few hill farms. Objective 5b is meant to make up for the decline in the importance of agriculture; to replace employment and income in areas where farming has been rationalised; and to counteract the movement of population away from rural areas. The objective is therefore to retrain and re-employ the former agricultural workers and to replace an economy dependent on farming with a new economy based on small businesses or tourism. Regions of the UK most affected by Objective 5b are Dumfries and Galloway, North, Mid and West Wales (bar Clwyd) and Cornwall.

Objective 2 regions

This objective has the aim of helping areas that were formerly dependent on traditional heavy industries such as coal, steel or shipbuilding. The decline of these industries has led to endemic unemployment and an industrial wasteland. Help is needed to attract alternative industries, to retrain the work force and to regenerate the environment.

These regions in Britain have always received funds from the EC, especially areas which were badly hit when a dominant industry closed down, as with Consett in County Durham, a former steel-town which was devastated by the closure of the steel works. This assistance has continued, and has possibly increased under the reformed structural funds, because Britain, as the first industrialised country in the world, is suffering disproportionately in the post-industrial world.

About 40 per cent of the total EC population living in Objective 2 regions are to be found in the UK. The regions concerned are the Central Lowlands of Scotland, West Cumbria, the North-East including Tyne and Wear and Cleveland, Yorkshire and Humberside, Greater Manchester, the West Midlands and South Wales.

Objective 1

These are the weakest areas of the Community, countries or
regions where the GDP is lower than 75 per cent of the EC average. Three countries are Objective 1 in their entirety – Greece,
Portugal and Ireland, as is most of Spain and the southern half of
Italy. In the United Kingdom the situation is less serious, and for
many years only Northern Ireland qualified for Objective 1 status.
But this was in some ways the fault of the UK government, which
was reluctant to apply for this status on behalf of any British
region, 'because they thought it would be interpreted as a signal
of Britain's economic decline'.[12] Another handicap was the reluctance of the UK government to put up money themselves, despite
it being a requirement that national governments should match
EC funds before Brussels will loose the purse-strings.

In the summer of 1994 two regions of Britain, which previously
had been concealed by being treated as part of a larger region,
emerged as recipients of Objective 1 funding. They were the
Highlands and Islands of Scotland and Merseyside. The award of
this status to Merseyside was delayed by the failure of the British
government to satisfy Brussels that the Treasury would not take
advantage of European money to withdraw British state funding
for the area, the Merseyside Task Force bidding for European
funds having to appeal to Europe directly over the heads of the
British government. Apparently the UK government had wanted
to use 40 per cent of the European money to fund schemes that
would have manipulated the unemployment figures. Their plan
was rejected by Brussels.

The Merseyside Objective 1 package will bring in £1.28 billion
over six years, the money provided by Brussels and London, with
the possibility of private sector money being added to it later. The
package is intended to provide for a massive programme of sustainable measures to cut unemployment, build up the infrastructure and regenerate the environment. In comparison, the
Highlands and Islands will get £245 million from the EU, £320
million from London and £295 million from the private sector,
also over six years. The renewed Objective 1 status for Northern
Ireland is worth £970 million from the EU, £397 million from

the Treasury and £719 million from the private sector.

The environment

At the Dublin European Council of June 1990 the Community's commitment to environmental issues was confirmed in a declaration signed by all twelve heads of state or government:

The environment is dependent on our collective actions; tomorrow's environment depends on how we act today ... We intend that action by the Community and the Member States will be developed on a co-ordinated basis and on the principles of sustainable development and preventive and precautionary action.[13]

The EC was late in becoming involved with the environment. The Treaty of Rome contained a commitment to improve the quality of life for member states, but that this might apply to the environment was not accepted until the late 1960s and it was 1973 before the first Action Programme on the Environment was announced. In the 1980s came the realisation that the environment, and specifically the pollution of the environment, is very much a Community matter, because pollution pays no heed to national boundaries. Pollute the upper reaches of the Rhine and the pollution will affect France, Germany, the Netherlands and, ultimately, the seaboard of the North Sea. Air pollution in Britain can create acid rain over wide stretches of Northern Europe. Concerns such as these led the Community to take preventative measures, leading to a total of 280 environmental legislative measures, 200 directives issued and four Action Programmes approved between 1973 and 1991.

Two factors led to a change of emphasis in 1987. One was the work involved in setting up the Single European Act. Environmental requirements on factories and industrial plants, if it were left to national governments to administer them, could lead to differential costs and a loss of competitiveness in some national industries compared to others. There was the need for a co-ordinated approach by all governments so as to provide a level playing field for the various member states involved in the Single

Market. Also in 1987, the World Commission on Environment and Development (WCED) produced what is known as the Brundtland Report, drawing attention to the way in which economic growth was leading to the destruction of finite resources. The WCED called for 'sustainable' growth. These two factors together produced the communiqué of the Dublin Summit, the establishment of a European Environmental Agency in 1990 and the introduction of a fifth Action Programme, named '*Towards Sustainability*', to run from 1993 to the year 2000.[14]

The main targets of EC environmental legislation have been pollution of the air, water and soil, together with the problem of waste, particularly toxic waste. Since the emphasis has shifted to sustainability the Community has laid great emphasis on issues such as the conservation of finite energy sources such as fossil fuels, saving energy through insulation and other means and the generation of energy from renewable sources like wind, sun and tide. There has also been a growing interest in the protection of wildlife, both flora and fauna. One ruling of the EC has been to say that any major engineering project must take into account its effect on the environment, particularly on the habitat of wildlife.

Community directives have laid down strict emission standards for the release of pollutants into the air and water. Directives have concerned the release of sulphur dioxide (1980), lead in exhaust gases (1982), nitrogen dioxide (1985) and ozone levels (1992). There has also been a continuing programme curbing the emission of carbon dioxide, held responsible for global warming. Key directives have also been issued concerning the quality of drinking water, the pollution of rivers and waterways and the quality of bathing water at seaside resorts.[15]

A major environmental initiative was the 1992 Habitat Directive, which builds on a 1979 directive on the protection of birds and is intended to preserve or restore the habitat for species of flora and fauna whose existence is threatened by intensive farming or pollution. In legislating for this directive the British government has joined proposals for wildlife habitat with the 'set-aside' provisions of the reformed CAP to produce the *Habitat Scheme*. The scheme, launched by the then Agriculture Minister, Gillian Shephard, seeks to persuade farmers to restore the natural environment in three areas:

1 Any set-aside land which is managed for the nurture of endangered species of plants, butterflies, birds, etc. will be subsided at the rate of £275 the hectare.
2 Along the fringes of certain key waterways farmers would be paid to maintain a strip twenty metres wide from the water's edge within which farmers could not use artificial fertilisers and pesticides. This will allow safe areas for colonisation by wildlife, while preventing the pollution of the water by nitrates and other toxic substances, with their consequent effects upon fish life and the food chain of water-birds. Farmers will be paid for these water fringes at a rate of £360 a hectare if the land is used for crop production, or £240 if the land is under grass.
3 Certain areas of land reclaimed from the sea or marsh and maintained by expensive and potentially damaging coastal defence or drainage schemes will be allowed to revert to natural water-meadows, marsh or wetlands at a subsidy of £525 the hectare if withdrawn from crop production of £196 if under grass.[16]

Environmental schemes are expensive and therefore unpopular with governments and industry. As a result there have been many disputes between national governments and the Commission about non-compliance with Community directives on the environment. The British government's first attempts to privatise the water industry had to be abandoned because the Community refused to accept the suggestion that the privatised water companies should regulate themselves. It was only after the institution of the National Rivers Authority to police the activities of the water companies that privatisation could go ahead. There are still continuing disputes over drinking water quality.

A long-standing dispute has concerned the standard of bathing water on British beaches. This dates back to a directive of 1975, which demanded that national governments should designate bathing beaches which would be required to meet strict guide-

lines on water quality by 1985. The British government was first
in trouble because they wanted to designate no more than twenty-
seven beaches for this purpose; after discussion this number was
raised to 446. The British government then pleaded for more time
to comply with the set standards and was granted an extension
until 1995. Yet a report by the National Rivers Authority in 1994
showed that fifty-five beaches in Britain could well fail to meet
the required standards by the 1995 deadline and might remain
with waters unsafe for bathing because of raw sewage and other
pollutants.[17]

Another high-profile dispute between Britain and Europe has
been over the directive requiring civil engineering projects to
have regard to the environment. In 1991 the then Commissioner
for the Environment, Carlo Ripa di Meana, officially warned the
UK government that it was in breach of Community regulations
in seven engineering projects, the most famous of which was the
building of the M3 across Twyford Down, an area of natural
beauty and historical and scientific interest near Winchester. The
Commission was persuaded to withdraw its objections to
Twyford Down in 1992, but disputes over the Government's
road-building programme continue.

Disputes between the Community and Britain have a high
profile because environmental pressure groups such as Friends of
the Earth learned very early that the open nature of European legislation allowed for greater involvement of interest groups in the
decision-making process. And while the Commission would not
intervene on its own initiative, it was much more ready than
national governments to respond to complaints. The Commission
receives more complaints about Britain than any other member
state: in 1990 there were 125 complaints registered.[18] And it is not
only interest and pressure groups who intervene in this way.
Local authorities, who often have to implement the environmental legislation, have begun to make direct contact with the Community. In July 1993 Lancashire County Council successfully
took the British government to the European Court of Justice for
failure to clean up the bathing beaches at Blackpool, Southport
and Morecambe.

Because of this high profile it should not be assumed that Britain is the worst offender. In 1991, in terms of non-compliance with Community directives, Britain, with twenty-three offences, was the fourth most compliant, with only Denmark, Luxembourg and the Netherlands having a better record. That twenty-three compares favourably with Greece's fifty, Italy's fifty-three and Spain's sixty-six.[19]

Social issues

Most directives and regulations emanating from Brussels relate to economic issues and concern some aspect of the Single Market. The TEU introduced a comparatively new element in the emphasis it placed on social issues, specifically as they concerned employment policy. This was the so-called Social Chapter of the Maastricht agreement, which regulated matters like workers' health and safety, working conditions, a minimum wage, rights to consultation through Works Councils and the rights of women in the workplace. The social dimension in the Maastricht Treaty was against the instincts of Mrs Thatcher and her successors; as one of those successors expressed it: 'The government will not tolerate unwarranted interference in people's lives from Brussels which would put extra costs on employers, make firms less competitive and reduce the number of jobs. We have decided not to be part of the social chapter and that position will not change'.[20]

As a result of British objections, the Social Chapter is not integrated within the TEU but is added as a protocol subscribed to, at the time, by eleven members – in other words by all members apart from the United Kingdom. This has meant that in subsequent Council meetings that have discussed social matters the British minister has had to sit on the sidelines as a mere spectator. The procedure has been that the Commission proposes the social legislation as general Community legislation; the UK then applies the veto to the legislation; and it is later re-introduced under the Social Chapter Protocol as a measure applicable only to the Community minus Britain under Maastricht rules. This was the procedure adopted in September 1994 when Michael Portillo, as Employment Secretary, vetoed a proposal before the Council of Ministers to permit men to take three months' unpaid paternity leave on the birth or adoption of a child. At the same Council meeting Portillo gave notice that Britain would similarly force proposed legislation on the rights of part-time workers to be brought under the Maastricht protocol, rather than as legislation for the whole Community.

Nevertheless, there are aspects of social legislation that have, or will, become enforceable in the UK, despite the disapproval of the British government.

Children working

In November 1993 the Commission brought forward a directive designed to prevent the exploitation of child workers by limiting the hours that can be worked by children under sixteen to two hours a day or twelve hours a week. Conscious of the numbers of school-age children in Britain who might have a weekend job as well as delivering newspapers on a daily basis, the UK sought exemption from this directive. Despite opposition from Spain, Italy and Greece and an adverse vote in the European Parliament, this was finally agreed by the Social Affairs Council of Ministers in 1994. This was claimed as another successful opt-out by Britain, but those claiming it as such were immediately contradicted by the Irish Social Affairs Commissioner, Padraig Flynn. The concession granted to the UK was for a four-year period only, and was not renewable as the British had claimed. After four years the exemption will lapse and will not be renewed by the Commission.

Trade union rights

In March 1994 the European Court reversed British anti-union legislation by finding that, in the privatisation of the Health Service and local government services, the government had ignored a directive of 1977 concerning workers' rights when public enterprises are transferred to new ownership. Under the terms of the court's ruling, the British government could be fined if it did not introduce legislation to re-impose collective bargaining on those privatised companies that had set up non-union agreements.

Equality for pensioners
Again in March 1994 the Commission took action against the British Treasury, which was proposing to issue grants for home insulation to old-age pensioners in order to offset the effects of VAT on heating bills. The Commission took action under sexual equality rules because, in Britain, men and women could not apply for these grants at the same age. The government was obliged to accept that 60 would be the age at which application for the grants could be made, even though men would not be pensioners until they were 65. Later that same year a decision by the European Court against the Dutch government, but applicable to all member states, ruled that part-time workers should have equal pension rights to full-time employees, back-dated if necessary. However, in order to gain that equality, British pensions for part-timers would be payable only at 65, for women as well as for men.

Women's rights
Perhaps the greatest beneficiaries of European social legislation or judgments are women: 'All the most progressive legislation on women's rights is coming from Europe. The British government is continually being pushed to act by European directives and court decisions'.[21] The cases with the highest profiles have been those of women who were dismissed from the armed services when they became pregnant. As a result of a ruling from Europe the British courts are having to award substantial damages to the women affected, who could number in excess of 5,500.

These rulings over sexual equality have little to do with the Social Chapter of the TEU. Most are a result of Article 119 of the Treaty of Rome, which states the principle that men and women should receive equal pay for equal work. In 1984 the European Court ordered the British Government to amend the Equal Pay Act so as to read 'equal pay for work of equal value', which meant that employers could no longer justify inequalities in pay by claiming that men and women were doing different jobs. In one case a female speech therapist was allowed to claim equality with a male pharmacist because they had a similar health service grade, although he earned very much more than she did.

European rules have also helped women in cases of equality of retirement, maternity benefits, compensation to pregnant women for unfair dismissal, Invalid Care Allowances, sexual harassment in the workplace and so on. It is through actions such as these, from the Commission and the European Court, that some measure of social legislation is forced on to the UK government despite the British opt-out from the Social Chapter.

Economic policy

The Intergovernmental Conference at Maastricht agreed a timetable for achieving economic and monetary union (EMU). This was to include economic convergence on inflation, interest rates and currency stability, the introduction of a single currency and the setting up of a Central European Bank. The programme set out at Maastricht saw a Stage 2 in this process that would begin in 1994 and end in 1999 at the latest, leading into the final Stage 3 of complete union. Britain originally intended to be part of the EMU, albeit reluctantly as far as many members of the Conservative government were concerned. In September 1992, however, the events which culminated in the so-called 'Black Wednesday' led to the UK's withdrawal from the ERM and a negotiated opt-out for Britain from the EMU timetable. However, Britain agreed to continue to accept macro-economic objectives issued by the European Commission, intended to inform EU members as to the action on convergence required of them to meet the criteria for economic and monetary union before the deadline set.

When Stage 2 opened in 1994, Luxembourg had already met the convergence criteria, while Germany, the Netherlands and Denmark were due to hit the target during 1995. It was felt probable that France, Spain and Portugal would follow suit in 1996. The same forecasts indicted that the UK might well satisfy the convergence criteria at some time during the 1996–7 financial year, at which point Britain would be free to rejoin the EMU if the government so wished.

The EMU timetable had no formal regulatory position in the UK, which, through the opt-out negotiated at Maastricht, is free to rejoin the EMU at whatever time suits the country best. British economic policy is constrained by European factors such as the Single Market and the strength of the Deutschmark, but is otherwise not obliged to heed the Commission. As the Chancellor, Kenneth Clarke, said when the Commission prepared its convergence statement in 1994, 'I'll wait to see what the Commission recommends. I'll follow it if I agree with it and not if I don't'.[22]

Competition policy

European legislation on competition in industry and commerce has been in existence for some time but gained greater importance after the establishment of the Single Market.

The continuing integration of the Community and the ever-present need for the protection of the consumer from competitive abuses, ensures that competition policy will always play a vital role in Europe.[23]

Competition legislation in Europe has had its effect on Britain in a number of spheres, including anti-monopoly and cartel legislation, selective distribution systems and action against restrictive nationalised industries.

Cartels
The aim of European legislation here is to prevent companies in various countries getting together to fix prices, or rigging the market against the interests of the consumer. One area that has concerned Europe for years is the high fare structure on European airlines, where routes are assigned to specific companies and competing airlines are not permitted to fly those routes. Prices have notably fallen on routes where competition has been introduced, such as London–Amsterdam or London–Dublin.

In another well-publicised case, the Commission fined British Steel several million pounds for joining in a price-fixing cartel with other European steel companies.

Selective distribution

This is where multinational companies prevent customers in one Community country from buying a product in another where the price is cheaper. The most noticeable example of this is in the car industry, where the same model of car can be many times cheaper in another EC country compared to the UK. At one point the Ford Motor Company was taken to the European Court because it was refusing to supply right-hand drive models for British use to Belgian dealers when British buyers had discovered that they could get an identical car in Belgium at anything up to 40 per cent less than they would have to pay in Britain.

Removing national monopolies

The Community is interested in opening up national monopolies to competition when it is suspected that the monopoly is protecting inefficient practices. A principal target is the large state monopolies in the telecommunications field like Deutsche Bundespost Telekom or France Télécom. These cannot affect Britain domestically because the privatisation of BT took place some time ago, but the removal of the state monopoly in the mainland EC does open up opportunities to British telecommunications companies. In the reverse direction, the Dutch Post Office, among others, is acting competitively to secure international mail services that the Royal Mail in Britain is prevented from offering by the current monopoly position.

Internal security

One of the three 'pillars' of the European Union is a new deal on the policing of internal security through the Europol system, which would mean the abolition of border checks within the boundaries of the EU. The main advocate for the removal of internal borders is the Schengen Group, of France, Germany and the Benelux countries, so-called because of a meeting at the small Luxembourg town of Schengen in 1985. The five countries came to a formal agreement in 1990 and were joined by Italy (1990), Spain and Portugal (1991), Greece (1992) and Austria (1995).

The original five signatories, together with Spain and Portugal, abolished their internal borders on 26 March 1995. Italy, Greece and Austria confirmed their intention to follow suit as soon as certain technical difficulties were removed.

Denmark, Finland and Sweden were deterred from joining the Schengen Agreement because these three countries already have a Scandinavian free-movement agreement, which includes non-EU members Norway and Iceland. The agreement made at Schengen links the abolition of internal frontiers with the strengthening of external frontiers, and the three EU members value the Scandinavian agreement too much to erect strong border controls against Norway and Iceland. The reluctance of Britain and Ireland to agree to the removal of immigration controls for visitors entering one of the two countries from another EU country has a great deal to do with the problem of terrorism and the need to control the movement of terrorists and their weapons. But it has also a great deal to do with the insular nature of both the UK and Ireland and the two countries' lack of land frontiers. Both countries prefer to check thoroughly at the point of entry and then allow the visitor to move freely and unchecked within the country. In this way the UK can avoid the system of identity cards and residency permits demanded by most countries in the mainland EU.

This drawing back from the removal of border controls is not unique to the British Isles, however. As the numbers of immigrant workers and asylum seekers in countries like France and Germany increase, even signatories are looking again at the Schengen Agreement.[24]

The disharmonies of harmonisation

Earlier in this chapter we discussed the concept of harmonisation and the extent to which the Community is willing to allow for national variations to avoid over-regulation. This does lead to certain anomalies where British practice differs from the European standard.

- Non-approved additives. Certain colouring agents and flavourings in food are not approved by the EC and do not receive an 'e' number as a result, but are nevertheless accepted as legal in British foodstuffs because of traditional practice. Examples are the green colouring added to mushy peas and the red dye add to Red Leicester cheese.

- American programmes on TV. The Commission laid down a directive for television broadcasting, which states that at least 50 per cent of the material broadcast within the EU must be of European origin. Britain, however, issues two types of licence to television companies: one to domestic broadcasters using terrestrial stations on a frequency assigned to the UK, and another to non-domestic satellite broadcasters using international frequencies. The former are bound by the European-content rules but the latter are not, and can broadcast material which is 100 per cent American, even if the television company is British-owned, based in Britain and aimed at a British audience.

- Metrication. For a long time Britain has been adjusting to the metric system in weights and measures, and the UK has accepted for most purposes the standard metre or litre as laid down by the EC. For some time now the temperature has been quoted in degrees Celsius without having to quote the Fahrenheit equivalent, motorists appear willing to buy petrol sold and priced in litres, while products in the supermarket are packaged in grams. Yet for traditional reasons certain measures remain unaltered, instead of, or alongside, the metric equivalent. Milk in bottles on the doorstep and draught beer in pubs are still sold by the pint, even though their equivalent in the shop is sold by the litre. Athletes may now run the 1500 metres but distance by road is still measured in miles. And small shopkeepers and market stallholders are usually prepared to sell in pounds and ounces. In one other respect the UK is unusual, even when using the metric system. The British practice appears to be to divide metres and litres into thousandths as millimetres and millilitres, where the Continental European practice is to divide into hundredths with centimetres and centilitres.

- Taxation. Another area that is supposedly subject to harmonisation is taxation. However, each member country is left free
  as to the extent and severity of the tax. In this way there is a
  Community ruling that the principal tax on goods and services should be VAT, but the UK is free to set its own rate
  of 17.5 per cent and to allow certain goods such as children's
  clothes to be zero rated. However, the Community does issue
  directives on VAT from time to time, and whether the nation-
  states adopt the directive as it stands or not, they have to
  adjust their national policies accordingly. For example, the
  Sixth VAT Directive referred to financial services, as a result
  of which the UK government imposed VAT on insurance
  premiums and considered its applicability to the purchases of
  shares and on bank transactions.

In another sphere, the UK's individual application of excise
duties is creating difficulties. The duty on drink and tobacco in
the UK is far higher than it is in the rest of the EC; for example, the British duty on a pint of British beer was around 30p at
the time the Single Market was introduced, as against about 8p
in France. The difference in duties on spirits was even greater.
Since the Single Market removed many of the restrictions on the
personal import of beer and other alcoholic drinks, it became
commonplace for consumers to cross to France to purchase their
drink. The trade became so regular that Sainsbury and Tesco set
up their own outlets in Calais to cash in on the trade. British
breweries and distilleries have suffered, and, of course, the Treasury has been losing millions of pounds in lost duties each year.

Summary

The rulings of the EC have had their effect on all aspects of life
in Britain, even though some of the horror stories about Euro-
cratic interference are little more than modern mythology. The
impact of the Common Agricultural Policy on both British farming and the British economy has maybe not always been beneficial

but the process of reform of the CAP continues, with benefits for the consumer and taxpayer, if not necessarily for the farmer. For many economically depressed parts of the country considerable assistance has come from regional aid.

The impact of environmental legislation has been most marked, and environmental groups operating in Britain have found their causes considerably helped by the accessibility of the EC's legislative process and by the support of the European Court. Social issues have had their effect, despite the fact that the UK has officially opted out of the Social Chapter. Britain has also opted out of the EMU and the Schengen Agreement, but one lesson of the Community as it has developed is that it has become a community in all senses of the word, and no member can be totally isolated from community actions.

Notes

1 Jonathan Lynn and Antony Jay, 'Party Games' in *Yes Prime Minister*, vol. 1, BBC Enterprises Ltd., London 1986.

2 The European Commission in the United Kingdom, *Do You Believe All You Read in the Newspapers? The Euro-myths*, London, February 1994.

3 European Commission, *Consumer Rights in the Single Market*, European File Series, Luxembourg 1993.

4 Christiane Scrivener, EC Commissioner for Consumer Affairs.

5 Figures quoted by Larry Elliott, 'Year of living dangerously', in V. Keegan and M. Kettle (eds.), *The New Europe*, Fourth Estate, London 1993. The sums paid under the reformed CAP and 'set-aside' have increased since then, the figures quoted are those obtaining in 1993.

6 *Ibid.*

7 European Commission, *Our Farming Future*, European File Series, Luxembourg 1993.

8 Richard Norton-Taylor and Kevin Cahill, 'This land is their land', *The Guardian*, 13 August 1994.

9 Elliott, 'Year of living dangerously'.

10 European Commission, *Helping Europe's Regions*, European File series, Luxembourg 1992.

11 Figures produced by the European Commission in 1990. The GDP is expressed in PPS (purchase power standard), which is a cost of living index based on a common 'shopping basket' of goods and services.

12 John Carvel, 'Merseyside wins record Euro-grants', *The Guardian*, 13 July 1994.

13 European Commission, *Protecting our Environment*, European File series, Luxembourg 1992.

14 Stephen C. Young, 'Environmental Politics and the EC', *Politics Review*, February 1993, pp. 6–8.

15 Department of the Environment, *Protecting Europe's Environment*, HMSO, London 1992.

16 Paul Brown, Environment correspondent, *The Guardian*, 16 May 1994.

17 Reported in *The Guardian*, 16 May 1994.

18 Young, 'Environmental Politics and the EC'.

19 'The Dirty Dozen', *The Economist*, 20 July 1991.

20 Michael Portillo, Employment Secretary, speaking on 27 July 1994, commenting on the issue by the Commission of a six-year social programme.

21 Jane Grant of the National Alliance of Women's Organisations, reported by Sarah Rutherford, 'Europe, my Europe', *The Guardian*, 17 May 1994.

22 Kenneth Clarke, at the informal council of EU finance ministers, Lindau, Germany, September 1994.

23 Sir Leon Brittan, Commissioner for Competition Policy, in *Competition Policy in the European Community*, European File series, Luxembourg 1992.

24 'Open to us, closed to them', *The Economist*, 13 August 1994.

III

Participation

7

Representation – elections and the European Parliament

Article 138 of the EEC Treaty included the following provision: 'The Assembly shall draw up proposals for elections by direct universal suffrage in accordance with a uniform procedure in all Member States'. The Assembly approved such proposals as early as 1960, but found itself frustrated by another Article 138 requirement which stated: 'The Council shall, acting unanimously, lay down the appropriate provisions ...'[1]

From the above passage it can be seen that it had been the intention from the first for the Community to have its own democratically elected parliament, but that this objective was thwarted for twenty-two years by the Council of Ministers, led by the more intergovernmental and anti-federalist states: France originally but Britain and Denmark thereafter. The cause of the delay was quite simply that direct elections would give increased legitimacy and credibility to the deliberations of the European Parliament. Such increased legitimacy would confer an improved status and authority on the EP, and such an improvement could only be at the expense of the stature and authority of national parliaments. It was in the interests of all those who valued parliamentary sovereignty that the European Parliament could be dismissed as no more than an empty discussion chamber with no constitutional purpose or authority.

After Britain's entry in 1973, the UK was allocated thirty-six seats in the European Parliament, the MEPs being nominated members of the British Parliament, both Commons and Lords, and with the thirty-six seats distributed between political parties in proportion to those parties' representation in the national parliament. This meant that all members of the European Parliament had what is known as the 'dual mandate', in that they were, at one and the same time, members of both the European and their national parliaments. The main disadvantage of the dual mandate was that parties not represented in the national parliaments could not get representation in Europe, however large their support. In addition, critics of the European Community were not represented in the Parliament because only Euro-enthusiasts tended to put their names forward for nomination. There was, naturally, also the question of how effective members holding the dual mandate could be in either capacity, given the pressure of work the dual role laid upon them.

The dual mandate largely disappeared after 1979 and the introduction of direct elections. Indeed, in Belgium, Germany, Greece, the Netherlands, Portugal and Spain the dual mandate is not now permitted, while many parties in other countries, such as the British Labour Party, do not allow their members to exercise the dual mandate. Even if the dual mandate were permitted by country or party there is one factor which inhibits members of national parliaments from seeking election to Europe, and that is the ruling that ministerial office is held to be incompatible with membership of the EP, and any national member of parliament who is also an MEP would therefore find promotion to ministerial rank denied them.

The one area within the UK where the dual mandate still finds favour is Northern Ireland, where John Hume and Ian Paisley have both been MEPs since 1979, as well as being members of the Westminster Parliament. But then they are used to the dual mandate in Northern Ireland: Ian Paisley was a member of the Northern Ireland Parliament at Stormont between 1970 and 1973, despite concurrently being the Westminster MP for North Antrim since 1970. In the Conservative Party there are no members of the House of Commons holding the dual mandate with the European Parliament, but it is not uncommon for members of the House of Lords to stand for election to the European Parliament, and to be elected. In the European Parliament which stood down in 1994 there were four Conservative British peers who were MEPs: the Lords Bethell, Inglewood, O'Hagan and Plumb. But, of the four, only Lord Plumb survived the 1994 elections, winning his Cotswolds seat with a majority of just over 4,000, compared with the majority of more than 45,000 in 1989. Lord Plumb is, however, a very distinguished MEP, having been President of the European Parliament from 1987 to 1989.

Electoral systems

Although the Council of Ministers was forced to concede the direct election of the European Parliament, by universal suffrage, as of 1979, the Council still proved unwilling to grant the other provisions that were laid down in the Treaty of Rome so as to create a uniform procedure in all member states. There is, for example, no uniform eligibility for candidature as an MEP; the age qualification in the various member countries ranges from 18 to 25, and with some countries barring the dual mandate as mentioned above, while other countries welcome it. It is only since Maastricht, and therefore as of the 1994 elections, that non-nationals have been able to stand as candidates in Euro-elections, although it is now permissible under the EU's citizenship rules to stand and vote in one's country of residence rather than one's country of national origin. Even here there is no uniformity, since Luxembourg, which has a very high proportion of non-nationals in its resident population, demands a five-year residency before allowing access to the electoral system.

The EU countries cannot even agree on the day on which elections are held. For European elections, the UK chooses to use Thursday, which is the day normally used for Westminster or local elections. In 1994 this was also the case in Denmark, Ireland and the Netherlands. The other eight countries voted on Sunday, again as they do in national elections. Since the election results are declared at the same time across the Community it means that voters in the four countries which voted on the Thursday had to wait until Sunday evening to find out whom they had elected.

The most serious failure to standardise the procedures of European elections is, however, in the electoral system used. It was originally envisaged that all the member countries would choose a common electoral system which would presumably be some form of proportional representation. However, despite all the arguments levelled at the debate, the UK stood out for the British 'first-past-the-post' electoral system for constituencies in Great Britain and that has been the system used since 1979. The Labour Party, as a result of the Plant Enquiry into electoral reform for the party, has now agreed that a future Labour government will introduce proportional representation for European elections, but it was a Labour government which originally insisted on FPTP for the 1979 elections. The Conservative Party are, of course, totally committed to the FPTP system for all elections, even though they were disadvantaged by it in 1994.

However, even the UK itself does not have a uniform system. The most diehard supporters of FPTP recognise that the sectarian nature of Northern Ireland politics would cause considerable problems if a majority system of voting failed to give representation to the Catholic minority. The Province of Northern Ireland, entitled to three MEPs, is not divided into three constituencies but exists as one three-member constituency, with its three representatives elected by the Single Transferable Vote system of proportional representation.

Great Britain is the only member state, or part-state, which uses a majority rather than a proportional system of voting. Yet, because the UK broke ranks, there has been a consequent general failure among the other states to agree a common system. They all use proportional systems but of many different types, Germany, Greece, Spain, France and Portugal use straightforward list systems, while Belgium, Denmark, Italy and the Netherlands have a preferential vote element. The Republic of Ireland, like Northern Ireland, uses the Single Transferable Vote, and Luxembourg, with six MEPs, has a system whereby each voter is entitled to six votes, which they can split between the candidates as they wish.[2] In a number of countries employing a list system of proportional representation there is a threshold, usually 5 per cent of the vote, which parties have to reach before they are granted representation.

The European Parliament has repeatedly shown that it wishes to see a uniform system of voting throughout the EU. In the autumn of 1991, and again in March 1993, the Parliament voted overwhelmingly in favour of a common system, although the decision was taken in principle rather than agreeing on the actual system to be used. Any scheme, however, would have to have the unanimous consent of the Council of Ministers before it could be adopted. And so far such an agreement, even in principle, has not been forthcoming.[3]

There is a significant difference in the populations represented by MEPs in the various member states. As with Qualified Majority Voting in the Council of Ministers, seats in the EP are allocated to member states for political reasons as much as for strict proportionality. Before 1994 Germany had eighty-one MEPs like France, Italy and the UK, despite having a much larger population. After the increase in the number of seats in 1994, because of the rise in population brought about by German reunification, the approximate distribution of seats meant that the larger member states had one MEP for each 500,000 electors. In contrast, at the other end of the scale, the smaller member states are probably over-represented, in an attempt to prevent them being overwhelmed by the larger states in the decision-making process. For example, compared with the larger states' allocation of one seat per 500,000, Denmark has an MEP for approximately each 250,000 registered electors, while Luxembourg has an MEP for every 37,000 electors.[4]

Proportionality

It appears strange that the UK should cling to the first-past-the-post system of voting in European elections when one of the main arguments in its favour does not apply. One of the main complaints levelled against proportional representation for Westminster elections is that whereas one of the functions of an election is to choose a government, PR does not deliver a clear-cut decision, resulting in permanent coalition governments. The European elections, however, do not exist to choose a government, but to send a body of members to the EP that is representative of the member state's people. And, by the criterion of fair representation, the FPTP system clearly fails. Another argument used against proportional representation within Britain is that PR removes the link between representative and constituent. Yet, despite the constituency link being maintained in Britain, it is hard to see the link as being anything other than extremely tenuous when an MEP is required to represent up to 600,000 voters in a constituency made up of seven or eight Westminster constituencies combined.

The faults and unfairness of the FPTP system, already well-known through arguments over representation at Westminster, are multiplied tenfold when applied to the massive constituencies of the European elections. Even more than is the case in national elections, the smaller parties have difficulty in gaining representation. The Liberal Democrats won two constituencies in the 1994 election but this was the first time they had gained any seats in the EP, despite the Alliance having achieved 19.5 per cent of the vote in 1984, 3 per cent more than the LibDems achieved in 1994. The Green Party gained 15 per cent of the vote in 1989 but won no seats, even though the Conservatives, with little more than twice the share of the vote at 34.7 per cent, won thirty-two seats. Regional concentrations of votes can bring success, just as they do in national elections, but here again it is exaggerated. It was their concentration in the South-West that won the Liberal Democrats their two seats in the 1994 election, while the regional factor created the situation whereby the Scottish National Party is the one minor party to have been represented in Europe since 1979.

It is not only the third or minor parties that are affected by the anomalies inherent in the first-past-the-post system. For the two main parties as well, FPTP exaggerates small changes in opinion with no regard to proportionality. In the first direct elections of 1979, the Conservatives gained 48.9 per cent of the vote, but with sixty seats out of eighty-one, 74.1 per cent of the seats available. Compare that with 1994, when Labour received 44.24 per cent of the vote but 71.26 per cent of the seats (sixty-two out of eighty-seven). Yet despite these glaring discrepancies, all the government can find to say in defence of the first-past-the-post system is that it would confuse the electorate if they had to vote in a different way in the European elections to that with which they are familiar from national elections.[5]

Turn-out and apathy

One aspect of European elections that has attracted a great deal of attention is the low level of voter participation in the elections. In three countries, Belgium, Luxembourg and Greece, voting is compulsory and their turn-out figures can be regarded as respectable, Belgium and Luxembourg managing a turn-out of around 90 per cent while that of Greece approaches 80 per cent. In most other countries of the Community the turn-out is little more than 50 per cent, while three countries in 1994 had turn-outs that represented not much more than a third of the electorate. Of those three, the United Kingdom achieved a turn-out of 36.4 per cent in 1994, which nevertheless represented the highest turn-out for the UK since 1979. On the other hand, the other two countries with percentage turn-outs in the thirties, Portugal and the Netherlands, had previously had higher turn-outs: Portugal, with 35.5 per cent in 1994 had achieved 51.2 per cent in 1989, while the Netherlands, with 35.6 per cent in 1994, had managed 47.2 per cent in 1989. In other words, in a Europe where turn-out is generally poor, that of the UK is the poorest of them all and this has been true since direct elections began in 1979.

The UK has always had a poor turn-out record for anything other than Westminster elections, and the level of voting in European elections is very much in line with the turn-out for local elections. The principal reason for this is probably very much the same. No matter what other reasons there may be for voting for one's Westminster MP, the main motivating factor for the voter is the choice of the government that will rule the country for the next four to five years. Even the important responsibilities of local councils are seen as of no great matter in comparison to this. How much more irrelevant, therefore, is an election seen to be which does not form a government, which does not select a legislature and which does not affect policy decisions? The British public do not understand the European Parliament, do not see that it has any relevance to their lives and therefore see no reason why they should vote.

Thanks to the indifference of the British electorate to European elections, the people who ought to be working to overcome that apathy – the politicians, parties and the media – are equally indifferent. The media are only interested in what interests their readers, listeners or viewers, and therefore cannot be bothered with what apparently leaves the public cold. The parties are not going to devote precious resources to European politics when their resources are already limited for the more important field of national politics. And, with a few notable exceptions, politicians of ability and public appeal are not going to become involved in an activity so far removed from influence and power in the national arena.

The role of the European elections in the UK political process is also very similar to that assumed by local elections. The campaign and the reasons for people voting as they do are founded on national rather than European politics. The fact that only 27.83 per cent of British voters voted for the Conservatives in 1994 had far less to do with dissatisfaction at Conservative performance in the EP than with a protest at a Conservative government in the UK at the mid-point in a parliament. And this is not only true of the UK. Throughout Europe in 1994 there was evidence that the movement of votes from left to right or vice versa in the EP was very much to do with the movement of opinion in the various member states as regards their national politics; this was particularly true of significant swings of allegiance in Spain, France, Italy and Denmark. 'In effect the elections were fought as twelve different national votes with distinct domestic flavours, rather than on common issues or programmes.'[6]

The supreme irony about the apathy and indifference in the Community over EP elections is the 'chicken and egg' nature of the arguments. Voters would be more interested in the European elections if the 'democratic deficit' were removed and the European Parliament was given more power and its importance was made more clear, runs one argument. But the EP will not be given that power or importance because the perception of the national governments on the Council of Ministers is that the European Parliament lacks significance since so few electors are seen to be interested in it.

The role of an MEP

Among the many aspects of the European Parliament that are unknown to the average British citizen is any conception of what an MEP actually does. As is the case with the British Parliament, one obvious assumption is that members spend most of their time in the debating chamber, but if this is not the case at Westminster, it is even less true of Strasbourg or Brussels. Even when Commissioners are summoned before the Parliament to answer for their area of responsibility or to make a policy statement, very few bother to listen to them or question them. One British journalist described Leon Brittan's appearance before the Parliament, to announce the new world trade agreement that would replace GATT, in these terms, 'In the whole vast near-circular debating chamber there were, officials and flunkeys aside, only a dozen people. The press gallery was almost empty ... This was not a particular comment of Sir Leon or his subject ... It is always like this. No one goes to debates, except to speak. No one listens except the interpreters'.[7]

The point about interpreters is important, since there are nine official languages in the Community and it is very hard to make an impact with a speech in the EP when one's words cannot be understood directly by most the people present: even the finest speech-making cannot survive the intermediary of an interpreter. As Engel says, 'oratory, rhetoric and invective all fall flat'.[8]

In the European Parliament all the real work is done in committee, even more so than is the case at Westminster. All MEPs serve on at least one of the nineteen committees, the membership of which is proportional not to national representation but to the political groupings in the Parliament. The Committees are very much bound up with the Community legislative process, spending up to nine months on items of legislation entrusted to them and ensuring that about one-third of all legislation originates from the Parliament. Maastricht gave MEPs a considerable say in certain policy areas related to the Single European Act, such as education, culture, public health, consumer protection and action programmes on the environment.

There are nineteen specialist committees within the EP:

Rules and Procedure deals with interpretation of parliamentary procedure and verifying the credentials of new members.

Culture, Youth, Education and the Media

Civil Liberties and Internal Affairs deals with any aspects of human rights and is also concerned with the new 'internal security pillar' of the TEU, including Europol.

Legal Affairs and Citizens' Rights covers both Community Law and co-ordinating aspects of national legislation.

Agriculture, Fisheries and Rural Development

Budgets, which includes not only the annual Community Budget but all aspects of the financial framework of the Community.

External Economic Relations

Women's Rights

Regional Policy and Planning and Relations with Regional and Local Authorities

Transport and Tourism

Environment, Public Health and Consumer Protection

Development and Co-operation largely concerns help for the Third World, including the Lomé Convention.

Budgetary Control which basically means auditing Community expenditure.

Social Affairs, Employment and the Working Environment

Institutional Affairs overlooks all aspects of integration and the committee looking for a uniform electoral system.

Foreign Affairs and Security

Economic and Monetary Affairs

Petitions receives and analyses petitions received from EU citizens.[9]

It is appropriate that there should be a Women's Rights Committee, because an increasingly significant element in the composition of the EP is the proportion of women members when compared to the composition of national assemblies. In the EP elected in June 1994, 145 of the 567 members were women, more than a quarter of the total. Women also filled prominent positions in the Parliament, most notably Pauline Green, MEP for London North since 1989, already leader of British Labour MEPs, who was elected leader of the Party of European Socialists, the largest grouping in the new Parliament.

MEPs are paid the same salary as is paid to members of their national parliaments, ranging from the lowest, which is the £21,436 paid to Spanish MEPs, to the substantial £73,051 paid to Italian members. British MEPs elected in 1994 had a salary of £31,687. Expenses and allowances are uniform for all MEPs and are often very much better than national allowances. For the expense of running their offices and employing secretarial assistance they are paid £71,951 a year. Subsistence and travel allowances cater for the considerable amount of travelling MEPs must do, not only between Brussels, Strasbourg and Luxembourg but also between the EP and their home constituencies, and total £28,459 a year. There are frequent complaints about the amount of money paid out to MEPs and the comfortable lifestyle they are said to enjoy; the tabloids make great play of the 'Brussels gravy-train'. Nevertheless, the costs of the European Parliament, even with its heavy expenditure on interpreters and translation, are less than half what is spent in the USA on the House of Representatives.[10]

One area in which some suspicion lingers is in the extent of payments made to MEPs by lobbyists and interest groups. There is a register of interests supposedly completed by MEPs, copies of which are kept in Brussels and Luxembourg. However, the register is not kept very assiduously and not many MEPs are particularly scrupulous in declaring their interests: only Dutch and

British MEPs make any serious attempt to declare all their external interests and allowances. Klaus Hänsch, the new President of
the Parliament, is seeking to change this, 'determined to
strengthen the public's confidence in the integrity and impartial-
ity of the elected representatives'.[11]

Political groupings

Members of the European Parliament do not sit or associate as
national groups but as members of a variety of political groupings
based on an approximation of ideological similarity. The largest
of these groupings form transnational federations for mutual
assistance at election-time, creating propaganda and campaigning
material based on an agreed manifesto. None of these federations
and few of the other groups have the cohesiveness or discipline
of national political parties, but there is a certain feeling of
common interest, the groups have more influence than individuals or small national groupings would have and the groups receive
financial support from the Parliament for administrative and
research purposes, dependent on their size. According to the EP
rules of procedure, a group has to have a minimum of twenty-six
MEPs if all the members come from a single state, but the minimum number of members required reduces as the number of
countries increases, so that a minimum of just thirteen members
is required if four or more states of origin are involved, sixteen if
from three states or twenty-one if from two.

There are two major groupings or party federations in the EP
which have at least one MEP from each member country in their
ranks. The larger, and possibly more cohesive of the two is the
Party of European Socialists (PES), with 198 members in July
1994. Representing the broad left in European politics, the group
ranges ideologically from the 'hard-left' of the state intervention-
ists to the more moderate 'centre-left'. The majority, including
British Labour Party members, belong to the latter category,
being more social democrats than pure socialists. In the 1994 elections there was a considerable loss of votes by parties of the left,
not only in Italy but also in France and Spain, and the result was

a domination of the PES by the Labour Party, who, in association with John Hume of the SDLP, had sixty-three of the PES' 198 seats in the EP, representing 32 per cent. This is why a British MEP was chosen as leader of the PES and the concerns of the PES increasingly became areas of interest to UK members.

On the right the major grouping is the **European People's Party (EPP)**, with 157 members in July 1994. In origin this group was made up of Christian Democrats but the DC party of Italy has collapsed in recent years and the ideological identity of the group has suffered as a result. British Conservatives and the Ulster Unionists are associated with the EPP albeit very loosely, since the British parties find the strongly pro-federal approach of the EPP hard to live with. Until very recently the Conservatives formed their own group in the EP, the **European Democratic Group**. This group was entirely British except for two anti-Europe Danish MEPs, although the Spanish Popular Party also belonged for a time between 1987 and 1989. After the departure of Mrs Thatcher in 1990 the Conservatives felt able to join the EPP, finally affiliating officially in May 1992, although this does lead to Conservative MEPs being mostly out of step with party policy on Europe.

All other political groupings in the EP are smaller and do not represent all countries in the Community. Largest of these groups is the **Liberal, Democratic and Reformist Group (LDR)**, with forty-three members in July 1994, including the two British Liberal Democrats. Despite the presence of Liberal members with leftish tendencies, the European Liberal parties are still very much rooted in the *laissez-faire* liberalism of the nineteenth century and the LDR as a whole is much more a party of the right than its British component.

The remaining groupings are all much smaller. The **European United Left (EUL)**, with twenty-eight members in July 1994, contains the remnants of the former Communist Parties of France, Italy, Greece, Spain and Portugal. Also on the left are the **Greens**, with twenty-three members in July 1994. Until 1989 the various Green parties formed part of the so-called Rainbow Group, but an upsurge of support for green politics in 1989 pro-

duced sufficient representation for them to create a group of their
own; in fact, with twenty-seven members they were the fifth
largest group in the Parliament. Ironically, the 15 per cent vote
for the Green Party in the UK, which provided no seats because
of the British electoral system, was a larger national vote than that
for any of the Green parties which did gain representation. In
1994 the Green vote fell back, but with members for seven different countries, the group was still large enough to stand alone.
Finally on the left there is the **European Radical Alliance
(ERA)**, with nineteen members, thirteen of whom belong to the
French *Energie Radicale* party, known as the 'Tapie List' after it
leader Bernard Tapie. The remainder of this group belong to
what used to be called the Rainbow Group and includes regional
members, such as the two MEPs of the Scottish National Party.

On the right, the largest of these smaller groups is that rarity,
the one-country party. This is *Forza Europa (FE)*, with twenty-
seven members, all of them members of the *Forza Italia* party of
Silvio Berlusconi. Like many of these right-wing splinter groupings, *Forza Europa* is sceptical of European integration. The
European Democratic Alliance (EDA), with twenty-six seats,
represents an alliance between the French Gaullists and the Irish
Fianna Fail Party, two parties which have little in common except
a general centre-right outlook and a total dedication to the
Common Agricultural Policy. The **Nations of Europe Group
(NE)** is a new grouping created out of a dislike for the Maastricht
agreement. Of its nineteen members, thirteen are members of the
French party, *Majorité pour l'Autre Europe*, led by Philippe de
Villiers and Sir James Goldsmith. Another four are anti-Maas-
tricht Danes.

The remaining MEPs, who do not belong to any grouping and
are regarded as **Independent**, can be numbered at twenty-seven,
twenty-five of whom belong to the Far Right and are largely non-
attached because other European groupings fight shy of association with parties that are openly neo-fascist, such as the Le Pen's
Front National from France (ten members) and the *Alleanza
Nazionale* from Italy (eleven members). There are just two independent MEPs who do not associate with the Far Right, one of

these two being Ian Paisley of the Democratic Unionist Party.

The European elections of 1994

The elections were hailed in advance as being of some importance, the British government going so far as to issue a booklet urging people to vote and reverse Britain's record as the most apathetic of the member states.[12]

- The European Parliament had been enlarged by the reunification of Germany, increasing from 518 to 567 members, with a further increase to 639 foreseen for the 1995 enlargement.
- The elections were the first since the Maastricht agreement had given new powers to the Parliament, and both the main party groupings of the EPP and PES were looking to achieve a decisive majority so as to be able to control the policy direction of the new EP.
- There was a consciousness that recent events such as the post-Maastricht referendums in France and Denmark suggest that faith in an integrated Europe was an élite-led movement, more favoured by the politicians than the ordinary people of the member countries. The integrationists wanted the elections to counter this suspicion, legitimising the integration movement by a diminution of the democratic deficit.

Immediately prior to the elections the signs were not good for those pro-Europeans expecting reassurance from the elections. A pre-election opinion poll in all member countries showed a continuing apathy, or even hostility, to the idea of European unity within a federal structure. A majority in eight of the twelve member states were opposed to any idea of a federal Europe and any further loss of sovereignty. The only comfort for pro-Europeans in the survey was that a majority in all states were in favour of remaining in the EU, even though on a functionalist rather than a federalist basis.[13]

In the event the election results seemed to bear out the poll findings. The apathy of many citizens of the EU was shown by the turn-out of 56.8 per cent, the lowest yet, comparing with 57.2

per cent in 1989, 59 per cent in 1984 and 62.5 per cent in 1979.[14] The three major party groupings of the PES, EPP and LDR remained with much the same representation as they had had before, although that had been in a smaller Parliament. Both the Socialists and the Centre-Right were denied dominance of the new Parliament by fragmentation into a number of splinter groups, many of which were openly anti-federal and anti-Maastricht in their policy platforms. Everything seemed to point to a considerable degree of confusion on the part of voters as to how the main parties stood in relation to Europe integration. A typical example is the British Conservative Party, which in the European context campaigned on the strongly integrationist EPP platform and manifesto, but which within Britain represented a strictly functionalist, anti-federal stance.

The one thing that was very clear was that however much the propagandists might have hailed these elections as truly European and fought on pan-European issues, the fact was that 'the elections were fought as twelve different national votes with distinct domestic flavours, rather than on common issues or programmes'.[15] It therefore seems most logical to look at the 1994 elections on a country-by-country basis.

Belgium

Belgium had twenty-five seats, one more than in 1989. Because of the country's language problems those seats were divided into fourteen seats for Flanders, ten for Wallonia and one for the German-speaking area around Malmédy. All the major parties have French and Flemish divisions and there is one party exclusively for the German speakers. Flanders tends to be more right-wing than the old mining districts of Wallonia. Within Belgium there was the complication of a corruption scandal which affected the French-speaking Socialist Party.

With voting being compulsory in Belgium the turnout was 90.7 per cent, the highest in the EU. The Socialists lost two seats compared to 1989, both in Wallonia, while the Christian Democrats lost one in Flanders but regained that deficit by taking the newly created seat for the German-speaking region. The Liberals and the neo-fascist Far Right both gained in votes and seats in all parts of the country.

Denmark

For Denmark's sixteen seats (unchanged since 1989) the turn-out was 52.9 per cent. The most significant trend was the success of anti-Europe parties, of which there were two, and which gained 25.5 per cent of the vote and four MEPs, confirming Denmark's status as the most Euro-sceptical of all the members states, more so even than Britain. The Centre-Right made gains at the expense of the Centre-Left.

France

As with the UK, France's eighty-one seats were increased to eighty-seven. The European election was complicated by party manoeuvrings in advance of the presidential elections of 1995. The Socialist leader, Michael Rocard, needed to do well in order to give credence to his candidacy for the presidency, while the breakaway left-wing group led by Bernard Tapie was seen as a 'stalking horse' for Jacques Delors to present himself as a presidential candidate.

Turn-out was 52.73 per cent which was a 4 per cent increase on 1989. Both the Centre-Right and the Socialists suffered, with impressive gains being made by the 'Alternative Europe' list of de Villiers and the radical-left party led by Bernard Tapie. One result of this fragmentation is that France is very much under-represented in the two main party groupings of the EP. With only fifteen Socialist MEPs France's standing in the PES is dwarfed by Germany's forty Social Democrats and the UK's sixty-two Labour Party members. The twenty-eight French MEPs elected as Centre-Right candidates are split, leaving only thirteen as members of the EPP, overshadowed by Germany and Spain.

Germany

Because of reunification Germany is now the largest country within the Community and representation has increased from eighty-one to ninety-nine seats. Turn-out was 60 per cent, which represents a slight fall on 1989, although the electorate now is much larger than it was then. There was, however, an element of election weariness since, with regional elections and so on, there had been nineteen elections in one part of Germany or another before June and the country was facing federal elections for the national government in October. Chancellor Kohl's CDU/CSU party increased its representation substantially, but the Social Democrats and the Greens also made progress. Compared to the fragmentation in France and elsewhere Germany moved in the opposite direction. The two smaller groupings, the Liberal Free Democrats and the Far Right Republicans, both lost votes to fall below the 5 per cent threshold and failed to gain representation in the EP.

Greece

With twenty-five seats, an increase by one on 1989, Greece had a turn-out of 71.2 per cent, which is almost 9 per cent down on 1989 and a fairly low figure, given that Greece is one of the three member states where voting is compulsory. There was little change in the overall position of the parties, although the Communist Party put forward a separate list from the rest of the Far Left, and there was a new party in the form of POLA, representing Macedonian nationalism, which gained two representatives.

Ireland

Unchanged at fifteen seats, 44 per cent of the electorate voted. Domestically the election was seen as a vote of confidence in Albert Reynold's government and its handling of the Northern Ireland peace process. That vote of confidence was duly given by Fianna Fail increasing its representation from six seats to seven. Two of the smaller parties represented in 1989, the Democratic Left and the Progressive Democrats, failed to win seats, to the benefit of the Green Party, whose share of the vote rose from 3.8 per cent to 7.92 per cent and gained them two seats for the first time. Sinn Fein remained without representation on less than 3 per cent of the vote.

Italy

With eighty-seven seats contested, the turn-out was 74.8 per cent, very high for a country where voting is not compulsory. However, it is the lowest figure yet for Italy: in the previous three elections turn-out had been more than 80 per cent. Like Italy's national politics, the electoral map was in turmoil with the old-established parties crumbling. The Christian Democrats, who had held twenty-six seats in the old Parliament, split into two new parties and only managed to gain eleven seats. The Socialists, most discredited by the corruption scandals, slipped from twelve seats to just two, while the former Communist Party also split and the Democratic Left just managed to hold on to sixteen of the Communists' former twenty-two seats. Main beneficiaries of this collapse of the old parties was Berlusconi's *Forza Italia*, although the Northern League and the neo-fascist National Alliance also made strong gains. With no threshold on Italy's regional list system a huge number of parties are represented in the EP, often by single representatives and based on less than 1 per cent of the vote.

Luxembourg

As the smallest Community member state Luxembourg has six seats in the EP for an electorate of just 224,031. Turn-out was 86.6 per cent, a high figure not only because voting is compulsory but because the national general election was held on the same day. Luxembourg is the country most affected by the Maastricht provision that EU citizens can vote where they are resident: 30 per cent of Luxembourg residents are non-native EU citizens. The Christian Democrats continued to gain most votes, but lost one seat to the Greens.

Netherlands

With thirty-one seats, an advance on twenty-five in 1989, the turn-out in the Netherlands was only 35.6 per cent. This was by far the lowest turn-out in the Netherlands for a European election, but the turn-out has been steadily declining over the years. From 57.8 per cent in 1979 it fell to 50.6 per cent in 1984 and

47.2 per cent in 1989. There is also the factor of election weariness since this was the third set of elections in the year, and at
the time of the European elections, the country was still without
a prime minister and government after the May general election.

The leading two parties, Christian Democrats and Labour,
both maintained the same number of seats held, but only because
of the extra seats in the Parliament. The main gains were made
by two Liberal parties, the VVD and D66, who between them
increased their representation from four to ten.

Portugal

With twenty-five seats, an increase of one, Portugal had the very
low turn-out of 35.5 per cent compared with 51.2 per cent in
1989, and 72.4 per cent in 1987 on accession. The explanation was
that the election took place in the middle of a series of national
bank holidays. The Socialist Party edged ahead of the Liberal
Social Democratic Party by one seat, the reverse of the 1989 situation, but this reflects national politics since the SDP government is very unpopular and had already lost badly in local
elections.

Spain

With sixty-four seats as against sixty in 1989, Spain had a turn-
out of 59.1 per cent. Like the situation in many other countries,
Spain's results reflected public opinion over national politics. The
governing Socialist Party, severely damaged after twelve years in
power by corruption scandals, dropped from twenty-seven MEPs
in 1989 to twenty-two in 1994, while the conservative opposition
Popular Party rose from fifteen seats to twenty-eight. Those
Socialist Party voters who did not move right to the Popular Party
transferred their allegiance even further left to the former Communists, who more than doubled their representation to nine
seats. A total of eight minor centre and regional parties, who were
represented in the 1989 Parliament, failed to gain any seats in
1994.

United Kingdom

With six extra seats at eighty-seven, like France and Italy, the UK turn-out was 36.4 per cent, actually not the lowest turn-out in the Community, but unlike the Netherlands and Portugal, very much in line with previous low turn-outs. Turn-out in Great Britain was actually 36.1 per cent, with a turn-out in Northern Ireland of 48.67 per cent.

The Conservatives suffered considerably, dropping from thirty-two seats to eighteen, most of the seats going to Labour, whose share rose from forty-five to sixty-two, including seats in formerly Conservative areas such as Suffolk and Kent. The Liberal Democrats made a breakthrough in the South-West, taking two seats and coming within reach of a third, which they failed to win because of a 'spoiler' candidate who stood as a '*Literal* Democrat' and captured 10,000 votes despite not campaigning. The result is the subject of a legal challenge by the LibDems. If the LibDem vote had been only 1.5 per cent higher the Conservatives would have been reduced to a mere eight seats.[16] In Scotland the SNP took a record 32.6 per cent of the vote to win their second European seat, but although Plaid Cymru took 17 per cent of the vote in Wales they did not make the breakthrough to representation. The Green Party dropped from 15 per cent to 3 per cent of the vote. An anti-Europe UK Independence Party came fourth in England, having gained about 4 per cent of the vote, which did affect some closely contested seats in the South of England.

In Northern Ireland the system of proportional representation ensured that the three seats were neatly divided between the Ulster Unionist Party, the Democratic Unionist Party and the Catholic Social and Democratic Labour Party.

1994 and the democratic deficit

Despite the fragmentation of the main political groupings the Parliament elected in 1994 showed early signs of wanting to exercise parliamentary power. The driving force came from the PES, which remained the largest party group, reinforced by the choice of the dynamic Pauline Green as leader of the group and the election of German Social Democrat Klaus Hänsch as President of the European Parliament.

In July 1994 the European Parliament challenged the nomination of Jacques Santer as President of the Commission, the way in which Santer was chosen being denounced by Pauline Green as 'squalid, shabby and ill-judged'.[17] Santer would have been rejected if the Greek and Spanish socialist parties had not been persuaded to switch their votes at the last minute. As it was the nomination was approved by 260 votes to 238, with twenty-three abstentions. The need to escape another crisis forced the German presidency to announce the need to extend the powers of the EP, including a review of Article 158 of the TEU, which allows the Council of Ministers alone to choose the President of the Commission. In future the Parliament is likely to have a say in major constitutional decisions. As Klaus Hänsch said, 'The European Parliament has for a long time insisted on playing an equal role with national governments to ensure that normal decisions be taken by majority decisions'.[18]

Summary

Despite the eagerness of the European Parliament to increase its democratic voice in the Community, the elections of 1994 seemed to show that the people of the Community as a whole are less enthusiastic about Europe than many of their leaders. Turn-out in European elections has always been poor in the UK, but is also declining in other member states. Even when people vote, they tend to vote on domestic rather than European issues, mostly in order to show their displeasure with national governing parties. The problem seems to lie in how personally involved the people feel, because the electorate of the Community tends to show more interest in referendums than in elections for the European Parliament.

Prior to the enlargement referendums of 1994, there had been seven referendums in the EC. In two countries, Ireland and Denmark, it is a requirement of the constitution that constitutional changes should be put to the people in a referendum. Both countries referred the question of accession to the EC in 1972, 71 per cent of the Irish voting and a massive 90 per cent of the Danes. Twenty years later, both countries held referendums on the ratification of the Maastricht Treaty, the Danes most famously having to hold a second referendum in May 1993, after having voted 'No' the first time. The Irish voted in much the same numbers, 69 per cent voting in this referendum. The Danes, however, dropped back a little, 82 per cent voting in the first Maastricht referendum and much the same in the second.

Britain has only had one referendum on European matters and that is the one called by Harold Wilson's government in 1975. As is the case in European elections, the UK showed itself the most apathetic member state with 64 per cent voting, although that represented almost twice the number who vote in European elections.

France also has had just one referendum, on the Maastricht Treaty in September 1992. Then the turn-out was 70 per cent, a low figure compared with Denmark but comparing well with the 50 per cent normal to French European elections.[19]

The difference in participation between referendums and elections for the EP shows that people appear to be more willing to vote in referendums, when it is over a matter that can be seen as important to them, than they are in elections to a parliament which seems to have no direct effect on their lives.

Notes

1 Neill Nugent, *The Government and Politics of the European Community*, Macmillan, London 1991, p. 142.

2 The source of this information, and indeed for much of the information contained in this chapter as a whole, is the Directorate-General for Information and Public Relations, Central Press Division, of the European Parliament, as circulated through their UK Office, 2 Queen Anne's Gate, London SW1H 9AA.

3 Duncan Watts, *Reluctant Europeans*, PAVIC Publications, Sheffield 1994, pp. 55–6.

4 Figures taken from *Facts through Figures*, Eurostat, Luxembourg 1994. Note that the figures relating to the numbers represented by MEPs

refer to qualified voters, not to total populations. In terms of population, Germany, with ninety-nine seats, has 1 MEP for every 818,000 people, while Luxembourg, with its six seats, has 1 MEP for every 66,000 people.

5 Foreign and Commonwealth Office, *The European Elections – Why They Matter to You*, the COI for HMSO, London 1994.

6 Philip Lynch and Stephen Hopkins, 'Europe Decides', *Politics Review*, September 1994.

7 Matthew Engel, 'Parliament of Snoozers', *The Guardian*, 25 January 1994.

8 *Ibid.*

9 European Parliament, *Working Together for a Better Europe*, The European Parliament UK Office, London 1994.

10 Salaries and expenses are those paid in 1993, quoted in *The Observer*, 29 May 1994, p. 13.

11 Reported by Rory Watson, *The European*, 30 September–6 October 1994.

12 FCO, *The European Elections*.

13 MORI poll conducted for and published in *The European*, 13–15 May 1994.

14 Figures for the 1994 election are taken from the Results Tables published by the Central Press Division of the European Parliament, as document PE 177.791/fin, 6 July 1994. For all countries except the United Kingdom the figures are based on official statistics, although the results for Italy and Luxembourg were still subject to adjustment when the statistics were compiled in July.

15 Lynch and Hopkins, 'Europe Decides'.

16 John Curtice in *The Guardian*, 14 June 1994.

17 Reported by Mark Frankland in *The Observer*, 24 July 1994.

18 Reported by John Palmer in *The Guardian*, 22 July 1994.

19 Figures based on *Keesings Contemporary Archive*, for various dates.

8

British political parties and Europe

The area of British political life which has been most affected by membership of the European Union is, without doubt, the position of the political parties. The Labour Party split over the question of Europe, while the Conservative Party lost a leader and very nearly lost power over the issue. In the development of British political parties the argument over Europe and European integration has assumed the same importance as the Repeal of the Corn Laws or Home Rule for Ireland did in the nineteenth century – as a contentious issue which has dominated the political agenda and redrawn the political map.

The Liberal Party and its successors

Of all the parties, the Liberals, followed by the Liberal–SDP Alliance, and, latterly, the Liberal Democratic Party, have been the most consistent in their attitude to Europe. Membership of what was then still known simply as the Common Market was the policy of the Liberal Party at the start of the Liberal revival in the early 1960s, and they remained consistently supportive of a pro-European policy throughout the successive applications and rejections of the 60s, even while the Conservative and Labour Parties blew hot and cold over the matter.

The 'Gang of Four' who formed the SDP broke away from the Labour Party over a number of issues, by Labour's policy on Europe was a major factor and the SDP was solidly pro-European

from the first. It could hardly have been anything else since one
of the 'Four', who became the SDP's first leader, was Roy Jenkins, who had been President of the European Commission
between 1979 and 1981, leader of the Britain in Europe campaign
during the 1975 referendum, and who had resigned from the
Deputy Leadership of the Labour Party in protest at Labour's
stance on Europe. Indeed, the formation of the SDP and its
Alliance with the Liberals was the product of ideas first put forward in the Reith Lecture given by Roy Jenkins on his return
from the Commission presidency; the lecture speculated on the
future development of British politics, and advocated not only a
strategy that would 'break the mould' of bi-partisan British politics but one which would involve increasingly closer integration
with Europe.

The Liberal Democrats, in deference to its antecedents, are
wholeheartedly pro-European. Indeed there are those who would
claim that the LibDems are too uncritical in their attitude
towards Europe. In the view of these critics the party will accept
without question policies emanating from Europe which perhaps
ought to be questioned, and will ignore possible tactical advantage in the British political arena if, by adopting those tactics,
they compromise their pro-European status. On 5 November
1992 there was a vote in the House of Commons on a Labour
amendment to the 'paving motion' for the Maastricht Ratification
Bill. With a substantial number of Tory rebels ready to vote with
Labour there was a real prospect of defeating the government and
possibly forcing the resignation of the Major administration. But
a vote against the Maastricht provisions could be interpreted as a
vote against Europe and the LibDems were unwilling to risk that.
As a commentator wrote, 'The Liberal Democrats, though opponents warned them that they might save the life of an unpopular
government, declared that the cause of Europe ought to come
first, and voted with the Conservatives'.[1]

The Liberal Democrats were heavily criticised by the Labour
Party and others for their part in supporting the Conservatives in
that critical vote, but the point made by Paddy Ashdown and his
party was that sufficient damage had been done to Britain's place

in Europe by the actions of the two major parties, and Britain could no longer afford to send ambiguous messages to Europe by appearing to reject a pro-European measure.

Yet despite the overwhelmingly pro-European stance of the Liberal Democratic Party, the party does have one Euro-sceptical MP in Nick Harvey, elected for North Devon in 1992, who either abstained or voted against all pro-Maastricht measures during the ratification process, despite his own party's policy.

The Nationalist parties

The Scottish Nationalist Party was once bitterly opposed to Europe and campaigned vigorously against membership during the 1975 referendum. Their position then was basically that a party campaigning for independence for Scotland could hardly advocate yet another level of government to which the people of Scotland would be subject. Since 1983, however, the position of the SNP has changed to one of advocating a strong and federal European Union. The reasoning now is that it would make sense for an independent Scotland to be a full member of a federal European Union, thus eliminating any control of Scotland from Westminster, replacing domination by London with direct relations between Brussels and Edinburgh, in the true spirit of John Major's advocacy of subsidiarity. The European dimension reduces the doubts about economic viability which used to be advanced against full Scottish independence.

'An independent Scotland within Europe' has been the slogan of the SNP in recent years. After all, the SNP claims, with an electorate of 3.9 million, Scotland is many times the size of Luxembourg, a third as large again as Ireland and about the same size as Denmark. The SNP has been helped in coming to this conclusion by being the only minor party in mainland Great Britain to have had a representative in the European Parliament since the start: Winnie Ewing has represented the Highlands and Islands since 1979.

The position adopted by the Welsh Nationalists, Plaid Cymru, mirrors that of the SNP, from initial hostility to current enthusiasm for Welsh independence within Europe. As is the case with the Scottish party, the Welsh position on Europe is reinforced by seeing the position accorded in Brussels to the regions of other member states. Wales now has its own office in Brussels in order to promote the interests of the Principality.

In Northern Ireland the Unionist parties are largely hostile to Europe, Ian Paisley's Democratic Unionists more so that the official Unionist Party. This has not stopped the Unionists from campaigning vigorously in the interests of the Province and Northern Ireland has done well out of Objective One and other EC regional funding. The Social and Democratic Labour Party under John Hume is fully supportive of Europe because it is possible for politicians of Northern Ireland to work alongside the politicians of the Republic of Ireland within the European context.

All these minor parties, with the exception of the Liberal Democrats' solitary rebel, have maintained a united policy front on Europe throughout, even if that policy has changed over the years, as it has done with the SNP or PC. When we turn to the two major parties, however, it is a very different story. For both parties the relationship with Europe has been turbulent, with major and potentially fatal divisions in both parties over their European policy.

The Labour Party – the hostile phase

Historically the Labour Party was opposed to Britain's membership of the European Community. This stance dates back to the start, with the complete rejection of the idea of European integration expressed by Attlee's government when the first proposals for a Coal and Steel Community were put forward in 1949, and the Treaty of Paris was signed in 1951. The attitude of the Labour Party at that time was governed by the attempts of the 1945–51 Labour administration to bring about change in Britain through a programme of nationalisation and the introduction of the Welfare State. In order to bring about what the party saw as these vitally necessary changes the government needed to be in full and independent control of the British economy and social legislation. A true reforming government could not afford to dilute its programme through the need to co-operate with other countries. For many on the left of the party, the EEC, as it was established in the mid-1950s as a business-orientated Common Market, was little more than a capitalist club, membership of which was inimical to socialist principles.

It was a Marxist, Tom Nairn, writing about Europe at the time of Britain's accession to the Community, who pointed out that Labour's opposition to membership was not solely on ideological grounds. There is, in fact, an old-fashioned strain of British nationalism in grass-roots Labour thinking and a strongly xeno-phobic, vaguely jingoistic, attitude underlying working-class values.[2] It was that nationalistic thread which split the party over what their attitude should be towards the Macmillan govern-ment's first application to join the EEC in 1961. Most of the party was bitterly opposed to the idea, but no one could be certain as to the attitude of the leadership. In the summer of 1962, the Labour leader, Hugh Gaitskell, seemed to define his own stance, claiming that to join Europe would mean that Britain had to throw out 'a thousand years of history for the sake of a marginal advantage on the price of a washing machine in Düsseldorf'. Yet only a few weeks later, in replying on television to a talk by the prime minister, Gaitskell seemed to hedge his bets, saying that he would wait to see the terms of entry before he committed him-self. Macmillan had great fun at Labour's expense, telling the 1962 Conservative Party Conference that Labour's policy on Europe reminded him of the old popular song:

> She didn't say 'yes', she didn't say 'no',
> She didn't say 'stay', she didn't say 'go',
> She wanted to climb but dreaded to fall,
> So she bided her time and clung to the wall.[3]

Shortly after this Macmillan's application was rejected by de Gaulle and Labour's scepticism seemed to be vindicated.

Nevertheless, it was Gaitskell's successor, Harold Wilson, who initiated Britain's second application to join the Community in

1966. Wilson was always a pragmatist and he was ready to weigh the ideological and nationalistic objections to Community membership against the penalties of being excluded from the then economic success of the six EC members, and to conclude that membership was desirable. The second rejection of Britain by de Gaulle dented Wilson's confidence and publicly he reverted to a position critical of Europe. However, he had become convinced of the need for Britain to be involved in the development of the Community, and this would inform his thinking after Labour's re-election in 1974.

The Labour Party – renegotiation and referendum

Labour was in Opposition when the Heath government negotiated the terms for Britain's entry into the Community in 1971, and it was decided that Labour would oppose the government in the motion accepting the principle of EC membership. But Wilson was still playing it canny by avoiding outright condemnation of membership itself. The Labour stance was that the terms negotiated by Heath's team were wrong for Britain and would have to be renegotiated before Labour could accept them. In a free vote of the House of Commons the principle of EC membership was passed by 356 votes to 244. Significantly, in the light of future divisions, thirty-nine Conservatives voted against the government motion, and as many as sixty-nine Labour MPs went against party advice to vote with the government.

Wilson's main concern was to keep his party united despite the deep divisions that had opened up over Europe, and in order to avoid giving offence to anyone, he gave no clear guidance as to the leadership's stance on Europe. The party entered the first general election of 1974 with senior members of the party advocating at least three different approaches:

1   Those who believed the party should accept membership now that Britain was in the Community and that the party's energies should be devoted to getting the best possible deal for Britain out of the Community (Wilson's private position);

2   Those who wanted immediate withdrawal from the Community and the full restoration of British parliamentary sovereignty;

3   Those who believed that Britain should probably stay within the Community but that the terms needed to be renegotiated (Wilson's public position).

The party made no attempt to paper over these cracks but rather chose to flaunt them, as when they decided to devote their last party political broadcast before polling day to the issue of Europe: 'About half the team then talked about the Common Market. Michael Foot claimed British housewives were paying high prices in the shops to subsidise French farmers; Shirley Williams said Labour would re-negotiate the terms of Britain's entry and Denis Healey added "we can get out altogether if we don't get what we want".'[4]

Between the February and October elections of 1974 Harold Wilson, at the head of his minority government, determined his strategy for dealing with divisions within the party: the split was very deep. The Party Conference was overwhelmingly opposed to European membership, the Parliamentary Labour Party was split fifty-fifty, whereas the Cabinet was divided two to one in favour of continued membership. The device adopted by Wilson to keep all shades of opinion in his party sweet was to fight the October election with the manifesto promise that membership terms would be renegotiated, and that the government would take no further action until the public had given their verdict in a referendum.

This programme was put into effect with the European Council meeting in Dublin in March 1975, when the British government formally requested a revision of the terms agreed in 1971. By June 1975 Jim Callaghan was able to announce changes in the terms that were cosmetic rather than substantive, but which were sufficient for Wilson and Callaghan to be able to endorse them when placing the matter before the electorate in the referendum. The referendum itself was so worded as to encourage a 'yes' vote, the question put being 'Do you think the United Kingdom should stay in the European Community (the Common Market)?'

The referendum campaign was not fought by the political parties but by two all-party umbrella groups – Britain in Europe supporting a 'yes' vote and the National Referendum Campaign in
favour of a 'no' vote. Wilson wanted to remain aloof from the
campaign, pretending that he was completely neutral and that the
government had no interest in the outcome of the vote. He was
left, however, with the problem of a deeply divided Cabinet, all
of whom were eager to take part in the campaign but with sixteen
cabinet ministers wanting to support a 'yes' vote and seven ministers wanting to advocate a 'no'. To escape his dilemma, Wilson
took the unusual step of suspending the convention of collective
responsibility so that prominent ministers such as Barbara Castle,
Peter Shore, Tony Benn and Michael Foot could campaign
against government policy while remaining members of that government.

At first Wilson tried to prevent cabinet ministers on opposing
sides from appearing on the same platform or on the same television programme. But this was relaxed towards the end and
Panorama was allowed to screen a head-to-head confrontation
between Roy Jenkins and Tony Benn. Wilson maintained his neu-
trality, but his preference for a 'yes' vote was known and may
have been influential in persuading 66 per cent of the electorate
to vote in favour of membership. Certainly Tony Benn thought
so when he said 'I regard it as the third election in which the
Labour Party was defeated and Wilson won'.[5]

The Labour Party – renewed hostility

The defeat of Labour in 1979 led to a resurgence of anti-European thinking in the party. The left, as exemplified by Tony
Benn, blamed the Conservative victory on a lukewarm attitude
towards socialism in the Labour leadership. And advocacy of
European policies was seen as one of the hallmarks of that luke-
warm attitude. With the hard left in control of many constituencies and exercising their influence on Conference, Labour policy
began to move to the left also and therefore to an anti-European

stance.

In 1981 the party finally split at a special party conference, with David Owen, Shirley Williams and Bill Rodgers joining Roy Jenkins to form the 'Gang of Four' which issued the Limehouse Declaration and brought the SDP into existence. The immediate cause of the split was the matter of voting rights within the party, but the breakaway group also felt very strongly indeed about Europe. The Labour MPs who followed the Gang of Four into the SDP comprised the most pro-European sections of the Labour Party. Their departure, combined with the leftward drift of the party led to a renewed rejection of and sustained opposition to European integration.

In the run-up to the 1983 general election the Labour Party, under Michael Foot, adopted the alternative economic strategy (AES):

The AES assumed that it was possible to revitalise the ailing British economy through a programme of socialist economic expansion which would include domestic reflation and the use of import controls. An essential prerequisite was full economic sovereignty. In other words, a potential Labour government would need to have full control of the British economy. This was not deemed to be possible with continued membership of the EC.[6]

The Labour Party fought the 1983 election on the policy of complete withdrawal from Community membership. It was the most extreme position to be adopted by Labour in opposition to Europe. Yet at the time it seemed that Labour had irrevocably adopted an anti-EC position and that nothing was likely to change. A decade ago two of our more distinguished political commentators could confidently write: 'It is quite possible that a future Labour government will want to take Britain out of the EEC, or demand such fundamental structural changes as the price of staying in, that withdrawal becomes inevitable'.[7]

The Labour Party – the change of direction

In the decade since those words were written such a change has been effected within the Labour Party that it could be described at the start of the 1990s as 'the more European of the two major parties'.[8] Yet the change only really began in 1987, when Neil Kinnock set up the party's policy review in the light of the election defeat of that year. In that review process a great deal of attention was paid to the European dimension and there are those cynics who say that Labour's change of direction was little more than a political device in order to offer a clear alternative to the perceived direction of Conservative thinking. The cynical view seemed to be supported by Labour's actions over the Maastricht debate in the Commons, when the party seemed ready to vote against acceptance of the treaty in the hope of bringing down the government.

The change of thinking in the Labour Party was, however, more deep-seated than a mere search for electoral advantage. It was based on a number of premises that became clear after Labour's third successive general election defeat.

- The economists in the party recognised the interdependence of economic processes in the modern world and came to doubt the viability of the AES in isolation from the powerful economic blocs such as the EC.
- There was a realisation that the continued success of Mrs Thatcher and the Conservatives meant that there was no scope in Britain for advancing the policies of the left but that those policies were still prominent in Europe and that it was still possible to impose social policies on Britain via the Commission – what Mrs Thatcher called 'Socialism by the back door'.
- Exposure of the faults in the British political system by groups such as Charter 88 made advocacy of parliamentary sovereignty less acceptable, removing one of the props from the nationalistic arguments against Europe.

The real turning-point, and the equivalent to Labour's light on the road to Damascus, was the visit to Britain in 1988 of the President of the Commission, Jacques Delors. Delors came to Britain to address the Trades Union Congress and received a standing ovation for a speech in which he laid out his thinking on a Social Chapter for Europe, which guaranteed certain minimum standards for pay, working conditions and social benefits across the whole Community. This was so much in line with Labour thinking that the party enthusiastically endorsed the direction being taken by Delors and the Commission. To that extent the change in Labour from an anti-European to a pro-European stance is less a change in the nature of the Labour Party than a change in the nature of the European Union. When the Community was seen as little more than a trading area for the benefit of commercial interests, the Labour Party felt quite naturally obliged to oppose it; when the Community is seen as a body promoting improved social and environmental standards, then it is seen as natural for Labour to support it. It is, in many ways, a mirror image of the change in Conservative attitudes to Europe.

The policy review initiated by Neil Kinnock accepted as desirable the social policies advocated by Jacques Delors, which later became the Social Chapter of the Maastricht Treaty. To the Labour Party, which had been denied any hope of power in Britain since 1979, Europe seemed a logical way by which, indirectly, the social policies desired by Labour could be introduced into Britain, despite a Conservative government. The opt-out on the Social Chapter of the TEU was a disappointment to Labour but the acceptance of a pro-European stance was adopted successively by Neil Kinnock, John Smith and Tony Blair. The Labour Party retained its anti-Community faction, but once Bryan Gould retired from British politics, the members of the Labour Party opposed to the European project were very much an ageing, and increasingly peripheral, group. The young, modernising tendency in the party who were associated with the rise of Tony Blair were virtually all pro-Europeans. The final irony in the Labour Party was to see Neil Kinnock, who had campaigned against Europe in 1983, accept the post of European Commissioner in 1994 and go to Brussels, where his wife was already a prominent MEP.

The Conservative Party – the decline of support

In the same decade which has seen the Labour Party move from antagonism to support in its attitude to Europe, the Conservatives have moved in the opposite direction, from support to a situation where leading members of the party can advocate withdrawal from the Union. The trigger for this change is the same for both parties and is the belief that Europe should be something more than just a mere club of trading partners. But whereas the common market aspect of Europe was the thing that Labour found most objectionable, for many Conservatives that remained the sole justifiable reason for membership. Once the Single Market was established the European Community had served its purpose and senior Conservative politicians became determined not to let the movement towards European integration proceed any further.

During the 60s and 70s, while Labour wavered between luke-warm support and outright opposition, the Conservatives became dedicated to British membership and participation in the Community. Ted Heath, appointed negotiator by Macmillan in 1961, was converted by his involvement and, as the prime minister who finally took Britain into the EC, became and has remained an enthusiast for European integration. While Heath remained leader, opposition to Europe within the Conservative Party was muted, the only prominent party member to raise his voice against the policy being Enoch Powell, who urged fellow-Tories to vote Labour in 1974 as a way to extricate Britain from the Community.

When Mrs Thatcher replaced Heath as leader of the Conservative Party in 1975 and then became Prime Minister in 1979, she was critical of Europe. But her criticism was levelled at what she saw as faults in the operation of Community institutions such as the Common Agricultural Policy, rather than at the basic principle of membership. During the first half of the 1980s Mrs Thatcher was involved in the British Budgetary Question and the restructuring of Community finances: in effect she was attempting to re-launch the EEC on free market principles. She was particularly concerned about the influence of the Commission, which she referred to dismissively as the 'Eurocracy', and what she saw as its tendency to over-regulate economic activity through devices such as the CAP, at the expense of the free operation of market forces.

Despite the strong feelings which Mrs Thatcher aroused in her colleagues within the European Council, she would seem to have been successful in her European aims, not only in resolving the BBQ but inasmuch as commentators like Michael Heseltine credit her with being a principal architect of the Single European Act. Up until that point Mrs Thatcher was perceived by her European colleagues as bloody-minded and confrontational but working in her own idiosyncratic way towards some vision of Europe. That this was not the case, and that Mrs Thatcher was going to lead an increasingly vocal Euro-sceptical movement within the Conservative Party, only became clear as a result of the same event that caused the major change in the Labour Party – the advent of Jacques Delors as President of the Commission.

The impression created by Mrs Thatcher has always been one of single-minded dedication and undeviating steadfastness of purpose. In reality her views were an uncomfortable marriage of two contradictory nineteenth-century ideologies – nationalistic conservatism and economic liberalism. The economic liberal could take pride in the creation of the Single Market but the nationalist in her reacted against the consequences of that act, namely against the imposition of a single currency and a European Central Bank, and at the whole social dimension which formed part of the Delors Plan.

Mrs Thatcher seems to believe that the Community will introduce socialism by the back door. She has been particularly vitriolic in her attacks on the 'social dimension' of the Community, whether in the form of the social charter or the social chapter discussed at Maastricht. At her 1988 speech in Bruges Mrs Thatcher argued that she would not allow the frontiers of the state to be rolled forward by the EC when she had spent nine years rolling them back in the UK.[9]

The Bruges speech led to the formation of the Bruges Group

and an identifiable faction within the Conservative Party opposed to any suggestion of European federalism, political or monetary union or any measure which might lead to any further diminution of British sovereignty. Under the influence of this group, the Conservatives treated the 1989 European elections with indifference or, at best, lukewarm enthusiasm. The party was punished for its attitude, Labour taking forty-five seats in that election, as against the Conservatives' thirty-two.

As has been reported earlier, the attitude towards Europe adopted by Mrs Thatcher was ultimately one of the major factors in her downfall and resignation. The challenge to her leadership was an almost immediate response to Geoffrey Howe's resignation speech, which castigated the Prime Minister for her approach to Europe; one of the central arguments put foward by Michael Heseltine in his leadership challenge was his positive attitude towards European issues. By that time, such was her hostility to Europe that once out of office and freed from the restrictions of her position, Lady Thatcher, as she had become, became the leading voice and propagandist of the Euro-sceptical tendency. And that tendency was rapidly assuming the characteristics of a party within a party. In Parliament there were a number of Conservatives of ministerial rank who were unable to criticise Europe too openly because of the constraints of office, but a sizeable group of backbenchers grew up under the unofficial leadership of Bill Cash, MP for Stafford.

The Conservative Party – Maastricht and after

When John Major became Prime Minister he was immediately plunged into the negotiations of the IGC, which led to agreement at Maastricht in December 1991. He had some trouble with his backbenchers because the Euro-sceptics in the party shifted their position. Up to this point Conservative reservations about Europe had centred on what was perceived as a bureaucratic centralism in the Community, or were directed against 'creeping socialism'. Now the main line of attack switched to one of outright nationalism in defence of British sovereignty, and 'federalism' became the 'f-word' that was not to be mentioned in polite society.

At Maastricht John Major succeeded in cutting out the word 'federal' where it had appeared in the draft treaty, as well as negotiating opt-outs for Britain on both EMU and the social chapter. During the negotiations, debate within the party had been largely stifled and Major may have felt that he had done enough to satisfy the Euro-sceptics with the deal he had negotiated over the Treaty. In fact, the most bitter debate within the party was about to follow as Major sought to obtain approval for the Maastricht Treaty. In so doing the Prime Minister was suffering from one major disadvantage. In the 1992 election the overall government majority had been reduced to twenty-one, while there were known to be at least thirty Euro-sceptics dedicated enough to be ready to vote against the party line. The government had become very vulnerable to any backbench rebellion.

The European Communities Amendment Bill 1992 began its passage through Parliament on 7 May 1992, reaching its second reading on the 21st and 22nd of that month. Contrary to popular opinion, it was not intended to ratify the Maastricht agreement; treaties with foreign powers can be ratified by the government without reference to Parliament. The bill was for the purpose of absorbing the Maastricht provisions into British law. This the rebels were determined to prevent, while the government were equally determined to put down any dissent. Prior to the vote on the second reading the party whips did everything to persuade reluctant Tory backbenchers to vote with the government, from persuasive talk about how subsidiarity had removed the threat of federalism on one hand, to outright threats on the other. Those threats in turn ranged from reminders that rebels could forget any hopes of promotion, to hints that scandalous details of the rebel MPs' private lives might be leaked to the press. More than one MP was seen to have been reduced to tears by the attentions of the whips. Even so, twenty-two Conservatives voted against the government on the second reading, although the decision by Labour to abstain led to the government having a comfortable majority of 336 votes to 92.

At that moment, when the bill was about to move into its Committee Stage, its progress was halted by the Danish referendum, which rejected Maastricht. Suspended until the position of Denmark had been resolved, the bill remained in limbo until after the summer recess. In that intervening period the Euro-sceptics were reinforced in their thinking both by the anti-Europe feeling revealed in Denmark and France, and by the set-back to monetary integration provided by Black Wednesday and the collapse of the ERM. As the confidence of the rebels increased the government gave a hostage to fortune by agreeing to a Labour suggestion that they should subject the suspended bill to a paving motion, which would give the Commons' permission for the bill to proceed. Constitutionally there was no requirement for such a motion and there had been no precedent in the passage of other controversial measures.

As the 1992 conference season began, there was a reminder that Labour was also still divided when Bryan Gould resigned from the Shadow Cabinet over the issue of Europe. Even so, the Conservative Conference reminded the government that grassroot opinion in the constituencies was very Euro-sceptical. Speakers like Norman Tebbit received standing ovations for anti-European speeches. 'Let's launch the drive for Maastricht Two,' he said, 'a treaty with no mention of economic and monetary and political union.' Lady Thatcher was persuaded not to speak, but her very presence reminded conference representatives of her continuing opposition, made explicit in an article in *The European* newspaper. The rebel Tory MPs left Brighton convinced that they had the support of the party in the country for their opposition to Europe.

When the Commons voted on the paving motion on 5 November twenty-six Conservatives voted against the government, and another sixteen abstained. The government would almost certainly have been defeated if the Liberal Democrats had not voted with them. Even so, the bill went into Committee Stage with the most vigorous opposition to the Conservative government coming from the Conservative backbenches. As is required for constitutional issues, the Committee Stage was taken by a Committee of the Whole House, which guaranteed that the progress of the bill would be slow. There were now forty or more identified Tory rebels who did not mind the delays they caused and who had declared that they were ready to bring down the government rather than see an extension of Brussels' influence.

In March 1993 the government was defeated over the composition of the Committee of the Regions, which the government wanted to be composed of nominees but which Labour wished to be made up of elected councillors. Forty-two Conservatives voted with Labour on that amendment. Further threats of rebellion caused the government to back down on the question of accountability over negotiations on economic union. The most serious threat of defeat came over a Labour amendment that would reverse the government's opt-out on the Social Chapter. The rebels were as opposed to the Social Chapter as the government, but would vote for it in the belief that the government would then withdraw the bill rather than let it go through in its amended form. The government escaped on that point by persuading the Labour Party to withdraw its amendment in favour of a new amendment (known as 'clause 75'), which meant that between the bill becoming law and the government's ratification of Maastricht there had to be a separate debate and vote on the Social Chapter.

It was with this clause included that the bill received its third reading on 20 May 1993, exactly one year after its second reading. Labour abstained again and the government received 229 votes in favour, with 112 against, forty-one of whom were Tory rebels. The bill then passed to the Lords where another struggle was foreseen, largely because two of Europe's most vocal opponents were now members of the Upper House – Lord Tebbit and Lady Thatcher. Yet the expected struggle did not actually happen and the bill made rapid progress. The showpiece debate and vote was over the issue of a referendum, with Lady Thatcher espousing a course that she was once the first to condemn. As it happens the government packed the Lords with its supporters, loyal backwoodsmen being drafted in from the remotest of locations. The referendum amendment was lost by 445 votes to 176, the largest vote in the Lords during the twentieth century.

The bill received the Royal Assent on 20 July 1993, but the

Commons immediately moved to the Labour amendment which stated that Britain must accept the Social Chapter before ratifying Maastricht. The debate was fixed for Thursday 22 July and all the attentions of the Whips' Office were concentrated on winning over the rebels, while other government supporters worked on gaining allies from the Ulster Unionist MPs. It was during this time that feelings within the Conservative Party became particularly bitter. 'These people are going to be hated for all time', said Edward Heath about the rebels. Some of the Euro-sceptics came back into the fold but others became even more entrenched in their position by the pressure being brought to bear on them.

There were two votes on the question of the Social Chapter. On the first, which was on the Labour amendment for acceptance of European social policies, eighteen rebels proved willing to vote against the government, resulting in an apparently tied vote of 317 to 317, which was resolved by the Speaker's traditional casting vote for the government. But on the second vote, which was on a government statement merely noting the existence of the Social Chapter, the number of rebels rose to twenty-five and the government was defeated by 324 votes to 316. The government had to re-present the motion on the following day, this time making it a vote of confidence which would have required the government to resign if defeated. Despite the rebels' earlier promise to bring down the government if necessary, they gave way at this point and the government had a majority of forty. The government were then free to ratify Maastricht, but it was only after incalculable damage had been done to relations within the Tory Party.[10]

The Conservative Party – after the Maastricht debate

In March 1994, Martin Kettle wrote an article in the Guardian[11] bemoaning the fact that the common terminology employed by the media tended to divide opinion on the issue of Europe into just two groups, the Euro-enthusiasts and the Euro-sceptics, whereas he claimed that he could distinguish at least four different attitudes:

Euro-enthusiasts are those who welcome membership of the Community and the moves towards integration. In their way they are somewhat uncritical of European measures and are typified by the Liberal Democrats or Ted Heath and his supporters.

Euro-phobes is the more accurate term for those known at the moment as Euro-sceptics, such as Bill Cash, Michael Spicer or Teddy Taylor, who are rather more than merely sceptical and are in fact against anything European and who would quite gladly welcome a British withdrawal from Europe.

Euro-sceptics, in the true sense of the term, are what Kettle describes as people 'who doubt the wisdom of the European project but who are prepared to go cautiously along with it'. They accept that in a few areas, such as the Single Market, the European Union has its uses but are highly sceptical about any European involvement in areas like social policy, defence or internal security.

Euro-progressives or **Euro-positives**. This is the group no one mentions but who, according to Kettle, probably form the majority, not only in Britain but throughout the Community. They are people who 'are basically in favour of the Euro-project but who don't want to endorse change indiscriminately'. These are the people who voted two to one to remain in the Common Market in the referendum of 1975 and who would probably vote in the same proportions today. It is also, broadly speaking, the position adopted by the Labour Party.

The point that Kettle was making in his article was that John Major, at the time he took over from Lady Thatcher, was a Euro-positive, eager to put Britain 'at the heart of Europe' and able to say at the European Council in Edinburgh, 'the majority of people in this country want us to make a success of our membership'. The conflicts of the debate over Maastricht have dragged Major out of the Euro-progressive camp into that of the Euro-sceptics. In order to accommodate the Euro-phobes in the party the Prime Minister has had to adopt a highly critical attitude in European circles, appearing in the eyes of many observers to block measures that seemed to be integrationist, not for the sake of Britain or Europe but in order to keep the favour of his party at home.

During the spring and summer of 1994 the British blocked a number of measures, to the annoyance of their Community partners. At Janina Britain attempted to block changes to the requirements for Qualified Majority Voting, and at Corfu the UK was the one member state to veto the choice of Jean-Luc Dehaene as President of the Commission. On both issues Britain persisted, in defiance of majority opinion, even though the arguments on both occasions put at risk the timetable for negotiations over the accession of the three Scandinavian countries, and despite enlargement of the Community having long been a favoured policy of the Major government. Both disputes enraged Britain's partners, not least because they were seen and perceived by those partners as moves that had little to do with principle or government policy but everything to do with the internal disputes of the Conservative Party.

The moves by the leadership of the party from a positive to a sceptical perspective does not seem to have appeased the Europhobes in the party. Rather, they have become more and more openly phobic as Major has changed his position. Very much a backbench movement at the time of the Maastricht debate, the phobes have attracted government ministers and even members of the Cabinet to the cause. Prominent Cabinet ministers, including Michael Portillo, Peter Lilley, Michael Howard and John Redwood, have not only spoken openly in a critical manner about aspects of the Community but have used the increasingly phobic reactions of the Tory grassroots to form a power-base for their own ambitions and career prospects. Major has recognised this fifth column in the Cabinet and was overheard to refer to them as 'bastards'.

From the moment that the Maastricht debate finished, the Conservative Party had hoped that the arguments within the party were over and the process of healing the wounds could begin. In fact, the contrary was more the case and anti-European sentiments became common among the party activists at constituency level. At the 1994 Conservative Conference the former chancellor, Norman Lamont, made a speech openly advocating British withdrawal. The Employment Secretary, Michael Portillo, made a speech containing a catalogue of what he believed was wrong with Europe, to be greeted with wild applause each time he made an anti-European statement, true or not. A survey of backbench Conservative MPs showed that 87 per cent were against any increase in the supranational powers of EU institutions, 78 per cent were for increasing the power of national parliaments to scrutinise European legislation, and about 40 per cent were in favour of permitting Westminster to overrule any Commission directives or regulations.[12]

Summary

It is interesting that the only European policy on which there is a difference of opinion *between* parties is over the Social Chapter. On all other policies there appear to be far greater differences *within* the parties than there are between them. In 1975 politicians campaigned for their viewpoint in cross-party groups; Conservative pro-Europe campaigners serving alongside Liberals under the leadership of Labour's Roy Jenkins. On the other side of the divide Teddy Taylor and Tony Benn shared the same anti-Europe platform. Labour seems to have forgotten those years and settled their internal differences in broad support of Europe. But in the Conservative Party the situation continues to pose a serious threat to party unity. The Extreme Right/Bruges Group, anti-European Tories grow steadily more extreme and more opposed to Europe for a variety of reasons, invoking memories of the Hard Left of the Labour Party in the early 80s, even down to the factional in-fighting common to extremist wings of parties.

So the hope that there may be a consensus between the parties on European matters is as far away as ever. In order to distinguish between party attitudes it might be productive to look at the three main parties and their attitude to Europe and European issues, as expressed in statements made about European institutions in June 1994.[13]

Conservative At Britain's insistence the Maastricht Treaty enshrined the principle of 'subsidiarity' or minimum interference. This means *less* European law and *better* European law. We want to make sure subsidiarity becomes even more effective in the years ahead. The European Parliament now has the real power to influence decisions taken in Brussels. Conservative MEPs will use the Parliament's legislative powers in the service of an open, thriving, free enterprise Europe. They will vote for an outward-looking, decentralised Union, committed to free trade.

Labour Labour will work to ensure that decision-making in the European Union is developed in an open and democratic way, in contrast to the present ministerial way of operating in secret. Labour supports greater powers for elected representatives to share in the decisions that are binding on Europe. Whenever they make laws, Council meetings must be open, with all votes recorded and published.

Liberal Democrat The Liberal Democrat vision of Europe is not a centralised superstate but one which is democratic, decentralised and diverse. The Commission should be smaller, with its members appointed by, and accountable to, the Parliament. Parliament should be strengthened to give it equal legislative rights to the Council and to allocate seats proportionately to population. The Council of Ministers should take its decisions in public. European institutions should exercise power only over policies which cannot be effectively dealt with at local, regional or national level.

Notes

1 David McKie, *The Guardian Political Almanac 1993/4*, Fourth Estate, London 1993.

2 Tom Nairn, *The Left Against Europe?*, Penguin, London 1973.

3 The exchanges between Gaitskell and Macmillan are quoted in Michael Cockerell's excellent book about relations between television and politicians, *Live from Number 10*, Faber & Faber, London 1988.

4 Cockerell, *Live from Number 10*, p. 202.

5 Reported by Cockerell, p. 222.

6 Ben Rosamond, 'The Labour Party and European Integration',

Politics Review, April 1994, p. 21.

7   Bill Jones and Dennis Kavanagh, *British Politics Today*, 2nd edn., Manchester University Press, Manchester 1984.

8   Stephen George, *Britain and European Integration since 1945*, Basil Blackwell, Oxford 1991.

9   Daniel Wincott, 'The Conservative Party and Europe', *Politics Review*, April 1992, p. 12.

10   A full account of the Maastricht debate, with analysis of the various divisions and the voting record of all MPs, is to be found in the *Guardian Political Almanac 1993/4*, edited by David McKie, pp. 199–224.

11   Martin Kettle, 'A leader lost amid the phobes and sceptics', *The Guardian*, 19 March 1994.

12   D. Baker, Fountain, A. Gamble and S. Ludlam, *Conservative Parliamentarians and European Integration: Initial Survey Results*, Economic and Social Research Council, with the University of Sheffield Politics department, October 1994.

13   Each statement is extracted from the relevant party manifesto issued for the European elections in June 1994.

9

The citizen of the European Union

The EU does not noticeably appeal directly to the individual. Euro-enthusiasts are always ready to quote opinion polls conducted by the statistical offices of the Community, claiming majority support for the EU among the public in all member countries. In 1991, for example, a Eurobarometer opinion poll found that 53 per cent of the population, across the twelve member states, claimed to feel a sense of belonging to Europe, 'sometimes' or 'often'.[1] In 1994, only 22 per cent of the British population questioned by Eurobarometer wished to see an end to the Union, while 25 per cent claimed they would feel 'profound regret' at such an end; an incredible 41 per cent actually said that they felt that European integration was 'too slow'. Yet although it is probably true that a majority of British electors would vote now, as they did in 1975, for continued membership, it would be an apathetic form of support, which basically means little more than that people think that now we are in we might as well stay in, and that it would be less of an upheaval to remain in the Community than to leave it. When it comes to European integration it is hard to find any real enthusiasm among the general public and that does not only apply to Britain. 'European integration has been promoted by political élites rather than by the electorate as a whole ... Elite-led advances in European integration may not correspond to popular wishes, as the 1992 Danish referendum demonstrated.'[2]

One reason for public indifference to Europe is ignorance.

Most people are unaware of the benefits of Community membership and they are not enlightened by a functionalist government that does not wish people to know just how many policy decisions are taken outside the control of national governments, and which is aided by a media far more interested in publicising the faults of the Commission and pouring scorn on the disadvantages of membership. A small proportion of the population have direct contact with European action, and acquire strong attitudes for or against Europe as a result: those working in agriculture or the fishing industry are examples of this. Others, perhaps living in depressed areas which are in receipt of Community funding, might also be aware of Community influence thanks to the placards announcing European funding for some improvement in the infrastructure such as the building of new roads. For the most part, however, the majority of people remain unaware of any benefits or penalties of EU membership, except for some peripheral benefits from relaxed Customs restrictions when travelling in the EU on holiday.

Nevertheless, aware of it or not, all British citizens have been affected to some extent by the UK's membership of the Community. Apart from the influences on British policy noted in Chapter 6, there are two main areas in which the individual is affected by Community membership: one is the EU citizenship provisions of the TEU, and the other is the rights given to citizens as consumers under the Single Market provisions of the SEA. To consider the first of these, it is worth remembering that, as far back as 1984, the European Council set up a committee chaired by Pietro Adonnino to consider the action required to create 'a people's Europe'. The work done by that committee prepared the ground for the citizenship provisions that make up Article 8 of the Maastricht agreement.

Citizenship of the Union

Article 8 of the Treaty for European Union states that 'Every person holding the nationality of a Member State shall be a citizen of the Union',[3] and then goes on in a series of sub-clauses to detail the rights of citizenship that are granted within the TEU:

- The right of freedom of movement within the territory of all member states.
- The right to reside in any country of the Union.
- The right to work in any member state, although subject to certain national restrictions.
- The right to vote and stand as a candidate in municipal and European elections, subject to the qualifications demanded of nationals of the state in question, in the country of residence. However, it has to be said that in the local and European elections of 1994, in the first elections under which such voters were eligible, the British government only made registration possible in March and most EU residents found it difficult to register in time for the elections.
- The right to have academic and/or vocational qualifications recognised throughout the Union.
- The right to parity of provision for welfare benefits.
- The right, when travelling outside the Union, to diplomatic or consular assistance from the Embassy or Consulate of any member state.
- The right to receive pension entitlement in whichever state the pensioner is resident, at a rate equal to that paid in the country where the entitlement was earned.
- The right to petition the European Parliament, to resort to legal action in the European Court of Justice or to apply to the Ombudsman.

All these rights came into force with the ratification of the TEU and the provisions are scrutinised and guaranteed by the Commission being required to report on their application to the European Parliament, and to the Economic and Social Committee, at three-yearly intervals.

Freedom of movement

The aims of Maastricht in establishing completely free movement of people, with the right to study, work and live in another country, have not been introduced without certain constraints upon their full application. The Single European Act should have done away with passport controls between member countries, just as it did away with checks by Customs. The UK, however, insisted that anti-terrorism measures meant that rudimentary passport checks must be retained for EU citizens, and with the passport union already existing between the two countries, the Republic of Ireland had to follow suit. Denmark also had to remain aloof because of the passport union existing between the Scandinavian countries, although the position alters significantly with the accession of Sweden and Finland. The nine other signatories of the SEA did, however, form the Schengen Group, which means that the EU, with the exception of Denmark, Ireland and the UK, had no internal borders for either passport or customs control.

It might be pointed out that citizens of the three countries outside Schengen, who have their freedom of movement impeded through their governments' failure to implement the SEA fully, are free to appeal to the European Court over that infringement of treaty provisions. There was talk at one point during the Irish troubles that Gerry Adams, or any other Sinn Fein representative who faced an exclusion order from the United Kingdom, might file a case against the UK government for this restriction of their movements.

Residence in any EU country is possible through 'freedom of establishment', by which EU citizens can settle in any EU country that they wish. All they need is a residence permit, which is valid for five years and is automatically renewable on request. Moreover, no EU citizen can be refused a residence permit except on the grounds of security or heath. On the right to work in another country within the EU the situation differs according to the member state, as do the individual's rights to unemployment benefit and pension rights.

Belgium EU citizens working in Belgium can bring in their marriage partner and their children, all of whom also gain the right to work and all social benefits. Any unemployed have the right to reside in Belgium, if registered as a 'job-seeker'.

Denmark An EU citizen has the right to work in Denmark as the employee of a Danish employer, or to set up their own business in Denmark if they are likely to employ Danish workers. All EU citizens have automatic pension rights and free treatment in the Danish Health Service.

France EU citizens have the right to reside and work in France but difficulties remain over the recognition of qualifications. Members of the families of registered workers have equal rights with native French citizens to welfare benefits.

Germany Unrestricted access to work and benefits for EU citizens on the basis of parity with native German citizens.

Greece A work permit is not required if the police are informed within eight days of arrival in the country. Three months' work qualifies the EU citizen to full national rights.

Ireland The UK and Ireland already shared full freedom of movement and the right to work before both countries joined the Community, although severely constrained at times by anti-terrorist legislation.

Luxembourg By far the most liberal of the EU countries in granting working rights, social benefits and assistance to EU immigrants since one quarter of the population are already nationals of other EU countries.

Netherlands No restrictions on EU citizens over access either to jobs or social benefits on an equal basis with Dutch nationals.

Portugal Still retains limits on access to work in Portugal. Also, Portugal does not possess a social security system.

Spain A five-year work and residence permit is required but this should be automatically available to EU citizens who apply.

United Kingdom Gives no guarantees on work, freedom of movement or access to welfare provision for EU citizens, although government claims that all rights are available on a reciprocal basis. The UK is the one country in the EU which does not recognise workers' rights under the Social Chapter.[4]

Pensions and Social Security

From the start there has been a commitment in the Community that citizens from one member state should not be disadvantaged in receiving social or welfare benefit simply because they are resident in an EU member state that is not that of their birth, nor indeed the country in which they have spent their working lives. Basically the rule is that a welfare recipient working and living abroad in another EU country receives the benefits payable in that country. This can produce some strange anomalies, such as a British citizen working in Luxembourg who receives family benefit for his or her children, even though those children have been left behind in the family's English home. The system can also benefit some people more than others: a waiter from Portugal where there are virtually no welfare benefits will do very well if he works in a restaurant in Germany and qualifies for full German benefit.

One welfare benefit which is not paid by the country of residence is unemployment benefit, if the person concerned entered the country while unemployed. This is a necessary precaution by countries such as Germany or the Netherlands which pay a noticeably better rate of unemployment benefit: they would otherwise be the target of hundreds of the unemployed, touring Europe in search of the best rate of pay. An unemployed EU citizen can, however, look for work in other member states and continue to receive unemployment pay from the home country, at the rate paid in that country. For the unemployed person to do so they must have the permission of their country's equivalent of the British Department of Social Security, who can also provide useful information and advice. On arrival in their new country of residence anyone who is unemployed must register with the local authority as a 'job-seeker' within one week.

As far as retirement or disability pensions are concerned the position is clear-cut, even if a little complicated at times. If, after a life spent working in Britain, a couple chose to retire to a villa they had bought in Spain, they would receive their pensions in Spain, although at the British and not the Spanish rate. The complication sets in when a pensioner's working life has been spent in more than one EU member state because then the pension is paid pro rata to the pension rates in those countries, according to the length of time spent in each of those countries. As an example, let us take a British citizen, a civil servant, who spent twenty years working in Whitehall but who then, for the last ten years of his working life, transferred to work for the EC Commission in Brussels. He would receive a pension two-thirds of which would be paid at the British rate and one third at the Belgian. This, however, only applies to state pensions and there are still problems over transferring entitlement to occupational pensions from one country to another.[5]

Health

All Community countries have some form of health service. In some countries treatment is free, in others the patient has to make some form of payment towards the cost, and in yet others the patient has to pay in full and then claim for a full or partial refund. For some time the member states of the EU have made their health service facilities available to citizens of other member states on a reciprocal basis, whether the service is that of a doctor, dentist, hospital treatment or the issue of prescriptions. In the 1980s the EC extended this reciprocal arrangement to temporary residents of the member states, as holiday-makers or business travellers, and a special form (E 111) was issued, possession of which entitles the holder to the reciprocal medical arrangement.

In addition to this routine assistance the EU is also involved in the health of the Community in the commitment of funds to supranational health research projects. The first such project was 'Europe against cancer', which was set up and funded with the expressed intention of reducing the number of deaths from cancer by 15 per cent by the year 2000. Similar programmes have followed that have been targeted on AIDS and drug abuse.[6]

Young people and Europe

In recent years the Community has set up a number of initiatives intended to foster a sense of belonging to a European Community among young people, particularly students and young workers.

- The 'Youth for Europe' scheme is a simple exchange programme whereby young people between the ages of 15 and 25 can extend their knowledge of the EU by going to live in another EU country for a time.
- The 'European exchange programme for young workers' is, as the name suggests, intended to allow young workers in the first ten years of their working lives to gain work experience or to follow a course of training in another EU member state.
- 'Erasmus' is the established project for encouraging exchange and mobility among EU member states for students in the university sector. The programme is also intended to encourage the provision of courses in European studies on the part of colleagues and universities, as well as encouraging a pan-European perspective in existing disciplines.
- 'Comett' is a project intended to improve technical training, specially in the new technologies, by placing students and young workers in firms and research establishments in other member countries.
- There are a number of schemes to promote education and training in specific fields such as science and economics, they include the 'Lingua Programme' intended to improve the teaching of languages and the 'Petra Programme' for improving vocational training.

The Commission also funds a body concerned with research and development into the field of training and vocational education. The European Centre for the Development of Vocational Training (CEDEFOP) is based in Berlin. For postgraduate university students interested in studying the processes of European integration there is a College of Europe, which offers one-year courses in economics, law and political science from a European perspective and which receives around 250 students each year. The College is a bilingual institution and students must be fluent in either English or French. Based in Bruges, the College gained some notoriety for being the body to which Lady Thatcher was speaking when she made her infamous Bruges Speech.

The individual as consumer

The Community's policy towards the consumer has already been dealt with in Chapter 6, but it should be repeated that EC policy since the establishment of the Single Market has been to allow the sale throughout the Community of goods lawfully produced in any one country of the Union, subject to regulation by the Community of standards affecting safety, hygiene and quality. Over the two years 1993–95 consumer action plans were set up to improve standards of consumer protection. Areas that have been affected are:

- Food safety, with legislation controlling the safety, quantity and technical necessity of food additives, preservatives, colourings and ingredients in general.
- Product safety in general, but with specific directives on children's toys, furniture, fireworks, prams and pushchairs.
- Pharmaceuticals, medicines and cosmetics, with specially rigorous requirements for adequate testing before use and the clear labelling of constituents. As from 1998 the testing of such products on animals will be forbidden.
- Packaging and labelling. Specific regulations deal with misleading statements about the nutritional value of foods; with the clear marking of perishable goods with 'best before' statements; and with which languages should be used in the labelling of goods.
- Protection from unfair trading practices, including misleading advertisements, doorstep selling, excessive rates of interest on credit sales, distance selling and package holidays that do not match brochure descriptions.

In tandem with these action programmes the Commission is

setting up a consumer guide to cross-border shopping, a practice which has increased considerably since the Single Market enabled EU citizens to import unlimited quantities of goods bought in another Community country, as long as duty and VAT had been paid at the local rate. The Commission is also responsible for consumer information centres located near national borders, which will give advice on prices and availability of goods on both sides of the border, pointing out any special offers that might be available in one country rather than another. These centres work best, of course, with land frontiers and there are, as yet, none within the UK.

The interests of consumers in the UK as regards the Community are looked after by an umbrella interest group known as Consumers in the European Community (CECG). They in turn have contact with EC institutions through the Consumers' Consultative Council (CCC), which acts as an advisory body to the Commission and which helps to organise the pan-European Consumers Forum, meeting once or twice each year.[7]

The right to protest

As the discussion in Chapter 6 of the role of pressure and interest groups in the Community suggested, access to decision-making bodies by individuals is possibly more open in the EU than in the UK. Complaints from the individual are actually welcomed by the Commission, since it is only on the receipt of specific complaints that the Commission can begin to take action against national governments for non-compliance with Commission directives. Britain has at least learned this lesson well, and since 1990, something in excess of 100 complaints have been received each year from individuals or groups resident in the UK. It has proved one way to circumvent the closed nature of British government.[8]

An individual who joins a pressure group and uses them, or sometimes is used by them, to pursue a cause that has run into a brick wall when faced with British bureaucratic obduracy, often finds success in Europe where they failed in the UK. This has been particularly the case over issues concerning women, the environment or consumerism.[9]

As well as the Commission, the individual is entitled to approach the European Parliament. The EP is obliged to receive a written request or complaint, known as a petition even if there is only one signatory. Such petitions are screened of course to weed out the frivolous or malicious, but if there seems to be good cause behind the communication the petition will be discussed and considered by a Parliamentary Committee, which will make a decision and take any action it sees fit, communicating the outcome to the petitioner. Under the same Article (138) of the TEU as granted the right of petition, an Ombudsman was appointed to consider any examples of bad management or maladministration by Community institutions or bodies. Any individual can take these actions by communicating directly with the Parliament or the Ombudsman but, naturally enough, for UK citizens who have constituency representatives in the EP, such approaches are more effective when conducted through the petitioner's own MEP.

The other main channel through which the individual EU citizen can seek redress is through the European Court. There are sufficient examples quoted in Chapter 6 to show the efficacy of this approach in certain matters, particularly over issues such as women's or workers' rights. Nevertheless, it has to be said that progress through the European Court suffers from the same disadvantage for the individual as do the national courts. The process is exceedingly slow – four years being the normal delay between claim and settlement – and extremely expensive, since legal aid is not readily available. Generally speaking an individual will only find legal redress a viable possibility if they have the backing and financial support of some interest group.

Summary

For much of the European Community's life the individual was often neglected, to the benefit of Community institutions. This has changed somewhat in recent years since the Single European Act has reinforced the status of the individual as consumer, and the Treaty for European Union has codified the rights of individuals under the provisions of EU citizenship.

Notes

1 European Commission, *A People's Europe*, European File Series, Luxembourg 1992.

2 Simon Bulmer, 'Britain and European integration', in Bill Jones (ed.), *Politics UK*, 2nd edn., Harvester Wheatsheaf, Hemel Hempstead 1994, pp. 632–51.

3 General Secretariat of the Council and of the Commission of the European Communities, *Treaty on European Union*, full text, Articles 8–8e, Office for Official Publications of the European Communities, Brussels–Luxembourg 1992, pp. 15–16.

4 Julie Wolf, 'The Single Market and you', in V. Keegan and M. Kettle, *The New Europe*, Fourth Estate, London 1993, pp. 29–41.

5 *Ibid*.

6 EC, *A People's Europe*.

7 European Commission in the United Kingdom, *Fact Sheet 7 – My Benefits as a European Consumer*, HMSO, London 1994.

8 Stephen C. Young, 'Environmental politics and the EC', *Politics Review*, February 1993, p. 8.

9 Sonia Mazey and Jeremy Richardson, 'Pressure groups and the EC', *Politics Review*, September 1993, p. 22.

Conclusion

The future of the European Union – integration or disintegration?

In 1994 the EU reached what should have been a plateau in its development, following the rapid changes of the late 1980s and early 90s. The reform of the Common Agricultural Policy, the passing of the Single European Act and agreement on the Treaty for European Union had all made radical changes to the nature of the Community, and it seemed as though the member states could rest for a while in a spirit of consolidation before the next round of review and reform began with the intergovernmental conference due to convene in mid-1996. Despite the often dissenting view of the United Kingdom it seemed that the European Union was set on a firm course towards political and economic union, led by the integrationist triumvirate of Chancellor Kohl of Germany, President Mitterand of France and Jacques Delors for the Commission.

In an article reviewing the EU's policy towards Eastern Europe the political journalist Martin Kettle identified five objectives of the EU, post-Maastricht:[1]

- Co-operation in foreign and security policy to provide a co-ordinated position for Europe in world affairs.
- Movement towards a federal political structure based on the principle of subsidiarity.
- Convergence on an economic union based on stable monetary policies within a deregulated and free single market.
- An agreed social programme to mitigate the effects of mone-

tary policy on the working conditions and living standards of the people.

- Enlargement of the Union by the potential inclusion of all nation-states west of the Russian border.

The problem, as pointed out by Kettle, is not only the well-known sceptical attitude of the United Kingdom, but the fact that no one member state, except perhaps Belgium and Luxembourg, is equally committed to all five of these propositions. As early as 1992, deep cracks had appeared in the facade of integration and it became obvious that further progress along the proposed lines was only going to be possible with difficulty, if at all.

- The recession, German unification and other economic factors wrecked the convergence criteria for the economies of many countries, destroyed the Exchange Rate Mechanism and threatened any real progress towards Economic and Monetary Union.
- Countries other than the UK, such as Denmark and Italy, became strongly anti-federal in their attitude, while large sections of the population in many countries, including even France and Germany, showed in referendums and the European elections that they are somewhat less enthusiastic about integration than their leaders.
- Unpopularity and electoral losses at home weakened the position of strongly integrationist political groupings, such as Kohl's Christian Democratic Party in Germany.
- The widening of the Community through the admission of new members has become hung up between two viewpoints. There are those who feel that the problems created by too many new members could be destructive, unless the institutions of the Union are reformed to cater for enlarged membership; and those who advocate a rapid extension of membership for that very reason: in order to block moves towards integration.

The response to these factors, especially in Britain, has been to reinforce scepticism about the movement towards integration.

There has been a growing tendency to talk about a multi-track, multi-speed Europe that is already partially in place, thanks to the British and Danish opt-outs written into the Maastricht Treaty. And indeed there is a minority, but growing, viewpoint that dares to advocate withdrawal from membership and the dismemberment of the Union.

The undermining of EMU

The original timetable for Economic and Monetary Union foresaw at least seven states of the union satisfying convergence criteria for their economies by 1997, so that EMU could move into its final phase with the introduction of a single currency and an indepenent European Central Bank. That timetable was seriously thrown into question by the events of September 1992, known in Britain as 'Black Wednesday', when turmoil in the currency market drove first Italy and then the United Kingdom to announce withdrawal from the Exchange Rate Mechanism. The troubles of the ERM did not end there: during the rest of that year, the Spanish, Portuguese and Irish currencies came under pressure, the former two having to devalue twice and the latter once. The French franc was only saved from collapse when heavy financial support from the Bundesbank enabled the French government to resist all calls for devaluation. While Britain and Italy could afford to relax, being outside the ERM, those countries remaining within it, and thereby constrained to maintain the parity of their currencies against pressures applied by speculators in the money markets, continued to suffer turbulence until late July 1993, when the French, Belgian and Danish currencies all dropped to the floor of the ERM band.

In August 1993 a Council meeting of EC finance ministers agreed to widen the ERM bands from 2.25 per cent to 15 per cent for all EC members, except for Italy and the UK, who remained with floating currencies outside the ERM, and also excepting Germany and the Netherlands, whose currencies were strong enough to remain within the 2.25 per cent narrow band. Two months later, in October, the finance ministers agreed that these new looser arrangements for the ERM could not be revised until 1996 and therefore movement towards a single currency looked unlikely before 1999 at the earliest.

As Europe climbed out of recession the convergence criteria were beginning to be met again and the original target of seven countries looked like being achieved, but no one country seemed eager to reactivate the EMS in its previous form. The British government, having said that Britain would rejoin the ERM as soon as possible, seemed unwilling to do so however favourable the economic indicators, and continued to insist that while re-entry was seen as a probability, it was only as a very distant prospect. Britain has also made it clear that no definite decisions have been reached as to whether Britain would be willing to participate when, or if, agreement should be reached on a single currency. A single currency remains the stated aim of the Community but several countries, including federalist Germany, are wary at the blow to national pride in allowing the ECU to supersede the mark, franc or whatever. Indeed, for many Europeans as well as the British, the concept of European monetary union is becoming one of those things affecting national sovereignty that everyone agrees would be good at some indefinite date in the future, but for which no one is willing to set an actual date.[2]

Doubts over membership

The first Danish referendum of 1992, which voted against ratification of the Maastricht Treaty, was an unpleasant shock to the advocates of European integration but was not totally unexpected, given the Euro-scepticism that Denmark was known to share with the UK. What did cause consternation among EC members, who had assumed a pro-integration consensus among the original Six, was what at one time looked like a very real threat that the French would also vote 'No' in their referendum. The French vote, taken in the midst of the economic troubles, just four days after 'Black Wednesday', could have upset permanently the move towards integration, in a country that was seen as being allied to Germany in advocating a federalist future for Europe. The narrowness of the vote in favour of Maastricht, 51 per cent against 49 per cent, coming so close on the heels of the Danish rejection, emphasised that the assumption of federalists as to the inevitability of integration was flawed and that the population at large were considerably more sceptical than their leaders. After this, it became abundantly clear that the development towards union in Europe had been essentially an elite-led movement, which had assumed a consent from the people that was not necessarily there. This was made even more clear when the people of Norway rejected membership, despite the enthusiasm shown for membership by the Labour government of Ms Gro Harlem Gruntland.

The process of disenchantment was compounded by a growing disillusion with the traditional political forces in many European countries. Government inefficiencies coupled with revelations of corruption led to swings of public opinion against the ruling party, most notably in Italy but also in Spain and France. This was a two-handed weapon, because not only were those parties most associated with European integration also those most tainted by corruption, but the parties which emerged to replace them were at the very least Euro-sceptical if not anti-Europe in their stance. In the German elections of 1994, the CDU/CSU was not tainted by corruption and there was comparatively little dissatisfaction with Europe, but the governing parties suffered considerable losses and deprived Chancellor Kohl of the strong majority he would have liked to support his European policies.

The growing scepticism over integration was reflected in the European elections of 1994. The Euro-sceptical *Forza Italia* party of Silvio Berlusconi won twenty-seven seats in the EP, sufficient to form a group of their own in the new Parliament, largely opposed to any strengthening of the integration process. In France the Gaullist RPR split from their former allies and won fourteen seats on a platform advocating the *Europe des Patries* ideas of de Gaulle. Also in France, the new *Autre Europe* party won thirteen seats on a programme of outright hostility to the idea of a federal Europe. These thirteen were joined by four Danish MEPs to form a Nations of Europe group in the EP, Denmark having given 25 per cent of its vote to parties explicitly anti-Maastricht in their policies.

Of course, this ground swell of opinion does not mean that there is an anti-European majority across the Community, but it does negate the belief of many Euro-enthusiasts that a vision of ultimate and inevitable integration was universally held. It also reinforced the view that the political leadership of member countries should look again to see whether they really did have popular support for integrationist policies. 'For the first time, the EP's federalist consensus may be significantly challenged by anti-federal forces who have the potential to upset the consensus on the centre-right.'[3]

Widening and deepening

Enlargement of the Union by the admission of new members is inevitable. Applications by Cyprus, Malta and Turkey remain on the table, even if in abeyance, while six former Soviet bloc countries have submitted applications for membership, with the hopes of at least three of them – Poland, Hungary and the Czech Republic – fixed on accession before the end of the century. There is no doubt that the applicants will be permitted to join ultimately, but the time-scale of their applications and the conditions under which they would be admitted are subject to considerable doubt, controversy and argument.

The convergence requirements, whereby applicant countries have to match the political and economic development of existing members, extended the transition period for Greece, Spain and Portugal to something like seven years. By the same criteria, the length of time for which even the most advanced of the Eastern European states, the Czech Republic, would have to wait for the convergence requirements to be right, would be twenty years, a delay that would be politically unacceptable. Yet there are very real difficulties in too rapid an expansion, which could lead to economic chaos. For example, it is estimated that the agricultural problems of just one country, Poland, would be sufficient to bankrupt the Common Agricultural Policy and make it completely unworkable.

Controversy therefore centres on whether the widening of the Community, through the admission of more members, should precede or follow a deepening of the Community, through a reform and strengthening of Community institutions. Even countries such as Germany, which are keen to see the extension of EU membership eastward concede that there are aspects of community membership that would be unworkable with much more enlargement. The argument over qualified majority voting, in the spring of 1994, and the retention of a national veto, proved almost insuperable on an extension of the Union from twelve to a proposed sixteen members. How much greater would the problem be if membership were extended to nineteen, twenty-two or twenty-five states? Indeed, it has to be asked how a Union of more than twenty member states could possibly conduct its affairs if the need for unanimous decisions remained. Likewise with the question over the Commission: the argument over the assignment of portfolios that took place in the autumn of 1994 emphasised the extent to which there are too many commissioners chasing too few jobs in a Community of only fifteen members. And what of the language problem? Can the Community afford the amount of time and money spent on translation when every piece of EC documentation has to be produced simultaneously in all the languages of the Community?

Many advocates of enlargement therefore say that enlargement cannot be pursued until there has been a fundamental reform of Community structures in the Parliament, Commission and Council of Ministers. Those reforms would necessarily involve the deepening of the Community through a strengthening of federalist structures. Because of this there are those advocates of enlargement, including large sections of the British Conservative Party, who advocate widening without deepening because they recognise that over-expansion of the Community will make any later moves towards integration impossible.

The widening and deepening controversy allows for two possible scenarios:

- one where the Union is widened by the acceptance of all

applicants without reform of the institution, and which rapidly becomes a very large, de-regulated free trade area, without political connotations.

- or one in which the structures and institutions of the EC are reformed and strengthened to provide a constitutional framework into which new members can easily be fitted.

There are, however, two further alternative scenarios. One is the withdrawal of member states from the EU, possibly ending in the Union's disintegration, and the other is a differentiated response in which the member states recognise different aims within Europe and differential speeds for member states in reaching those aims.

Withdrawal

During the 1970s, at the time of Britain's accession, there was talk among the critics of Europe advocating Britain's withdrawal from the Community. It was understood that a 'No' vote in the 1975 referendum would have meant withdrawal, and the Labour Party, under the influence of the Left, fought elections on a policy of withdrawal as late as 1983. Yet, as time went by, the arguments for withdrawal seemed to fade; or rather, the arguments against withdrawal began to seem unanswerable.

- With the Single Market in operation British trade and industry was part of a large internal market. Very few were ready to retreat from that, with the possible threat of European tariff barriers being raised against British goods and services.
- Britain received a great deal of inward investment from the United States, Japan and the Far East by firms who wished to set up a manufacturing base within the Community so as to avoid the external trade tariff. Withdrawal from the Community would mean the loss of these companies, with a consequent loss of investment, tax revenue and jobs.
- If Britain rejected her trading partners in Europe it is hard to see who would replace them. The old Commonwealth countries such as Australia and New Zealand have found new mar-

kets, especially in the Pacific Rim countries. And the United States has made it clear that their interest in Britain is solely as a link with Europe, and that if they were offered a choice between Europe and Britain alone, they would choose Europe.

Given these arguments the case for withdrawal seemed to disappear during the 1980s and the divisions in the political parties were not between membership and withdrawal but over the nature of the Community and the extent and depth implied in membership. However, the scepticism (or, more properly, the phobia) evident in the Conservative Party did not go away. Having failed to derail the Maastricht Treaty the most sceptical among the sceptics, such as Bill Cash or Lord Tebbit, deepened their distrust of Europe and their total opposition to a federal solution. The preferred option of the sceptics is to reduce the EC to little more than a free trade area, but if continued membership were to mean more than this then Britain should be prepared to contemplate withdrawal as the best way to protect British interests

The first leading politician to put this idea into words was the former Chancellor, Norman Lamont, speaking at a fringe meeting during the 1994 Conservative Conference. Withdrawal was not the main theme of his speech, which was demanding British resistance to any moves towards federalism, which if it were not rejected, he said, 'would continue to dominate our politics and poison the Conservative party for many years to come'. There were various alternatives to federalism, but if all these failed the British government should not be afraid to accept the alternative of complete withdrawal: 'One day it may mean contemplating withdrawal. It has recently been said that the option of leaving the Community was "unthinkable". I believe this attitude is rather simplistic'.[4]

Variable geometry

In order to overcome the many problems associated with progress for the European Union, compounded on one side by the economic weakness of certain applicant states, and on the other by states such as Britain who are reluctant to surrender any part of their sovereignty, the vision of variable geometry has re-emerged, whereby groups of countries at different levels of development move at different speeds towards an ultimate goal of union. John Major was almost the first to mention the concept, with a passing reference to a 'multi-faceted, multi-speed, multi-layered' Europe, but the first reasoned argument was produced by the French Prime Minister in August 1994. Edouard Balladur called for a three-tier Europe which he described as three concentric circles:

1 A strong central core of France, Germany and perhaps the Benelux countries, united politically, economically and militarily.
2 A middle tier made up of the other EU countries, unable or unwilling to join the political and economic union at the centre.
3 An outer circle containing the other European countries, not part of the EU but with economic and security links.

Only such an arrangement, it was claimed, could prevent paralysis of the Union by the problems inherent in enlargement.[5]

Just two days later, this French opinion was apparently supported by the Germans when the German Christian Democratic Union, Chancellor Kohl's party, published a policy document which wished, as its main aim, 'to strengthen the EU's capacity to act and to make its structures and procedures more democratic and federal'.[6] At the heart of this aim was the need to establish a form of constitution for the EU which would create a federal structure according to the principle of subsidiarity. Reform of Community institutions would mean that the EP became a genuine legislature, the Council evolved into a second chamber on the pattern of the US Senate to safeguard member states' interests, and the Commission would assume the functions of a European executive. However, recognising that movement towards union would be impossible if all countries progressed at the speed of the slowest, the Germans repeated the Balladur suggestion that there should be a fast-track central core of countries, which they proposed should be France, Germany and the Benelux countries, since 'they (together with Denmark and Ireland) are the ones which come closest to meeting the convergence criteria stipulated in the Maastricht treaty'.

Despite Kohl's immediate repudiation of the CDU document as not being government policy, the discussion paper was seen as having the authority of most senior figures in Kohl's party and therefore likely to be Germany's negotiating stance in the 1996 IGC review of Maastricht. Naturally enough, the notion of a central, fast-track 'first division' group of five countries alarmed the seven remaining countries, who saw themselves as being left behind, and caused even more alarm in the four applicant countries, who could see themselves being excluded from any important policy decisions before they had even joined. There was a certain irony in the fact that John Major had made great play of a 'multi-speed and multi-layered European Union' during the election campaign in June, but who, now a mechanism for creating such a layered institution had been suggested, was protesting because it seemed to relegate Britain to some second-class outer circle. On 6 September Major made a keynote speech in which he reiterated British adherence to the European ideal: 'Britain is irrevocably part of Europe', he said, 'but it must be the right sort of Europe'. And the right sort did not include an inner and outer core of member states. There was a wide range of policies within the EU and member states should be allowed to adopt differentiated approaches to these policies, as Denmark and the UK had adopted a different approach to monetary union. The key word was flexibility, which was 'essential to get the best out of Europe'.[7] Major concluded by attacking the idea of federalism and reasserting Britain's belief in the nation-state, seeing the European Union as an association of nation-states, co-operating but each at their own speed and in their own interest.

Major's criticisms seem to ignore the extent to which the German proposals can be seen to conform to British wishes. On many points advocated by Germany Britain would have no reason to withhold agreement: the priority to be given to subsidiarity, enlargement to the East, a need for agricultural reform, the denial of any form of unified super-state and support for the principle of variable geometry. In return, there is one idea put forward by Major, and largely overlooked, that fits in well with German thinking: the proposal that national parliaments and the EP should undertake scrutiny of European legislation as a joint exercise.

Where John Major and the British government do need to take care is that they do not reject so many ideas that the hard-core European countries wish to discuss that Britain is denied a place in the central discussions after 1996. 'It is well set to become the reality we do not want but may have to adjust to ... It would confront us with the choice we have so far avoided. Shall we be at the centre, or on the margin?'[8]

Summary

All these conflicting ideas are currently preliminaries to the argument that will follow between mid-1996 and late 1997 as the IGC seeks to define the next steps for European Union. How the differences will be resolved lies in the future, but progress of the EU in the form of deepening and widening cannot take place without full consideration of the issues discussed in this chapter. What is clear, however, is that John Major's hope – that further widening of the Community is likely to halt any further deepening of the Union – is doomed to failure. 'It is worth recalling that in the past widening has tended to go hand in hand with a deepening of supranational integration.'[9]

Notes

1 Martin Kettle, 'Europe confused by eastern promise', *The Guardian*, 5 November 1994.

2 Details of the sequence of events surrounding and following the currency collapse of September 1992 can be found in Philip Lynch, 'Europe's post-Maastricht muddle', *Politics Review*, November 1993, pp. 2–5.

3 Philip Lynch and Stephen Hopkins, 'Europe decides', *Politics*

Review, September 1994, pp. 9–11.

4   Norman Lamont, address to the Selsdon Group of the Conservative Party, Bournemouth, 11 October 1994.

5   Edouard Balladur, Prime Minister of France, in an interview with *Le Figaro*, 30 August 1994.

6   The policy paper of the CDU/CSU was presented by Wolfgang Schäuble, leader of the CDU/CSU parliamentary party, and Karl Lamers, CDU foreign affairs spokesman, on 1 September 1994, but was not approved by the CDU/CSU government, as was made clear by Chancellor Kohl.

7   John Major, address to the University of Leiden, Netherlands, 6 September 1994.

8   Hugh Young, 'Major takes the soft approach to a hard core Europe', *The Guardian*, 8 September 1994.

9   Simon Bulmer, *Britain and European Integration*, in Bill Jones (ed.), *Politics UK*, 2nd edn., Harvester Wheatsheaf, Hemel Hempstead 1994.

Appendix 1

**Composition of the European Parliament after the
election of 1994 but before the enlargement of 1995**

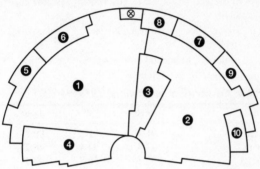

1: PES – 198	3: LDR – 43	6: ERA – 19
B – 6	B – 6	B – 1
DK – 3	DK – 5	E – 1
D – 40	E – 2	F – 13
GR – 10	F – 1	I – 2
E – 22	IRL – 1	L – 2
F – 15	I – 7	GB – 2
IRL – 1	L – 1	
I – 18	NL – 10	7: FE –27
L – 2	P – 8	I – 27
NL – 8	GB – 2	
P – 10		8: EDA – 26
GB – 63	4: EUL – 28	GR – 2
	GR – 4	F – 14
2: EPP – 157	E – 9	IRL – 7
B – 7	F – 7	P – 3
DK – 3	I – 5	
D – 47		9: NE – 19
GR – 9	5: Greens	F – 13
E – 30	B – 2	NL – 2
F – 13	DK – 1	P – 1
IRL – 4	D – 12	
I – 12	IRL – 2	10 & ⊗: Independent
L – 2	I – 4	B – 3
NL – 10	L – 1	F – 11
P – 1	NL – 1	I – 12
GB – 19		GB – 1

Source: Figures based on Statistical Document PE 177.791/fin issued by the European
Parliament, July 1994, with other information adapted from data included by P. Lynch
and S. Hopkins, 'Europe decides', *Politics Review*, September 1994.

Appendix 2

European elections:
Turn-out in the twelve member states, 1979–94 (%)

Country	1979	1984	1989	1994
Belgium	91.4	92.2	90.7	90.7
Denmark	47.8	52.4	46.2	52.9
France	60.7	56.7	48.7	52.7
Germany	65.7	56.8	62.3	60.0
Greece	78.6[1]	77.2	79.9	71.2
Ireland	63.6	47.6	68.3[4]	44.0
Italy	84.9	83.4	81.5	74.8
Luxembourg	88.9	88.8	81.5	88.5
Netherlands	57.8	50.6	47.2	35.6
Portugal	–	72.4[2]	51.2	35.5
Spain	–	68.9[3]	54.6	59.6
United Kingdom	32.3	32.6	36.2	36.4
TOTAL	62.5	59.0	57.2	56.8

Notes

Voting is compulsory in Belgium, Greece and Luxembourg.

1 First European election for Greece after accession, October 1981.

2 First European election for Portugal after accession, July 1987.

3 First European election for Spain after accession, June 1987.

4 General election held on same day.

Source Statistical Document PE177.791/fin., European Parliament, 6 July 1994

Appendix 3

The status of areas of the British Isles not part of the United Kingdom

There are certain anomalous areas within the geographical boundaries of the European Union. Some of these are independent or autonomous enclaves within, or attached to, the national territory of a member state, such as the miniature states of San Marino and Vatican City within Italy or the British territory of Gibraltar attached to Spain. Other anomalous bodies are outlying or dependent parts of the member state, which are often culturally or historically part of that state but which are not politically part of it; examples of this are the island of Greenland as an autonomous dependency of Denmark, or the Aaland Islands, which are part of Finland but, as a tax-free zone, remain independent of the mother country.

Within the geographical area of the British Isles there are two full members of the European Union – the United Kingdom and the Republic of Ireland. There is also the Isle of Man, which is subject to the British Crown but which is not part of the United Kingdom. It has its own administration in Tynwald, it has its own taxation system and indeed acts as a tax haven for individuals and companies, and it issues its own bank notes and postage stamps. The Channel Islands are not part of the British Isles but are subject to the British Crown, with much the same characteristics of autonomous sovereignty as the Isle of Man.

The position of the Isle of Man and the Channel Islands *vis-à-vis* the European Community was dealt with in Articles 25/27 and Protocol Three of the UK Act of Accession. It was also detailed, along with the other anomalous areas, in a report paper of the Commission issued in 1993 (No. 20/93). Basically, the situation is that neither the Isle of Man nor the Channel Islands are members of the EU politically and therefore are not eligible for any benefits of membership such as payments under the CAP, structural funds or regional aid. However, for goods produced in the islands and for Customs purposes, the territories concerned are regarded as being part of the Single Market.

Appendix 4
Allocation of portfolios to EC Commissioners

The allocation of portfolios to the Commissioners taking office in January 1995 presented two major problems to the President-elect, Jacques Santer. First of all there was the perpetual problem of there not being sufficient positions for the number of commissioners, a problem compounded by the admission of four further member states, each with its own commissioner. The available jobs have to be spread ever more widely, with obvious disappointments for established commissioners who find themselves with less important tasks in a re-distribution or with their responsibilities diluted by sharing the larger portfolios. In 1994 this resulted in an argument with the British Commissioner, Sir Leon Brittan, because relations with other countries which had previously been divided into separate economic and political portfolios were now divided geographically. Relations with potential member states in Eastern Europe was taken away from Brittan's Trade Relations portfolio and given to the Netherlands Commissioner, Hans van den Broek. Sir Leon's disappointment was obvious and there were threats of his resignation, as well as accusations that Sir Leon was being punished for Britain's attitude towards European integration.

The other major factor affecting Santer's actions was the 1996 IGC to review the Maastricht Treaty. The IGC was due to discuss foreign and security policy, the movement towards monetary union and reform of the Community's institutions. All these were seen as intergovernmental matters and concerns of the European

Union, while the Commission is only responsible for the European Community, within the Union. Santer could not give responsibilities for IGC concerns to rank and file commissioners since they would be unable to attend European Council meetings, where the nature of and timetable for these developments would be discussed. The President himself is the only commissioner who attends European Council meetings as of right, and Santer therefore had to take on these responsibilities, giving himself, as President, more powers than any of his predecessors.

Distribution of the portfolios

Jacques Santer (Luxembourg) – President with oversight of foreign and security policy, monetary affairs and the 1996 intergovernmental conference.

Manuel Marin* (Spain) – Relations with Mediterranean, Middle East, Latin America and Asia.

Martin Bangemann* (Germany) – Industry and technology.

Sir Leon Brittan* (UK) – International trade, relations with USA, Japan, China and the industrialised nations.

Karel van Miert* (Belgium) – Competition policy.

Hans van den Broek* (Netherlands) – Relations with applicant nations, including former Soviet bloc, foreign and security policy.

João de Deus Pinheiro* (Portugal) – Relations with Africa, Caribbean and Pacific.

Padraig Flynn* (Ireland) – Employment and social affairs.

Marcelino Oreja (Spain) – Institutional affairs, culture and media.

Edith Creson (France) – Science, research and training.

Ritt Bjerregaard (Denmark) – Environment and nuclear security.

Monika Wulf-Mathies (Germany) – Regional policy.

Neil Kinnock (UK) – Transport.

Mario Monti (Italy) – Internal market and taxation.

Emma Bonino (Italy) – Consumer affairs and humanitarian aid.

Yves-Thibault de Silguy (France) – Economic and monetary affairs.

Christos Papoutsis (Greece) – Energy, small and medium firms, tourism.

Thorvald Stoltenberg (Norway) – Fisheries.

Anita Gradin (Sweden) – Immigration, judicial affairs, anti-fraud measures.

Franz Fischler (Austria) – Agriculture.

Erkki Liikanen (Finland) – Budget and administration.

*Previously Commissioners in the 1993–94 Commission. Note that this Commission will serve for five years, coincident with the term of the EP.

In late December 1994 and early January 1995, during the last month before they took up their appointments, the commissioners-designate had to submit to examination by the European Parliament, under the terms of the Maastricht Treaty. MEPs were determined to make the most of one of the few rights of scrutiny they possess and many of the nominee commissioners had a rough ride. The MEPs do not have the ability to challenge any individual nominee but there was much speculation that if they did not extract some concessions from the Commission, with a promise of enhanced powers for the EP in the future, the MEPs could very well exercise the one right they did possess and reject Santer's chosen team as a whole. As it was, five of the commissioners-designate – Bjerregaard, Flynn, Gradin, Liikanen and de Silguy – were judged to be unsatisfactory. Most of their criticisms centred on the social affairs commissioner, Padraig Flynn, whose record on women's issues resulted in his being labelled a 'male chauvinist' by the MEPs. Flynn volunteered to step down as chair of the committee promoting women's rights while retaining his social affairs portfolio, and this largely defused the situation.

The potential crisis was ultimately resolved by a keynote speech made by Jacques Santer to the EP on 17 January 1995. In this the incoming president repeated his commitment to greater European integration and promised enhanced powers for the EP, including the right to vote on future amendments to the EU treaties by member states, such as Britain's opt-out from social policy. He also proposed that the European Parliament should have the right to elect his successor as president in five years' time. His actual words were, 'What about allowing parliament to elect my successor from a list put forward by heads of state and government?' It was enough to win the MEPs' approval for his team.

Another problem which arose between the distribution of portfolios and the new Commission taking office, was the question of Norway. A Norwegian commissioner, Thorvald Stoltenberg, had been nominated and had been awarded the fisheries portfolio. The Norwegians then voted 'no' in their referendum and withdrew from membership of the EU. The fisheries portfolio was transferred to Emma Bonino of Italy, who retained her consumer affairs portfolio in addition to the new responsibility.

Further reading and sources of information

This book has no bibliography, partly because texts referred to are fully listed after each chapter, and partly because the reason for writing this book was the lack of authoritative texts at this level dealing with Britain's place in the European Union. Of books dealing with the origins of British policy towards Europe the reader is referred to S. George (ed.), *Britain and the European Community* (Clarendon Press, 1992). For the impact of EC membership on British policy areas, useful information is to be found in S. Bulmer *et al.*, *The United Kingdom and EC Membership Evaluated* (Pinter, 1992). For an analysis of EC institutions and policy-making processes, the best technical account is in Neill Nugent, *The Government and Politics of the European Community*, 2nd edition (Macmillan, 1991). Nugent also edits an annual review of EC matters, as in *The European Community 1992: The Annual Review of Activities* (Blackwell, 1993).

There are several academic journals related to European Studies which concentrate on the EC, of which the *Journal of Common Market Studies* is probably the most prominent. Two journals which are specifically aimed at A-level and first-year undergraduate students (and their teachers) are *Politics Review*, published by Philip Allan Publishers of Deddington, Oxon., and *Talking Politics*, the journal of the Politics Association. Both journals deal with politics as a whole but the recently heightened profile of the European dimension has meant that they now regularly feature studies of European issues, as can be seen by the frequency of references to the journals in the course of this book. Among non-academic commercial journals. *The Economist* has regular features dealing with the economics, industry and trade of the European Community.

With the speed at which change takes place in the political world, the serious student cannot ignore the importance of the press in keeping up to date with developments in Europe. The four 'quality' broadsheets – *Daily Telegraph, Guardian, Independent* and *Times* – and their Sunday counterparts, all give adequate coverage of European issues on both their news and feature pages. It so happens that the newspaper most quoted in this book is *The Guardian*, but that is partly through my own preferences and partly because *The Guardian* was one of the first newspapers to base a special correspondent in Brussels to cover developments in the EC. Useful information can also be found regularly in the weekly newspaper, *The European*, and there is an English-language newspaper published in Brussels, the *Europa Times*.

The most prolific and most obvious source of information concerning the European Community is the European Commission itself. In Luxembourg the Commission produces a vast range of books and booklets covering all aspects of the constitution and workings of the European Union as well as a monthly journal, the *Bulletin of the European Communities*. All these are published in the various official languages of the Community. An idea of what is available can be gained from the publication *The European Community as a Publisher*, obtainable from the Commission's UK offices at Jean Monnet House, 8 Storey's Gate, London SW1P 3AT, or at Windsor House, 9/15 Beford Street, Belfast BT2 7EG, or at 4 Cathedral Road, PO Box 15, Cardiff CF1 9SG, or at 9 Alva Street, Edinburgh EH2 4PH. The UK Office of the Commission occasionally undertakes publication of literature aimed at Britain only, often in association with British government departments, and issued through the HMSO.

The Commission also maintains a network of information centres throughout the United Kingdom to serve the interests of small and medium-sized businesses, students and academics. There are twenty-four Euro Info Centres (EICs) for business information to be found within existing organisations in most major towns or cities. European Documentation Centres (EDCs) for students are found in academic institutions in forty towns or cities throughout the UK, some cities such as Birmingham, Coventry, Leeds and London having more than one EDC in different universities or colleges. Finally, to complement the above information centres, the EC maintains three depository libraries in Britain which receive copies of all EC documentation: their telephone numbers are – London 0171 798 2034; Liverpool, 0151 207 2147 and Wetherby 01937 546044.

As well as the Commission, the European Parliament also produces literature which can be obtained from the European Parliament UK Office, 2 Queen Anne's Gate, London SW1H 9AA. A mass of statistics about the EC, including an annual survey of statistical information and an annual electronic survey on CD, is produced by Eurostat, the Statistical Office of the EC. Eurostat publications should be available through the Commission, but if there is any difficulty, you can try the Office for Official Publications of the European Communities, 2 rue Mercier, 2985 Luxembourg.

Index

Figures shown in **bold** (e.g. **115–19**) indicate a main entry over a number of pages, rather than simple page references.

A number of politicians have been given peerages since the events described (e.g. Lord Jenkins, Lady Thatcher) but are listed here under their original names, without the title (i.e. Jenkins, Roy; Thatcher, Margaret).